LeConte Lodge

Contributions to Southern Appalachian Studies

1. *Memoirs of Grassy Creek: Growing Up in the Mountains on the Virginia–North Carolina Line.* Zetta Barker Hamby. 1998
2. *The Pond Mountain Chronicle: Self-Portrait of a Southern Appalachian Community.* Edited by Leland R. Cooper and Mary Lee Cooper. 1998
3. *Traditional Musicians of the Central Blue Ridge: Old Time, Early Country, Folk and Bluegrass Label Recording Artists, with Discographies.* Marty McGee. 2000
4. *W.R. Trivett, Appalachian Pictureman: Photographs of a Bygone Time.* Ralph E. Lentz II. 2001
5. *The People of the New River: Oral Histories from the Ashe, Alleghany and Watauga Counties of North Carolina.* Edited by Leland R. Cooper and Mary Lee Cooper. 2001
6. *John Fox, Jr., Appalachian Author.* Bill York. 2003
7. *The Thistle and the Brier: Historical Links and Cultural Parallels Between Scotland and Appalachia.* Richard Blaustein. 2003
8. *Tales from Sacred Wind: Coming of Age in Appalachia. The Cratis Williams Chronicles.* Cratis D. Williams. Edited by David Cratis Williams and Patricia D. Beaver. 2003
9. *Willard Gayheart, Appalachian Artist.* Willard Gayheart and Donia S. Eley. 2003
10. *The Forest City Lynching of 1900: Populism, Racism, and White Supremacy in Rutherford County, North Carolina.* J. Timothy Cole. 2003
11. *The Brevard Rosenwald School: Black Education and Community Building in a Southern Appalachian Town, 1920–1966.* Betty J. Reed. 2004
12. *The Bristol Sessions: Writings About the Big Bang of Country Music.* Edited by Charles K. Wolfe and Ted Olson. 2005
13. *Community and Change in the North Carolina Mountains: Oral Histories and Profiles of People from Western Watauga County.* Compiled by Nannie Greene and Catherine Stokes Sheppard. 2006
14. *Ashe County: A History; A New Edition.* Arthur Lloyd Fletcher. 2009 [2006]
15. *The New River Controversy; A New Edition.* Thomas J. Schoenbaum. Epilogue by R. Seth Woodard. 2007
16. *The Blue Ridge Parkway by Foot: A Park Ranger's Memoir.* Tim Pegram. 2007
17. *James Still: Critical Essays on the Dean of Appalachian Literature.* Edited by Ted Olson and Kathy H. Olson. 2008
18. *Owsley County, Kentucky, and the Perpetuation of Poverty.* John R. Burch, Jr. 2008
19. *Asheville: A History.* Nan K. Chase. 2007
20. *Southern Appalachian Poetry: An Anthology of Works by 37 Poets.* Edited by Marita Garin. 2008
21. *Ball, Bat and Bitumen: A History of Coalfield Baseball in the Appalachian South.* L.M. Sutter. 2009
22. *The Frontier Nursing Service: America's First Rural Nurse-Midwife Service and School.* Marie Bartlett. 2009
23. *James Still in Interviews, Oral Histories and Memoirs.* Edited by Ted Olson. 2009
24. *The Millstone Quarries of Powell County, Kentucky.* Charles D. Hockensmith. 2009
25. *The Bibliography of Appalachia: More Than 4,700 Books, Articles, Monographs and Dissertations, Topically Arranged and Indexed.* Compiled by John R. Burch, Jr. 2009
26. *Appalachian Children's Literature: An Annotated Bibliography.* Compiled by Roberta Teague Herrin and Sheila Quinn Oliver. 2010
27. *Southern Appalachian Storytellers: Interviews with Sixteen Keepers of the Oral Tradition.* Edited by Saundra Gerrell Kelley. 2010
28. *Southern West Virginia and the Struggle for Modernity.* Christopher Dorsey. 2011

29. *George Scarbrough, Appalachian Poet: A Biographical and Literary Study with Unpublished Writings.* Randy Mackin. 2011

30. *The Water-Powered Mills of Floyd County, Virginia: Illustrated Histories, 1770–2010.* Franklin F. Webb and Ricky L. Cox. 2012

31. *School Segregation in Western North Carolina: A History, 1860s–1970s.* Betty Jamerson Reed. 2011

32. *The Ravenscroft School in Asheville: A History of the Institution and Its People and Buildings.* Dale Wayne Slusser. 2014

33. *The Ore Knob Mine Murders: The Crimes, the Investigation and the Trials.* Rose M. Haynes. 2013

34. *New Art of Willard Gayheart.* Willard Gayheart and Donia S. Eley. 2014

35. *Public Health in Appalachia: Essays from the Clinic and the Field.* Edited by Wendy Welch. 2014

36. *The Rhetoric of Appalachian Identity.* Todd Snyder. 2014

37. *African American and Cherokee Nurses in Appalachia: A History, 1900–1965.* Phoebe Ann Pollitt. 2016

38. *A Hospital for Ashe County: Four Generations of Appalachian Community Health Care.* Janet C. Pittard. 2016

39. *Dwight Diller: West Virginia Mountain Musician.* Lewis M. Stern. 2016

40. *The Brown Mountain Lights: History, Science and Human Nature Explain an Appalachian Mystery.* Wade Edward Speer. 2017

41. *Richard L. Davis and the Color Line in Ohio Coal: A Hocking Valley Mine Labor Organizer, 1862–1900.* Frans H. Doppen. 2016

42. *The Silent Appalachian: Wordless Mountaineers in Fiction, Film and Television.* Vicki Sigmon Collins. 2017

43. *The Trees of Ashe County, North Carolina.* Doug Munroe. 2017

44. *Melungeon Portraits: Exploring Kinship and Identity.* Tamara L. Stachowicz. 2018

45. *Always Been a Rambler: G.B. Grayson and Henry Whitter, Country Music Pioneers of Southern Appalachia.* Josh Beckworth. 2018

46. *Tommy Thompson: New-Timey String Band Musician.* Lewis M. Stern. 2019

47. *Appalachian Fiddler Albert Hash: The Last Leaf on the Tree.* Malcolm L. Smith with Edwin Lacy. 2020

48. *Junaluska: Oral Histories of a Black Appalachian Community.* Edited by Susan E. Keefe with the Junaluska Heritage Association. 2020

49. *Boone Before Boone: The Archaeological Record of Northwestern North Carolina Through 1769.* Tom Whyte. 2020

50. *From the Front Lines of the Appalachian Addiction Crisis: Healthcare Providers Discuss Opioids, Meth and Recovery.* Edited by Wendy Welch. 2020

51. *Writers by the River: Reflections on 40+ Years of the Highland Summer Conference.* Edited by Donia S. Eley and Grace Toney Edwards. 2021

52. *Wayne Howard: Old Time Music, the Hammons Family and Mountain Lore.* Lewis M. Stern. 2021

53. *Lost Cove, North Carolina: Portrait of a Vanished Appalachian Community, 1864–1957* Christy A. Smith. 2022

54. *LeConte Lodge: A Centennial History of a Smoky Mountain Landmark.* Tom Layton and Mike Hembree. 2024

55. *D.D. Dougherty, Lillie Dougherty and the Early Years of Appalachian State.* Doris Perry Stam 2024

56. *Southern Mountain Music: The Collected Writings of Wayne Erbsen.* Wayne Erbsen. 2025

LeConte Lodge

*A Centennial History
of a Smoky Mountain Landmark*

TOM LAYTON *and*
MIKE HEMBREE

CONTRIBUTIONS TO
SOUTHERN APPALACHIAN STUDIES, 54

McFarland & Company, Inc., Publishers
Jefferson, North Carolina

ISBN (print) 978-1-4766-9603-4
ISBN (ebook) 978-1-4766-5454-6

Library of Congress cataloging data are available

Library of Congress Control Number 2024056594

© 2025 Tom Layton and Mike Hembree. All rights reserved

No part of this book may be reproduced or transmitted in any form or by any means, electronic or mechanical, including photocopying or recording, or by any information storage and retrieval system, without permission in writing from the publisher.

Front cover image: The 1939 dining hall built by Jack Huff is at the heart of the LeConte Lodge campus. The cabin on the left was built by Huff for his 1934 honeymoon (photograph by John Northrup).

Printed in the United States of America

*McFarland & Company, Inc., Publishers
Box 611, Jefferson, North Carolina 28640
www.mcfarlandpub.com*

LeContents

Acknowledgments	ix
Preface: A Roaring Twenties Birth Certificate	1
Introduction: Shrine of the Smokies	3
1. A High Calling and a Hermit's Job	13
2. A Man, His Mountain and His Mom	32
3. Almost a Motor Lodge	54
4. Extinction? Almost Lost in the Wilderness	80
5. Storms of the Century	91
6. Tragedy and Thanksgiving	101
7. "Ain't no mountain high enough"	108
8. From Moonshine to Moonshots	120
9. Llamas, Canines and Bears	141
10. How Does LeConte Measure Up?	153
11. The GOATs of Le Conte	166
Who's Who: A Biographical Index	181
Your Personal Logbook	189
References	193
Index	195

Acknowledgments

Hiking across mountains, up library steps, and into living rooms, we assembled a wealth of information and interviews to tell the story of LeConte Lodge. Along the way, we encountered many individuals who shared details about LeConte Lodge and deepened our understanding of the Smokies' most beloved mountain. You could call it our own personal Tour de Le Conte.

We are especially grateful to:

The proprietors and managers of LeConte Lodge, including John Northrup, Tim and Lisa Line, Jim Huff, Jr., and Myrtle Brown, plus Cookie Bowling, Neil Huff, and Barbara Brown Lindsey, who were raised at the lodge.

Cover designer Cameron Thorp for his expertise and his touch.

Our publisher McFarland, who believed in this book.

The photographers who were so generous with their images, especially Anne Thompson, great-granddaughter of photographer Jim Thompson, who frequented Mount Le Conte since the days of Paul Adams. Also, the guys at Up N' Adam Adventures (Adam Gravett, Adam Williamson, and Adam Ozment, plus "honorary Adam," Chris Maulden), Bennie Braden, Dewey Slusher, and lodge manager John Northrup for contributing photographs.

Our newspaper colleagues, including the late Dot Jackson, a gifted story-teller who reported so eloquently on the Wilderness Act debate that transformed the lodge in the 1970s; Tim Peeler, for ferreting out the story of "History's Most Significant Man" (Chapter 11); and the late Carson Brewer, sage of the Smokies, who wrote the first draft of LeConte history in the pages of the *Knoxville News-Sentinel*.

The keepers of the lodge blog, HighonLeConte.com, who have documented mountaintop tales since 2010.

Ash Walsh and Scott Gaskin for technical assistance with LeContest.com.

Ron Valentine and Ed Wright for their meticulous hiking records. Wright not only detailed his hikes but also preserved those of his peers, especially Paul Dinwiddie, Margaret Stevenson, and Tillroe Smith. Also, all the other pilgrims of Le Conte—those who not only keep climbing but also keep count, and especially those who share updates with LeContest.com (including Larry Russell, Tim Webb, Steve Odom, Steve Oliphant, Sandy Martin, Melissa Coatney, Tim Massey, P-Nut Clarkson, and Dewey Slusher).

Libby Kephart Hargrave, great-granddaughter of Horace Kephart.

Librarians and their archives, especially the University of Tennessee Libraries;

the Special Collections at Belk Library (Appalachian State University); Hunter Library Special and Digital Collections (Western Carolina University); and the King Family Library in Sevierville.

Archivists Michael Aday of the Great Smoky Mountains National Park Archives in Townsend, Tennessee, and Joanna Bouldin of the Calvin M. McClung Collection, East Tennessee History Center, Knoxville.

Peter Barr and Rick Shortt, our intrepid trail guides. Peter's tome, *Exploring North Carolina's Lookout Towers*, was an inspiration for this one.

Smoky Mountains Hiking Club, Knoxville, Tennessee. Happy centennial to you guys, too!

Fellow hikers who shared trails, meals, and good times on Le Conte, especially our loving and patient wives, Polly Hembree and Mary Layton, who not only walked extra miles with us but also have given us grace through the late nights and long hours associated with research and writing.

Preface

A Roaring Twenties Birth Certificate

When is the birthdate of LeConte Lodge? More than a year or a date, it's a riddle. The lodge sold T-shirts in 2024 that commemorate the 100th year of guest accommodations, but the 100th birthday party is planned for 2025. If you asked the founders, Paul Adams would have said 1925 and Jack Huff 1926. There's nothing wrong with those claims.

Yet without a series of events that began on Mount Le Conte in 1924, we might not have a national park in the Smokies—much less the lodge.

In 1924, the Great Smoky Mountains Conservation Association commissioned Adams, a 22-year-old naturalist, to host a mountaintop expedition for a federal national park commission. August 8–9, 2024, marked the centennial of that auspicious hike, which laid the groundwork for the park as well as the lodge.

In 1925, Adams discovered Basin Spring, pitched a canvas tent, and welcomed hikers to spend the night on beds cushioned with fragrant but bristly balsam boughs. So 2024 was indeed the 100th year of guest lodging on the mountaintop. Accompanied by his dog Smoky Jack, Paul became the first person to spend a winter on the mountaintop as he worked on a crude log cabin.

In 1926, Huff, also 22, the son of a Gatlinburg innkeeper, replaced Adams on Le Conte and began building the timber-and-stone campus we know today. As he opened a 32-bed bunkhouse, he hung a sign over the front door naming it "LeConte Lodge." Neither of those original cabins lasted 20 years, but the lodge itself grew and prevailed.

In 1934, Jack completed what is now called the "Old Cabin," where he and Pauline honeymooned after a sunrise wedding at Myrtle Point. Today, this cabin is not only the oldest structure at LeConte Lodge, but it also ranks among the oldest public accommodations in the entire national park system.[1]

That same year, on June 15, Congress formally authorized the development of the Great Smoky Mountains National Park. Consequently, the lodge had a long head start on the park.

---

1. Older national park inns in the East are Charit Creek Lodge (1817) in Tennessee's Big South Fork National Recreation Area; Skyland Lodge (1895) in Virginia's Shenandoah National Park; and Greyfield Inn (1900) at Georgia's Cumberland Island National Seashore. Charit Creek (90 miles northwest of Knoxville) once was managed by LeConte Lodge. The oldest park inns nationwide are Volcano House (1846) in the Hawaii Volcanoes National Park; Lake Yellowstone Hotel (1891) and Old Faithful Inn (1904) in Yellowstone; and El Tovar Hotel (1905) at the Grand Canyon.

Adams wrote two enchanting books about the founding years, Huff inspired a bluegrass ballad, and the lodge became a bucket-list destination—where hikers have crossed paths with astronauts, authors, movie stars, and sports heroes. Where else can you feast on such glorious sunrises, sunsets, rainbows, and family-style fellowship?

Over the course of a century, tall tales and adventures have accumulated like snowdrifts around LeConte Lodge. We've been making the hike for 40 years, and it's our pleasure to guide you through the legends and introduce you to some of the personalities who have flocked to the crown jewel of the Great Smokies.

Introduction

Shrine of the Smokies

One hundred years ago, the Great Smoky Mountains might as well have been the Great Wall of the Southeast, feared by flatlanders as the impenetrable lair of deadly rattlesnakes, belligerent bears, ghostly panthers, indomitable Cherokees, and feuding moonshiners.

Pigeon Forge had no hotels and was little more than a gristmill. Gatlinburg was more of a dead-end than a destination, because the roads didn't go much farther.[1] Sightseeing was not yet our national pastime.

Folks in eastern Tennessee recognized gigantic Mount Le Conte from a distance but rarely came close enough to visit. "Neither the white man nor the Indian hunter venture in this wilderness," wrote Arnold Guyot, a Princeton professor who surveyed Mount Le Conte before the Civil War.

"Few people have ever scaled it," said the *Knoxville Journal* in 1924, "and thousands of people have been born and reared under its very shadow, who have never tried to ascend it."[2]

Yet when the Great Smoky Mountains National Park was proposed in the 1920s, it was Mount Le Conte—not Cades Cove nor Clingmans Dome—that became the centerpiece of the campaign or, as naturalist Laura Thornburgh put it, "the shrine of the park's enthusiasts."[3]

Paul Adams, one of the founders of LeConte Lodge, called Le Conte "the most beautiful mountain in America." From the perspective of a preacher's kid, he considered the mountain a crowning achievement of creation: "Mount LeConte lies about four miles north of the state-line crest of the Great Smokies. It is as if the Maker of Mountains decided, as an afterthought, to build a spectacular annex."

Stephen Mather, the original director of the National Park Service, described Mount Le Conte as "one of the great mountain personalities of America." Horace

---

1. A 1933 guide published by the national park listed only two hotels in Gatlinburg and none in Pigeon Forge.
2. "Four Members of Park Commission Will Go on Tour," *Knoxville Journal & Tribune*, Aug. 6, 1924.
3. Mount Le Conte was not included in the original park proposal (probably out of deference to the timber owners) and was added in 1926 during negotiations among Secretary of the Interior Frank Maloney, Arno Cammerer of the National Park Service, Glenn Smith of the Great Smoky Mountains Conservation Association, and Tennessee senators Kenneth McKellar and Lawrence Tyson, who called Le Conte "the grandest mountain in the country." George H. Manning, "May Include Mt. Leconte in the National Park," *Johnson City Chronicle*, Dec. 19, 1926.

Albright, Mather's successor, visited LeConte Lodge in 1930 and declared the mountain to be "of national park grandeur," comparable in terms of "classic beauty" to national landmarks such as Pikes Peak, Mount Whitney, and Mount Rainier.

In 1925, the Great Smoky Mountains Conservation Association published a 32-page booklet to promote the natural wonders on Tennessee's horizon. "Almost at our door, though still without names and less known than the mountains of India or Tibet, seven majestic peaks in the Great Smokies rise to altitudes of more than six thousand feet. Eleven others are as high."[4]

Unreached by roads and unscathed by loggers, Mount Le Conte was way beyond the range of tourists—until the spontaneous development of LeConte Lodge during the Roaring Twenties.

Back when Prohibition was the law of the land, 14 years before President Franklin D. Roosevelt dedicated the Great Smoky Mountains National Park, LeConte Lodge was a log bunkhouse with a dirt floor and a tar-paper roof, carved out of a boreal forest owned by a North Carolina paper mill. Over the decades, it became a destination for adventurers, researchers, and romantics.

Leo Hershfield, a Tennessean working for the *New York Times* in the 1930s, offered this perspective on the Smokies:

> Twenty-five years ago, Le Conte was in the heart of a district as remote from the rest of the world as the middle of Mongolia. Therefore, if you are one of those hardy souls who have breathed the rarefied atmosphere of that mountain top, you may, with this writer's permission, wear a feather in your cap (after the manner of Swiss highlanders), carry a gold-tipped alpenstock and yodel from any peak the information that you are an amazing amateur mountaineer of high attainment; for, after all, isn't Le Conte one of the highest pinnacles east of the Rockies?[5]

Not only were the Smokies inaccessible by road, but getting from Knoxville to Gatlinburg in 1912 took two days by horse and buggy. Early Le Conte climbers took the train to Elkmont and then faced a six-mile bushwhack.

The Smokies became a hermitage for Horace Kephart, a restless librarian who left St. Louis and settled in a cabin on the North Carolina side of the Smokies, where he became a renowned outdoorsman and an unofficial ambassador for the national park movement. "When I prepared in 1904 for my first sojourn in the Great Smoky Mountains, which form the master chain of the Appalachian system, I could find in no library a guide to that region," he wrote. "Had I been going to Teneriffe or Timbuctu, the libraries would have furnished information aplenty; but about this housetop of Eastern America they were silent: It was *terra incognita*."[6]

---

4. *Our National Park*, The Great Smoky Mountains Conservation Association, 1925. Once the Smokies were surveyed, 12 peaks in the park made the South Beyond 6,000 list. Five of the "sixers" were still unnamed on the park's 1940 map.

5. Leo Hershfield, "An Idyll of the Great Smokies," *Chattanooga Times*, Sept. 2, 1934.

6. "Glories of Great Smokies Described in New Booklet," *Knoxville Sunday Journal*, Nov. 29, 1925. Kephart (1862–1931) did his best to bring the Smokies into libraries, as he wrote and published *Camping and Woodcraft* in 1907 and *Our Southern Highlanders* in 1913. The oldest published reference to "Mount Le Conte" in the newspapers.com archives is a letter from surveyor Samuel Buckley in the *Greensboro Patriot* in 1858.

Kephart never made it to the summit of Mount Le Conte, but on the opening page of *Our Southern Highlanders*, he dared his readers to lofty explorations with this quote from Rudyard Kipling: "Something hidden. Go and find it."[7]

Some mountaineers thought Le Conte might be the tallest mountain in eastern America (see Chapter 10), because of the way it towers so prominently a mile above Gatlinburg. That turned out to be an optical illusion—surveys found it shorter by 28 feet vs. Mount Guyot, 50 vs. Clingmans Dome, and 91 vs. Mount Mitchell—but those incremental feet did nothing to diminish the mountain that came to be known as the "Crown of the Smokies."

Le Conte or LeConte?

Should there be a space in the name? It depends—are you referring to the mountain, the lodge, or the family? Mount Le Conte (with a space) is the legal name of the mountain, according to the U.S. Board on Geographic Names. LeConte Lodge® (without a space) is the trademarked name of the inn. The National Park Service registered the trademark in 2011 and licenses it to the lodge for use on promotional materials and souvenirs.

When the Le Conte brothers were born (John in 1818 and Joseph in 1823), their family name was spelled with a space.[8] John LeConte eventually eliminated the space from his surname, as did Joseph's son, "Little Joe" LeConte, who succeeded John Muir in 1915 as president of the Sierra Club. Also, the space has disappeared from the name of the family homeplace, the LeConte-Woodmanston Plantation and Botanical Gardens near Riceboro, Georgia. Yet Joseph always spelled his name with a space. The Le Contes were of Huguenot descent.[9] In this case, the name may refer to their ancestral hometown in eastern France. In other cases, *le conte* can be a title, as in "count," or it may refer to a fable.

Speaking of fables, have you heard the one about how Arnold Guyot named the mountain in honor of Joseph Le Conte? That myth was debunked in 1998 by Smokies historian Ken Wise.[10] It's more likely that Guyot's associate, Samuel Buckley, bestowed the name as a token of thanks to Professor John LeConte for bringing a dependable barometer to help measure the peaks.

During an 1858 survey, John LeConte stayed at Colonel Joseph Cathey's farm at the Forks of the Pigeon River upstream from Canton, North Carolina, and monitored a stationary barometer to calibrate the mountaintop readings by Buckley and Thomas Clingman. In an 1858 letter to Clingman, John wrote that he calculated the

---

7. Horace Kephart, *Our Southern Highlanders*, 1913. Rudyard Kipling, *The Five Nations*, 1903.

8. The space was also omitted in the original name of the LeConte Memorial Lodge in California's Yosemite National Park. That lodge (actually a visitor center that does not accommodate overnight guests) was built in 1903 in memory of Joseph Le Conte, who died during a Yosemite hike in 1901. (The Yosemite lodge was renamed in 2016 because of Le Conte's association with slavery.)

9. The Huguenots were Protestants who came to the New World as refugees from France. Their descendants included Paul Revere, Davy Crockett, and Humphrey Bogart.

10. Ken Wise and Ron Petersen, *A Natural History of Mount Le Conte* (Knoxville: University of Tennessee Press, 1998), p. xxv.

The discrepancy between the spelling of Mount Le Conte and LeConte Lodge goes back to Jack Huff's original cabin, where he omitted the space on the sign over the door. The only space Huff worried about was the gap between the logs, which he chinked with moss and oxalis that were ice-coated in this scene, as demonstrated in this photo from 1929 (photograph by Dutch Roth, from the Albert "Dutch" Roth Photograph Collection, University of Tennessee Libraries).

elevations "based on the data furnished by the barometric observations of yourself, Mr. Buckley, and myself."[11]

Guyot and Joseph Le Conte were absent from the 1858 survey. Guyot (pronounced GHEE-oh) was a Swiss-born professor of geography at Princeton College who explored, mapped, and measured the mountains of eastern America. In 1856 and 1859, he surveyed many of the peaks in and around the Smokies. In a report in the *Asheville News* in 1860, he listed the mountains he had measured, including "Mt. Lecompte," a misnomer that implies a lack of acquaintance with the brothers.[12]

In Joseph Le Conte's 1901 memoirs, he included a photo labeled Le Conte Dome (the Yosemite peak now known as Half Dome), but he made no mention of a namesake mountain back East. In his role with the Confederate Niter and Mining Bureau, he said he visited all the niter caves in Georgia, Alabama, and Tennessee, so he may have investigated Alum Cave looking for saltpeter.[13] If so, that was probably the only time he set foot on the slopes of Mount Le Conte.

Joseph Le Conte was hailed in his generation as the greatest scientist the South ever produced, so it was no wonder that his name became associated with a great mountain. Buckley missed a chance to settle the question in 1859 when he wrote about the Smokies in the *American Journal of Science* and cryptically acknowledged "Prof. J. Le Conte of Columbia, S.C.," without specifying the first name.[14]

John LeConte was not without credentials. Trained as a medical doctor, he explored the Grand Canyon, the Great Lakes, and Central America. He became the founding president of the University of California—the *Macon Telegraph* called him "the father of the University of California"[15]—and also founded the American Entomological Society. Following Guyot's 1859 survey, John LeConte asserted that "Smoky Mountain" (probably referring to Clingmans Dome) reached 6,737 feet and outranked North Carolina's Mount Mitchell as the highest mountain east of the Rockies.[16]

Yet John was overshadowed by his younger brother Joseph, who followed him to California in 1869 aboard the brand-new transcontinental railroad. The *Knoxville Sentinel* wrote in 1922: "Mount Le Conte is named for Professor Joseph Le Conte, for years professor of geology at the University of California, whose work, entitled

---

11. *The Semi-Weekly Standard*, Raleigh, NC, Nov. 23, 1858. John LeConte calculated Clingmans Dome at 6,744 (compared to the modern measurement of 6,643). LeConte also reported "Jackson Peak (across the Tennessee line)" at 6,622. Based on the description, it seems likely that he was referring to the peak we call Mount Le Conte.

12. Arnold Guyot, "Guyot's Measurements of the Mountains of Western N.C.," *Asheville News*, July 18, 1860. Guyot measured Black Dome (Mount Mitchell) at 6,737 feet; Clingmans Dome at 6,600; Mount Guyot at 6,636; and Lecompte at 6,612.

13. Niter is potassium nitrate, an ingredient of gunpowder. In the 19th century, a rough road to the bluff was cleared by miners looking for saltpeter. Most of the excavations turned out to be epsom salts, which were sold for medicinal purposes.

14. Buckley wanted to put his own name on the highest peak in the Smokies, but Guyot insisted that it be named for Thomas Clingman, who funded the Smokies expedition and later became a U.S. senator and a Confederate general. Buckley letter, *Greensboro Patriot*, March 11, 1859. The names of Buckley and Samuel Love were given to subpeaks on the shoulders of Clingmans Dome.

15. H.B. Folsom, "LeConte Brothers, Founders of the University of California, are Gift of Georgia to Education," *Macon Telegraph*, Aug. 2, 1925. While John was a professor at the University of South Carolina, he wrote a definitive treatise on physics that was lost when Sherman's troops burned Columbia in 1865.

16. *The National Era*, Oct. 20, 1859.

'Mountain Building,' is the standard work on that subject today. Professor Le Conte did splendid work in determining the ages and methods of formation of the various mountain groups of this country and it is only fitting that this majestic peak should stand as a perpetual monument to his memory."[17]

As a charter member of the Sierra Club, Joseph Le Conte was also a distinguished conservationist. At the 1940 dedication of the Great Smoky Mountains National Park, park service director Newton Drury called Joseph "one of the most distinguished scholars and scientists in America, and one of those who, like John Muir, first brought the American people to realize the importance of preserving the beauties of mountains and forests and all the features of the native landscape."[18]

All of that certainly made Joseph a worthy namesake, but the park founders had an ulterior motive to honor him. As the Great Smoky Mountain Conservation Association was scrambling to raise funds to acquire park land in Tennessee, chairman David Chapman pursued a significant donation in memory of Joseph Le Conte.

National park proponents David Chapman and Horace Kephart believed the mountain was named for John Le Conte, as this telegram shows. The handwritten notes are presumably by Chapman after consulting with the Library of Congress (Great Smoky Mountains National Park Archives).

---

17. John Ogden Morrell, "Three Tops of Mount Le Conte Easily Visible from Knoxville; A Scenic Wonder of Smokies," *Knoxville Sentinel*, June 18, 1922.
18. Warner Ogden, "'Wonderful!' Exclaims Drury as Cars in Long Lines Wind Around LeConte," *Knoxville News-Sentinel*, Sept. 2, 1940.

Chapman asked Kephart if he could verify "that this mountain is named for Professor Joseph Le Conte." Kephart, who had assembled an encyclopedic knowledge of the Smokies, was certain Joseph was the rightful namesake, as he stated by telegram January 7, 1926.[19]

Uncertainty about the mountain's proper name was evident in Paul Adams' memoirs, published in 1966. The hand-drawn cover spelled the name as *MT. Le CONTE*, but the space disappeared on the typeset pages. Adams' spelling was often carefree,[20] and the space was probably superfluous to him. When Wise and Anne Bridges edited and republished Adams' book in 2017, they included the space in the mountain's name.

Huff, who married an English teacher and had an eye for detail, included a space in the lodge name in guest logbooks printed in the 1930s, though he kept the one-word spelling on his signs.

Knoxville newspapers have been inconsistent about the spelling. Pulitzer Prize-winning columnist Ernie Pyle made a precise distinction between "LeConte Lodge" in his dateline and "Mt. Le Conte" in his account of his 1940 visit (see Pyle's story in Chapter 2).

Even the national park has stumbled over the spacing: You will find a space on newer trail signs at Alum Cave (Mt. Le Conte Summit 2.7), Roaring Fork (Mt. Le Conte Summit 6.7), Rainbow Falls (Mt. Le Conte 6.6), and Trillium Gap (Mount Le Conte 3.8). But the space was omitted on other signs: the Alum Cave trailhead (Mt. LeConte 5.0), the Boulevard–Appalachian Trail junction (Mt. LeConte 5.3), Bullhead (Mt. LeConte 6.4), Brushy Mountain (Mount LeConte 8.1), and Porters Creek (Mount LeConte 9.1).[21]

This history uses both spellings, depending on the context. Quoted material—such as newspaper clippings, letters, and books—reflects the usage in the original publication.

Frog-town: A New Old Name?

Mount Le Conte's neighbor was officially renamed in September 2024. The U.S. Board on Geographic Names voted to restore the Cherokee name Kuwohi to the peak that has been known for more than a century as Clingmans Dome.

The name is ᎫᏬᎯ in the Cherokee syllabary and translates into English as "Mulberry Place." In an application requesting the name change, Cherokee chief Mitchell Hicks wrote: "This mountain has special significance to Cherokees. It

---

19. Henry Gannett (1846–1914) was the chief geographer for the United States Geological Service and was the namesake for Gannett Peak, the highest mountain in Wyoming. He dealt with Mount Le Conte when he wrote Bulletin 258 for the U.S. Geological Survey, *Origin of Certain Place Names*. Gannett omitted the space and accepted the premise that the mountain was named for geologist Joseph Le Conte.

20. "Paul talked better than he wrote," according to Carson Brewer, who edited the manuscript. *Knoxville News-Sentinel*, Dec. 17, 1978.

21. Most trail signs show the mileage to trail junctions rather than specifically to the lodge or the mountaintop. Exceptions are at the Myrtle Point-Boulevard junction (LeConte Lodge 0.7), the Alum-Rainbow junction (LeConte Lodge 0.1), and the Trillium-Boulevard junction (Mt LeConte Shelter 0.2). Many of the original park signs were lettered by Wiley Oakley's son, Harvey (1918–2007).

Long before the name was copyrighted, the iconic sign over the dining-room door spelled the name "LeConte Lodge," as shown in this photo from 1966. The office was in the dining room until the new office opened in 1971. The sign became a photo-op after dates were added about 1990 (courtesy Buzz Tatham).

was visited by medicine people who prayed and sought guidance from the Creator regarding important matters facing Cherokee people."

Kuwohi is the highest point visible from the Qualla Boundary, the Cherokee homeland on the North Carolina side of the Smokies.

The tribe has not challenged the name of Mount Le Conte, which the Cherokee called Walasi'yi, which means "Frog-town."

Clingmans Dome was named for Thomas Clingman (1812–1897), a North Carolinian who explored the Smokies before he became a general in the Confederate army. Clingman defended slavery as a U.S. senator, until he was expelled from Congress at the start of the Civil War. He helped fund the survey trips of Arnold Guyot, whom the Cherokees scorned for "scientific racism."

Like Clingman, the Le Conte brothers were sons of the antebellum South, came from slave-holding families, and held white-supremacist beliefs. Disillusioned by the prospects of Reconstruction following the Civil War, the brothers left the University of South Carolina and became professors at the University of California. In recent years, California has removed the Le Conte name from several landmarks, including the LeConte Memorial Lodge, a visitor center in Yosemite National Park.

Before the mountain was named Le Conte, early white settlers called it Bullhead, describing the profile of the ridge as seen from the Sugarlands. A member of Guyot's survey team, S.B. Buckley, originally mapped it as "Mount Jackson"—probably a nod to Andrew Jackson, the first Tennessean elected president.

Guyot reported no trace of the Cherokees on his explorations of what became Mount Le Conte. Kenneth Wise and Ronald Peterson wrote in *A Natural History of Mount Le Conte*: "It's doubtful that the mountain played a significant role in the culture of nearby tribes."

1

A High Calling and a Hermit's Job

When Paul Adams was growing up as a preacher's kid on the Illinois prairie, his whole world felt flat. Then his family took a vacation in the Ozark Mountains of Missouri. "There I climbed my first mountain and fished my first fast river," he wrote. "I wanted to stay forever."

Imagine the excitement he must have felt when his father answered God's call to become a missionary in the Southern Appalachians, working to improve mountain schools as a field secretary for the Presbyterian home mission board. In 1915, the Rev. Clair Stark Adams[1] moved his family to Burnsville, North Carolina (where teen-aged Paul explored Mount Mitchell), and they later settled in Knoxville, Tennessee (where he was enticed by views of towering Mount Le Conte).

Paul, the eldest of three children, grew up to become an Eagle Scout and an expert on birds, shellfish, and butterflies. He dropped out of the University of Tennessee for health reasons, yet the school employed him as a student instructor in bird life. So did Camp LeConte, a Boy Scout retreat adjacent to the Wonderland Hotel in Elkmont, two valleys west of Mount Le Conte.

Doctors recommended plenty of fresh air, so Adams took a job with florist Brockway Crouch and spent his days off exploring the Smoky Mountains. "I started learning the mountains in detail starting at the southwestern end and slowly working northeastward until I reached Davenport Gap," he wrote in his book, *MT. Le CONTE*. "Many of the main ridges were trail-less, so I learned them by trial and error."

Adams was just 16 when he first climbed Mount Le Conte in 1918. He subsequently explored as far north as the Shenandoah Mountains of Virginia, which prepared him well for his own mountain calling. In his case, the call came in 1924 from David Chapman, who invited Adams, 22, to join the Great Smoky Mountains Conservation Association in the campaign to establish a national park in Tennessee.

"The other members of the group were older, wiser, and considerably wealthier than I," Adams recalled. "When I mentioned this to him, he laughed and told me

---

1. The Rev. Clair Stark Adams (1862–1938) was a Presbyterian pastor in Paxton, Illinois, when his first son Paul was born in 1901. He later served churches in Bement, Illinois, 1904–15, Burnsville, North Carolina, 1915–18, and Alpine, Tennessee, 1926–38. He devoted Sunday afternoons to taking his children on nature walks and bird-watching expeditions.

that I would not have to be a paying member of the group. He said my knowledge of the mountains and my ability to carry my own provisions and live in the highlands would make me a valuable member of the organization."

Chapman sensed that Adams—being well traveled if not well heeled—could bring some trail credibility to the association. Specifically, Chapman trusted Adams to show off the Smokies to officials scouting the Southeast for a potential national park.

The "colonel," as Chapman was nicknamed for his stateside Army service during the Spanish-American War, was tough (he played football for the University of Tennessee in the unbridled 1890s era), resourceful (he inherited and managed a prosperous wholesale pharmacy business on Gay Street in downtown Knoxville), and charismatic. After Chapman died in 1944, local newspapers called him the "Father of the Great Smoky Mountains National Park."

As Carlos Campbell pointed out in his book, *Birth of a National Park in the Great Smoky Mountains*, Chapman might be better described as the foster father. The park was conceived by Anne and Willis P. Davis as they returned to Knoxville from a vacation in Yellowstone National Park.

David Chapman (center) from the Great Smoky Mountain Conservation Association meets with Horace Albright (left) and Arno Cammerer from the National Park Service, May 24, 1930 (Russell W. Hanlon Jr. Collection, McClung Historical Collection, East Tennessee Historical Society).

"Why can't we have a national park in the Smokies?" she wondered out loud. On that platform, she became the third woman elected to the Tennessee legislature, sponsored funds for the original purchase of land, and became known as "Mother of the Park."

Her husband (president of the Knoxville Iron Company) pitched the park concept to Hubert Work, secretary of the interior under President Warren G. Harding, and organized the Great Smoky Mountains Conservation Association, with Chapman as vice-chairman. There was already some talk of establishing a national park in the Southeast, and Virginia had a head start with its vision for the Shenandoah Mountains.

Chapman deputized Adams as the association's field secretary (the same title Paul's dad held in his noble outreach for the Presbyterians). Adams promised to do everything he could to promote the park movement. Though his assignment did not end happily, he accomplished Chapman's priority—to woo a national parks commission—and he established the mountaintop camp that became LeConte Lodge. Over the next two years, Adams hosted the first paying guests on Le Conte, cut the trail to Cliff Top, discovered Basin Spring, and became the first person to stay on the mountaintop all winter.

In 1924, Chapman traveled to Asheville, North Carolina, to solicit representatives of the Southern Appalachian National Park Commission, who had bypassed Tennessee as they evaluated possible locations for a new national park.

Massachusetts conservationist Harlan Kelsey was among the dignitaries who agreed to come see the Smokies. Kelsey was acquainted with the Southern Appalachians, as he had been president of the Appalachian Mountain Club in Boston in 1921, when a survey was commissioned to determine if Le Conte outranked Mount Mitchell as the highest mountain in eastern America (see Chapter 10), and his father was the founder of Highlands, a resort town atop the Blue Ridge in North Carolina.

The night before they climbed Le Conte, the commissioners stayed at the Mountain View Hotel in Gatlinburg, where they rubbed shoulders with innkeeper Andy Huff (and presumably his 21-year-old son Jack). Gatlinburg was still a rough settlement that had just opened its first school in 1912. In the hour before the commissioners checked in, a feud erupted into a shooting on the porch of a nearby store. "Probably over a still," the commissioners were told.[2]

Chapman wanted the commissioners to hear from Adams and Paul Fink, who had explored many of the Southeastern mountains that were also nominated for national parks—Grandfather Mountain and Linville Gorge in North Carolina, Roan Mountain along the Tennessee-Carolina border, and the Shenandoahs.

"We told them that all these places were beautiful," Adams said. "But we also told them that these did not compare with the Great Smokies for height of mountains, ruggedness, amount of virgin forest, lovely streams with cascades and waterfalls, and for having both grassy balds and timbered tops and slopes."

On a rainy Thursday, August 7, 1924, a group of 25 men—federal commissioners as well as local leaders—saddled up in Gatlinburg at 9:30 a.m. and rode horses for

---

2. L.W. Miller, "Famous Professors Laud Smokies to Party on Trip," *Knoxville News*, Aug. 12, 1924.

two hours up to Cherokee Orchard. Then they hiked up a freshly cleared path that was the forerunner of the Rainbow Falls Trail.[3]

They were hardly dressed for the wilderness or the weather. Some wore riding breeches with leggings or golf knickers with starched white dress shirts. Princeton professor Horace Longwell had the foresight to carry an umbrella. Newspaperman E.E. Burtt got soaked under his black felt hat, but an army campaign hat worked for World War I hero Cary Spence, as did a flat-brim straw skimmer for state forester R.S. Maddox.

Newspaperman Loye Miller described Chapman, 47, as the "Beau Brummel[4] of our party … caparisoned for the climb up LeConte in a flannel shirt barred in bright hues and with a kerchief of many colors knotted around his neck."

The delegation paused for lunch at Rainbow Falls. Burtt described the falls as "a miniature Niagara 75 to 100 feet high, the water running with a roar due to the heavy rains of the morning."[5]

Adams sized up the challenge before them: "Back then, one needed both strong arms and legs to gain the top of Rainbow Falls. The 'trail' went up a leaning tree near the bluff, about 100 feet west of the falls. Helpers at the base of the tree helped some of our less agile guests reach the first tree branches. Others at the top helped them from the tree branches to solid ground. But everyone had to climb the middle distance under his own power."

Above the falls, the original trail rock-hopped along Mill Creek, which is now known as Le Conte Creek. The hikers reached Cliff Top about 4 p.m. after ascending four miles in six and a half hours. "Far below, a panorama of clouds enveloped the mountain," Burtt wrote.

From Cliff Top, they scrambled down to a camp along the ridgeline toward West Point. The Alum Cave Bluff Trail did not yet exist, but the camp was near what upbound hikers call the Hallelujah Turn—where the trail crests and crosses the ridgeline, leaving an easy flat stroll to the lodge. Guide Wiley Oakley chose the location to take advantage of rainwater trickling off the rock ledges. Adams was certain there was a better spring nearby, but Oakley (raised at the foot of Mount Le Conte in a hollow called Scratch Britches) insisted that none of the Smokies had substantial springs near the top. The 1925 discovery of that spring would dictate the location for LeConte Lodge.

John Morrell, who was a law student when he first climbed Le Conte in 1913, described the campsite:

---

3. The national park commission included two Mayflower descendants—New Jersey's William A. Welch, 55, and Boston's Kelsey, 52. Others appointed by Secretary of the Interior Hubert Work were Pennsylvania congressman Henry Temple, 60; USGS engineer Colonel George Smith, 53; and Princeton professor Horace Longwell, 31. Representing the Smoky Mountains Conservation Association were Dr. R.N. Kesterson, 66; Willis P. Davis, 64; Carey Spence, 55; Gatlinburg mayor Wiley Brownlee, 54; David Chapman, 47; Jack Fisher, 45; Frank Maloney, 45; Si Sehorn, 40; Wiley Oakley, 38; Paul Fink, 32; Russell Hanlon, 31; and John Ogden Morrell, 23; Paul Adams, 22. Also on the trip were state forester R.S. Maddox, 48; state geologist Wilbur Nelson, 35; and several journalists, including *National Geographic*'s Milton Ailes, 57. "Park Commission Party Leaves on Inspection Tour," *Knoxville Journal & Tribune*, Aug. 7, 1924.

4. Beau Brummell (1778–1840) was a European dandy portrayed by John Barrymore in a 1924 silent movie.

5. E.E. Burtt, "Seasoned Hiker Finds Scaling of Towering Le Conte a Day's Work," *Knoxville Journal & Tribune*, Aug. 11, 1924.

1. A High Calling and a Hermit's Job

On the first of 120 Le Conte climbs, Dutch Roth visited the lean-to where the national park commissioners had stayed just a few weeks earlier. Roth had wired a remote trigger to his camera to take "selfies"; this one is from 1924, and he is at right, wearing the "21" shirt (photograph by Dutch Roth, from the Albert "Dutch" Roth Photograph Collection, University of Tennessee Libraries).

> A bark lean-to camp was erected just under the west end of Cliff Top of Le Conte about 1922. My guess is this was built by W.R. (Will) Ramsey and Wiley Oakley under direction of Andy Huff, as a camp for men he had swamping out and improving the old Rainbow Falls Trail to Le Conte.
> This camp was used as an overnight stay by the commissioners appointed by the Secretary of the Interior to ascertain whether the Smokies came up to national park standards as regards to scenery. The site was later abandoned, however, on account of an inadequate water supply.

Morrell cooked the meals and must have made a good impression—because he made his career in the park, and the headquarters building is named for him. "We had delicious baked beans, along with baked potatoes and ham for supper," Adams wrote.

The commissioners shared beds padded with balsam boughs, as a chilly rain fell all night and wild animals screeched in the darkness. Some guests had a sleepless night as they wondered: Was that an owl? Or a panther?

The temperature had been 66 when the commissioners left Knoxville but it was 52 at supper and dipped to 40 overnight. The coffee kettle was especially popular, and Russell Hanlon asked for donations of a dollar per cup, raising $25 in cold cash for the Great Smoky Mountains Conservation Association. In the long run, that would be enough to cover the average cost of an acre of park land.

Chapman worried that the overcast weather would ruin the sunrise panorama that he wanted to show off for the national park delegation.

Eastern Tennessee was then in the Central Time Zone, so the night passed quickly and sunrise on Friday, August 8, felt early. Adams woke up the camp with steaming coffee, bundled the VIPs in blankets, and lit lanterns to guide them through a dark fog toward Myrtle Point, the 6,534-foot promontory on the eastern flank of Le Conte.

As the commissioners arrived at Myrtle Point, the eastern clouds drew back like stage curtains, and they were treated to a dramatic cloud inversion that filled the valleys like a rippled bay, fringed by violet-colored ridges all the way to the horizon. Here is how Adams described it:

> The sky overhead was clear. But we looked down on billowing tops of thunderheads in the valleys. A south breeze touched us lightly. We knew that stronger winds were at work below us.
>
> Through a moderate haze in the east, we could see Mt. Guyot. And then the sun, a ball of red fire, rose over Guyot. Its rays sprinkled splendor on the cloud tops below us.
>
> The winds in the clouds grew more restless and began to agitate them more violently. Great chunks of clouds began to rip loose from the main mass and rise a thousand feet. As they arose, they sometimes briefly blocked the sun. A constant wind picked up those cloud chunks and hustled them off to the northeast.
>
> We were small spectators, awe-struck by the vast, primitive, beauty of an extra-special Myrtle Point sunrise.

From where the dignitaries stood, there was no doubt that they had found a worthy national park.

Unfortunately, cameras failed to capture the spectacle. A movie crew from Pennsylvania accompanied the commission, but instead of filming, it appears that they were flimflamming. They billed Southern merchants for the opportunity to promote their towns and businesses on the silver screen. However, no newsreel footage was ever seen, and the president of the company was convicted of mail fraud in 1940 and sentenced to a year in the federal penitentiary.[6]

The *Knoxville News-Sentinel* reported on how the moviemakers charmed their way into Knoxville society, including a golf outing at the Cherokee Country Club:

> They told society girls at the club that they would get them into the movies. Therefore, the four young men in a short while became very popular with the young ladies. They took the ladies out riding, and the young ladies took the new visitors and moving picture "magnates" out in their cars.
>
> It was now about Aug. 1. Word was received that a national park commission was coming to Knoxville to make a tour of the Smokies. Wouldn't it be a fine thing if movies could be made of the Smokies, to be exhibited all over the country?
>
> Yes, the Smoky Mountain Conservation Association thought it would be fine. It wrote out a check for $450 in favor of the Keystone Industrial Film Corporation.
>
> Two of the cameramen, Henry Clay and Adolph Leitheiser, went along as members of the party to make the inspection tour. For five days they hiked, climbed, ate, smoked, and slept with other members of the party. Mountain guides carried the heavy cameras up and down

---

6. "H-m! What About This? 'Knoxville Movies' Haven't Flickered," *Knoxville News-Sentinel*, Nov. 22, 1924. The scam was widespread, as Johnson City, Tennessee, lost $3,500 and Lynchburg, Virginia, $1,500. The president of Keystone was convicted in 1940 of mail fraud in 11 cities and was sentenced to a year in the federal penitentiary. "Number of Cases in Federal Court," *St. Lucie [FL] News-Tribune*, Feb. 6, 1940.

LeConte, Clingmans Dome, Mt. Guyot, and down to Elkmont. The cameraman and the director were for five days buddies of Col. Dave Chapman, W.P. Davis, Gen. Cary F. Spence— all Knoxville business men—and Loye W. Miller, managing editor of *The Knoxville News*, who went along to report the survey.

Knoxville newspaper accounts included no photographs, only some sketches drawn by Burtt, including a cartoon of a falling man captioned, "Jack Fisher of Maryville poses for the movies."

In the absence of photos, Miller described the scene for newspaper readers in Knoxville. "To anyone who has never seen the view from Mt. Le Conte, let me say here that it cannot be conceived in mere imagination. Fancy yourself on the highest of a series of peaks, hundreds of them covered with dark green forest, jutting up sharply here and there, not in regular formation but right and left in angles and curves; everywhere, as far as the eye can see. That's the Smoky Mountains as you see them from Le Conte."

After interviewing Kelsey, who was an influential voice for the commission, Miller wrote: "The Smokies are far different in their relief than the Blue Ridge of the Carolinas and Virginia. The Blue Ridges are smooth and curved with a perfect contour; the Smokies are rugged and sharp, jutting out in spires and cones and pyramids. The Smokies remind one of the Gothic-style cathedrals of Europe as compared to the Blue Ridge, formed in the same arched architecture as the oriental temples and mosques."[7]

After breakfast back at the camp, the group headed down the trail-less south face of Le Conte toward Alum Cave. At the time, this was a steep and treacherous bushwhack. The commissioners started down through the myrtle bushes between Cliff Top and High Top, bypassing the cliff face that was impassable until ledges were blasted out in the 1930s.

A traveling movie crew was hired to film the national park commission's 1924 visit to Knoxville and the Smokies. Unfortunately, no images were ever produced (photograph by Jim Thompson, courtesy Thompson Photo Products).

---

7. L.W. Miller, "Sunrise on LeConte; Peaks Look Like Gothic-Style Cathedrals," *Knoxville News-Sentinel*, Aug. 14, 1924.

"At Alum Cave, about halfway down, we got another thrill," Miller wrote. "Here we descended a cliff at an angle of some 60 degrees, aided only by such bushes and rocks as we could grab on to. No one was hurt, but we wondered why. Everybody had to sit down and slide a bit. Farther down, we got into a dense wilderness. The going got harder. Those difficult gulches in the mountains are many times called 'hells.' I don't know whether this was a hell or not. It ought to be called somebody's hell." Miller said they saw no water until they reached the Little Pigeon River, so they may have missed the modern route along Styx Branch and Alum Cave Creek.

And when the commissioners finally got down to the old Indian Gap Road, the horses that were supposed to take them to their cars were nowhere to be seen. Andy Huff had sent the horses to Grassy Patch (the modern Alum Cave trailhead), but the wranglers misunderstood and went to Grassy Gap (an early name for Trillium Gap).

While the bone-tired VIPs trudged down the valley to board cars for the roundabout drive toward Elkmont, Adams (being familiar with local paths) hiked across Sugarland Mountain through Huskey Gap and beat the cars to Elkmont. He estimated he walked 30 miles that day.

The delayed trip to Elkmont was providential for one mountain family. Paul Fink that he was walking with W.P. Davis and Knoxville dentist R.N. Kesterson, who were the eldest hikers who accompanied the commissioners. Kesterson was hobbled after a fall near the Alum Cave Bluff. Fink told the *Knoxville News-Sentinel*:

> Some of the members, footsore and weary from their long walk, were obliged to get lodging for the night at the cabin of a mountaineer farmer named Cole. Dr. Kesterson, W.P. Davis, and Paul Fink of Jonesboro ate supper and retired at the Cole house.
>
> During the night, Cole's young baby became desperately ill. Dr. Kesterson, altho without medicine or any equipment, administered relief to the babe as well as he could, while Fink hiked several miles thru the dark and treacherous trails to get a nurse for the child. The doctor's ministrations enabled the baby to survive its intense agonies and recover.
>
> The Cole home is back of Mt. LeConte, miles from the nearest house or settlement. But for the chance happening of Dr. Kesterson in the mountaineer's cottage that night, the Cole babe would surely have died, according to Paul Fink.[8]

In the following days, the national park representatives would see more of the Smokies—including Silers Bald, Gregory Bald, and Cades Cove, not to mention a persuasive reception with Governor Austin Peay at Elkmont's Appalachian Club, but the lofty sunrise on Le Conte had shown them all they needed to see. Even nature did them a favor: "We did not suffer a chigger bite nor see a snake the entire trip," Burtt wrote.[9] Nor did they encounter any bears or boars.

---

8. "Mountaineer Gives Lodging to Dr. Kesterson, Who Saves Life of Child," *Knoxville News-Sentinel*, Aug. 11, 1924. Cole is a common name in the Smokies, and this family has not been identified. This baby might have been a grandchild of Alex Cole (1879–1958), whose cabin was the last surviving home in Sugarlands, a settlement of 400 people. Cole's cabin has been relocated to the Roaring Fork Nature Trail. After working for the Little River Lumber Company in Elkmont, Cole became a hiking guide and led many tourists up Mount Le Conte.

9. "E.E. Burtt, Seasoned Hiker Finds Scaling of Towering Le Conte Quite a Day's Work," *Knoxville Journal & Tribune*, Aug. 11, 1924.

"Nothing else on the face of the earth like it"

Professor Longwell subsequently told the Knoxville Rotary Club: "You have one of the world's beauty spots within a stone's throw, and very few of you have seen it." The *Knoxville News-Sentinel* called him a "savant" for his global perspective:

> I was born in the Rocky Mountains and was reared to contemplate the glorious colors of its scenery. I have stood in the snow-crowned summits of northern Greece and watched rivers glide at their base, and can well understand how the ancient Greeks were the greatest lovers of beauty of all time. I have seen the Bay of Naples from Vesuvius, and reveled in the glory of the sunset which bathed the ships in gold, silver, and brass. I have looked upon the "Alps" of Japan and was entranced with the natural beauty of the Hawaiian islands. The Grand Canyon as it winds through Arizona overwhelmed me.
>
> After all these experiences, I looked from the top of Mount Le Conte. It was wholly unique; in its blending of color, its multiplicity of outline, enveloped in its fairy, ghostlike, veil and haze—there is nothing else on the face of the earth like it.[10]

Kelsey said the commission assessed more than 100 park proposals across the South, "and this was the most outstanding."[11]

Back in Washington, the commission made its recommendation to the administration of President Calvin Coolidge, who had succeeded Harding in 1923. Just before Christmas, Secretary of the Interior Hubert Work recommended the development of the Shenandoah National Park in Virginia while encouraging Congress to create a second park in the Great Smoky Mountains.[12] Congress subsequently nominated Mammoth Cave as a national park to ensure votes from Kentucky. It would be another 10 years before land acquisitions in Tennessee and North Carolina reached a threshold for Congress to officially authorize the national park.

As that August sunrise marked the dawn of the Great Smoky Mountains National Park, the mountaintop camp was also the cradle of LeConte Lodge.

The Basin Spring, and a New Camp

Here's how the *Knoxville News-Sentinel* profiled Paul Adams in 1925:

> He is a very young man, but he has a store of knowledge of God's outdoors and the life that inhabits it that would do credit to a hoary-bearded old man. Some day, we would not be surprised to hear that Paul Adams has become another John Muir or John Burroughs. He knows every bird to be found in the mountains of East Tennessee both by its common name and its long Latin one. And by occupation he is a florist with Flowercraft. He does that because he loves plant life and knows its lore just as he does bird life. A true son of Nature is Paul Adams.

---

10. "Savant Praises Le Conte View," *Knoxville News-Sentinel*, Aug. 27, 1924. Maude Waddell, "South Gives the Nation Its Most Beautiful Playground," *Charlotte Observer*, Jan. 18, 1931. Paul M. Fink, *Mountain Days: A Journal of Camping Experiences in the Mountains of Tennessee and North Carolina, 1914–1938* (Chapel Hill: University of North Carolina Press, 1960).

11. Warner Ogden, "'Wonderful!' Exclaims Drury as Cars in Long Lines Wind Around LeConte," *Knoxville News-Sentinel*, Sept. 2, 1940.

12. Russell Kent, "Blue Ridge Wins, Great Smokies First in Beauty," *Knoxville Sunday Journal*, Dec. 14, 1925.

Adams' expertise with birds was vital in the establishment of the mountaintop camp. In May of 1925, he led naturalists H.P. Ijams of Knoxville and Albert Ganier of Nashville on a hike to look for eagles soaring around Mount Le Conte. Excited by the possibility of sharing such a spectacle with others, they conjured up the idea of a permanent camp on the mountaintop. Ijams pitched the concept to David Chapman and recommended Adams to run the camp. Chapman liked the idea, and in July of 1925, he sent Adams back up the mountain to locate the spring, which Morrell had described in a 1922 story in the *Knoxville News-Sentinel*.

> Another peculiar feature of this mountain is what is locally known as "the basin." The basin is a perfectly flat piece of ground between the "cliff top" and the "far top." It is formed by the junction of a ridge called "the big lead"[13] which runs into Le Conte proper at this point. Here the ground is so flat that there is no drainage and the rain water collects in large pools where it remains until it is soaked up by the thick moss which carpets the rocky soil. The basin is densely wooded with a thick stand of mixed spruce and Canada balsam, which does not permit one to see more than fifty or sixty yards in any direction.[14]

The Basin Spring trickled under moss, roots, and boulders, so the stream was not self-evident. Thrashing through a thick stand of fir trees, Adams located the source about a half-mile east of the 1924 camp.

At an elevation of 6,300 feet, it's the highest perpetual spring[15] in eastern America—the source of Roaring Fork Creek, which pours over Grotto Falls, feeds into the West Prong of the Little Pigeon River in Gatlinburg, and drains toward the Gulf of Mexico via the French Broad, the Tennessee, the Ohio, and the Mississippi. Roaring Fork is the steepest creek in eastern America, falling 5,000 feet in six miles, with several seldom-seen cascades upstream from Grotto Falls.

Adams reported his discovery to Chapman on July 11, 1925, while Tennessee and the nation were transfixed by the spectacle of the Scopes Monkey Trial in the town of Dayton, 70 miles southwest of Knoxville. While Clarence Darrow and William Jennings Bryan debated evolution vs. creation, Chapman made a historic proposition of his own. He presented Adams with a letter authorizing him to establish a permanent camp on Mount LeConte.

Chapman's letter cast the vision for what would become LeConte Lodge:

> By an arrangement with the Champion Fibre Company and owners of Mt. LeConte, this organization has been authorized to appoint a custodian to take charge of the top and upper part of Mt. LeConte.
>
> Mr. Paul J. Adams of Knoxville has been appointed custodian by this organization. He is working in conjunction with Mr. Lewis McCarter, one of the patrolmen employed by the Champion Fibre Company.
>
> Mr. Adams is to protect the plant and animal life, look particularly after the sanitary conditions, and to do what he can to make the visitors more comfortable.
>
> In order to make this service self-sustaining, Mr. Adams is authorized to charge a

---

13. "Lead," pronounced "leed," is a mountain word for a ridgeline. Morrell was referring to Rocky Spur.

14. Far Top was a nickname for High Top—the easternmost peak visible from Knoxville. John Ogden Morrell, "Three Tops of Mount Le Conte," *Knoxville News-Sentinel*, June 17, 1922.

15. Mount Guyot has two intermittent springs along the Appalachian Trail at about the same elevation. On the south side of Le Conte, along the Alum Cave Trail, a gusher that feeds Trout Branch is at about 6,000 feet.

Early hikers at Basin Spring. In 100 years, the mountaintop spring has never run dry (photo by Jim Thompson, courtesy Thompson Photo Products).

reasonable fee to those who visit Mt. LeConte. Any assistance or courtesy shown him in carrying out his duties will be appreciated by this organization.

On July 13, 1925, as the *Knoxville News-Sentinel* broke the news, Adams began packing in the supplies to establish the camp that would become LeConte Lodge. He was accompanied by guide Will Ramsey, four young men, and a black German Shepherd called Smoky Jack. They hiked up an old logging-sled track from Cherokee Orchard toward Bullhead Mountain. Lavator Whaley, a strapping 17-year-old, volunteered to carry the heavy canvas tent. Also on the crew were Earnest Ogle, 19, and brothers Rellie Maples, 20, and Bruce Maples, 17. Hauling blankets, cooking utensils, an ax, a cross-cut saw, and a 10-pound sledgehammer, they made it in three hours to their chosen campsite near the spring.

They cut saplings into poles to frame the tent, lashed up a rough table and bed-frames (with fresh balsam boughs for mattresses), and built crude latrines they called "Johnnies"—holes dug between adjacent trees, with slats nailed to the trees to form a seat.

Day after day, Adams and the boys made double trips up and down the mountain to bring up more supplies from Charlie Ogle's general store in Gatlinburg. Adams paid Whaley up to $2 per day.

The outpost became known as the Basin Spring Camp, though some called it Camp LeConte, adapting the name of the Boy Scout camp in Elkmont.

The first guests arrived July 16, 1925. Orpheus Schantz, a naturalist from the University of Chicago, brought a group of 12 men and women, including guides Oakley and Ramsey. Schantz, the president of the Illinois Audubon Society, had been coming to the Smokies on scientific expeditions since 1918.

As members of the Audubon Society, it's likely that Adams and Schantz met at a 1924 convention in Nashville, when Chapman, Adams, and Ijams spoke before a meeting of the National Academy of Science. Adams' presentation was titled "Trips with the National Park Commission and Bird Check Lists Obtained."

Adams had not planned to serve meals at the camp, but he decided it would be proper to cook for his first guests. When they came back from sunset at Cliff Top, they were greeted not only by a hot meal but also by unexpected luxuries, including hot water for freshening up and mirrors hung on trees. Schantz paid Adams $36. They evidently stayed two nights.

The next day brought Knoxville photographers Jim and Robin Thompson, who documented scenes of the original camp. Founders of the Smoky Mountains Hiking Club arrived July 19. At the same time, some of the Gatlinburg youths employed by Adams told him they needed to go home for the weekend, so Adams had to scramble to have enough help to run the camp. That foreshadowed the perpetual challenge of staffing a backcountry inn.

Adams was authorized to keep the peace on the mountaintop. He was armed, but he did not allow loaded guns to be kept in the camp. Hunting for food along the trails was okay, but, as Adams wrote in his book, "I wanted no killing near camp."

The time was right for the mountaintop camp, as hiking was gaining popularity in the Southeast. The Carolina Mountain Club in Asheville was chartered in 1923, and the Smoky Mountain Hiking Club in Knoxville traces its roots to an October 1924 expedition to Mount Le Conte.

After returning to Chicago, Schantz organized a tour company offering guided trips to the Smokies, and a 1926 newspaper clipping credits him with his second trip

> **Would Build Cabin on LeConte; Keep Custodian**
>
> Negotiations are now on between the Great Smoky Mountain Conservation Association and the Champion Fibre Co. for the building on the summit of LeConte, of a cabin large enough for the accommodation of tourists, and stationing there a permanent custodian to prevent the destruction of property and the natural beauties of the mountain.
>
> A special committee headed by David C. Chapman is considering the employment of a custodian. Paul Adams, naturalist and mountain climber, will probably be employed if an agreement can be reached.
>
> Expenses for such improvements would be defrayed by making a small charge on all tourists climbing the mountain. The large number of travelers would make the sum merely nominal.

On July 13, 1925, the *Knoxville News-Sentinel* announced that Paul Adams would host a tourist camp atop Mount Le Conte.

1. A High Calling and a Hermit's Job

Paul Adams' camp in July 1925. Adams is holding the ax. This scene probably includes members of Orpheus Schantz' group, the first guests at Adams' camp. The bearded man on the left is Uncle Ike Carter, 76, who said he had climbed Le Conte as a boy, before the Civil War (Albert "Dutch" Roth Photograph Collection, University of Tennessee Libraries; the 1926 *Hotel Monthly* credits the photograph to Jim Thompson).

of the year and his fifth overall, so the tradition of counting hikes goes back to the start of the lodge. Schantz's party, guided by Adams and Ramsey, was credited with a new route, a loop up Rainbow and down Roaring Fork (the forerunner of Trillium Gap).

At that time, there were only two established paths up Le Conte—the Mill Creek Trail (forerunner to Rainbow Falls) from Cherokee Orchard and the Bear Pen Hollow Trail from the Indian Gap Road (which paralleled the modern route of U.S. 441). Adams blazed several trails atop the mountain, including the well-worn path that lodge guests still use to visit Cliff Top (which Adams called Main Top).

Adams built a lean-to for his home, so that he would have some privacy rather than sleeping in the same tent with his guests. In an average week, he welcomed 60–70 guests, although he once went 10 days without any visitors.

Guests that first summer included a group Adams derisively called "the Holy Rollers," who took over the mountaintop for a religious service. They banned other guests from the nightly campfire and posted guards on the Myrtle Point Trail the next morning to keep anyone from disturbing their rituals. Adams confronted the guards and threatened to "hiss" Smoky Jack on them unless they unblocked the trail. Jack was a menacing police dog, trained by Adams to go to the general store in Gatlinburg and fetch supplies (see his story in Chapter 9).

During that summer, Adams recorded a high temperature of 81 degrees—which stood as the lodge record for 87 years, until a digital thermometer hit 81.4 on June 29, 2012.

As the 1925 season ended, the conservation association authorized Adams to build a 15-by-20-foot log cabin, and he stayed through the winter to work on it. Park promoter Carlos Campbell guided *New York Times* correspondent Frank Bohn up to the camp. "At the very top of Le Conte there is a boy living alone in a cabin made of slabs," Bohn reported. He counted rings in the stump of a balsam fir that Adams had cut down and concluded that it had stood since the days of Christopher Columbus.[16]

Schantz made his sixth ascent in November, a 10-day trip after the Smokies were wracked by intense winds. "The camp maintained by Paul Adams, botanist and zoologist, assigned to duty on Mount LeConte by the Smoky Mountains Conservation Association, was laid low by the wind," Schantz reported. "Camp equipment was scattered in every direction, but the damage will be repaired by the immediate re-setting of the camp."

The gales of November ushered in the coldest winter ever recorded on Mount Le Conte. From a distance, Adams had seen Le Conte frosted with snow and ice, but he had never experienced such inescapable cold as he lived through that winter.

The first sleet came on October 9. In a report to Chapman dated October 25, Adams said, "Last night the wind was bad, way too rough for one to be comfortable in this shack."

"Snows fell, one on top of the other," Adams wrote. He and Smoky Jack were marooned for some time. "My mother worried about me," Adams wrote. "She occasionally called Col. Chapman about my welfare. He had no more information than she." Recalling how sickly Paul had been as a boy, his mother worried whether he could survive the winter up there.

Adams worked out a semaphore signal with pilot Bill Williams of the Army Air Service, who was photographing the terrain for the national park planners. Adams spread a black square of cloth on the white snow to say that he was okay. He also had a red square to signal trouble, but he never had to use it. After each day's flight, Williams would call Adams' mom on Kenyon Avenue in Knoxville and reassure her that her boy was fine.

Adams described the interior of his cabin as 12 by 15 by eight feet. The logs were not joined snugly, and though he tried to chink the gaps with moss and clay, he never succeeded in making it wind-proof. This cabin later became the site of Herrick Brown's sawmill, and the Tack House (staff housing) now stands there. The footprint of the cabin was pinpointed in 2024 by Frank March, an archaeologist who uses dousing rods to locate old homesites and graves.

Adams had lugged a typewriter to the mountaintop, so he spent some snowbound days typing letters to friends. Even though there was no way to mail them, this allowed him to "communicate with human beings."

Bunk beds were planned for the rear of the cabin. The cabin had an old drum heater and one window. Adams ran out of shingles and had to use the canvas tent from the original camp as a temporary roof. One night, the stove sparked a fire that charred a corner of the cabin.

According to a November 15, 1925, story in the *Knoxville Journal*:

---

16. Frank Bohn, "A New National Park," *New York Times*, Jan. 25, 1926. Bohn (1878–1975) hit the trail wearing a gray business suit, low-cut shoes with spats, a white shirt with a bow tie, and a derby. He was carrying two cameras but no backpack or supplies. When he reached Adams' shanty, he asked for directions to the summit hotel, and Adams told him, "This is it." Adams gave Bohn a tour of the mountaintop, but the reporter was unnerved by the precipitous heights, the windy weather, and the primitive conditions, and the next morning, Adams escorted Bohn safely off the mountain.

1. A High Calling and a Hermit's Job

Paul Adams ran out of shingles while building this cabin in the winter of 1925, so he reused canvas from his original tent as a roof (photograph by Jim Thompson, courtesy Thompson Photo Products).

> Paul Adams is the only man to live upon LeConte. He has accepted his hermit's job from choice and sometimes does not see or talk to a living soul for days at a time. His love of outdoor life and his familiarity with mountain birds has placed him in line for a position of responsibility with the national park commission. He hopes to be appointed study guide for the mountain.
>
> Adams is looking forward to the time when the government will take LeConte and the other lofty peaks of the Great Smokies over as a national park. He believes that the present campaign to secure the park will interest thousands of tourists to whom the beauties of nature are now unknown and who will have further incentive to visit the mountains when the park is under government supervision.[17]

Adams' thermometer plunged to minus 37 on New Year's Eve, the lowest temperature ever recorded on the mountaintop. Snow drifted five feet deep. Adams and his dog had plenty of food stowed away, and when the weather permitted, he worked to prepare for the 1926 season, improving the trails and building fireplaces and tables.

Adams wrote in *Smoky Jack*:

> I wanted to spend Christmas and New Year's with my family in Knoxville, but in November some University of Tennessee students asked for a hunting trip, so I spent the holidays on top of the mountain.
>
> On Christmas Eve, the crowd of university students hiked up the mountain to hunt. But

---

17. "'Young Man of Mountain' Is Title Bestowed on Paul Adams for Work at LeConte," *Knoxville Journal*, Nov. 15, 1925.

the snow was so deep and the weather so cold—several degrees below zero for most of their stay—there was no hunting. One young fellow drank from a bottle too often on his way up the mountain and came into camp with frozen hands and feet. It took three or four of his companions to hold him while the rest of us tried to bring back circulation into those parts of his body by keeping them in cold water and not letting him get too close to the hot stove. We were able to thaw him out in about two hours with no apparent after effects. This group stayed close to the fire, refusing even to go to Cliff Top to see sunsets, although I kept that trail open.

The next day brought a few fellows who wanted to celebrate New Year's Eve on Mount Le Conte. They came for one night only, saying that it was too cold up there to suit them, and that they could not understand why I wanted to stay up there all winter long.

When the spring thaw came, Adams got an unforeseen cold shoulder from his bosses at the Great Smoky Mountains Conservation Association. Some members of the board were not content with his work, and Chapman notified Adams by letter—delivered in Smoky Jack's saddlebag—that the association had decided to replace him as the mountaintop custodian.

Paul Adams and Smoky Jack in 1926, the year he was dismissed from his dream job on Mount Le Conte. Note Paul's wicker backpack and Jack's saddlebags (courtesy Paul James, Knoxville History Project).

Adams wrote about it in *Smoky Jack*:

After reading the letter, I cried. It was a letter of dismissal, effective as of May 10th. The colonel had been kind in his selection of words and told me how he had fought a one-sided battle for me to remain there until the coming season was over. But he was only one of five camp committeemen, and four of them thought it was best that I be dismissed. It was very disheartening to me. I had worked so hard in the interests of the association and had looked forward to the 1926 season.

What went wrong? There has been a century of speculation. When Ken Wise and Anne Bridges edited and republished Adams' memoirs in 2017, they included an introduction with insights from Adams' journals and letters. Evidently, the association had received some complaints from guests, perhaps from the "Holy Rollers." Some hikers had been bitten by Smoky Jack, who would snap defensively at anyone who tried to pet him while he was carrying supplies. The toilet conditions were less than sanitary. Also, there may have been some financial concerns—as the association had been billed for supplies from Ogle's general store in Gatlinburg, while the committee expected the camp to be self-supporting.

Wise and Bridges wrote that Adams likely never fully grasped the reasons for his dismissal from Le Conte. "I shall not write the causes of losing my job for I do not know them, at least all of them, but I do not think I have been given a square deal," Adams wrote.

Some hikers had voiced concerns about conditions on the mountaintop. Knoxville newspapers carried a dispatch from the Great Smoky Mountains Conservation Association about littering along the Rainbow Falls Trail. The *Knoxville News-Sentinel* said that Andy Huff was taking responsibility for the conservation of Mount Le Conte and that Jack Huff and William Ramsey would be based on the mountain and would build a new cabin. Hikers were reminded to bundle their trash and leave it on the trail, where guides would pick it up and dispose of it.

Adams went to Knoxville in an attempt to win his job back. Two committeemen refused to meet with him. "I talked to Colonel Chapman," Adams said, "and there were tears in his eyes as we conversed." Adams offered to resign immediately, but Chapman asked him to stay through May 10.

There may have been other personal or political considerations. The association had established the camp as a good-will gesture, and the last thing they wanted was a public-relations disaster that might derail the park movement. The committee anticipated a busy future for the camp, and perhaps they preferred someone with hotel experience to build and run the place.

In a letter dated April 13, 1926, Hanlon (representing the Great Smoky Mountains Conservation Association) asked Andy Huff (proprietor of the Mountain View Hotel in Gatlinburg) if one of his sons could take over the camp.

> I have just had a talk with Col. Chapman relative to supervision on the top of Mount LeConte this summer and while we think a great deal of Paul Adams and believe his intentions are good, and that he has done the best that he is capable of doing, still we realize that conditions could and should be greatly improved on top of the mountain.
>
> I told the Colonel what you said about building a horseback trail up the Roaring Fork Lead to LeConte, and he seemed to feel that this would be mighty fine, especially if the proper supervision of the top of the mountain could be secured. I also talked to the Colonel about the fact that the Champion Fibre Company had suggested that you build a cabin up there some time back, and that you seemed more receptive to doing that now, especially if the horseback trail is provided.
>
> We feel that if you would consider taking over the supervision of the top of LeConte, and put one of your boys up there, that it would be mighty fine. We have always been favorably impressed with the fact that you and your sons enjoy the full respect and regard of everyone in that community, and we know that some such person in charge of the mountain would be the most satisfactory arrangement that could be made, for, as you are aware, our only objective is to preserve the top of the Mountain, prevent its destruction, and supervise the sanitary conditions.

Hanlon anticipated a "huge influx of visitors to Gatlinburg this summer" and he proposed that "some nominal charge for the use of blankets and shelter, crude though it may be, and perhaps furnishing coffee, as has been done by Paul Adams, would provide sufficient revenue to justify some little preparation and pay anyone quite well for their time."

Andy Huff's oldest son, Jack, 22, took the job. Nine days later, Chapman asked Andy Huff to go to the camp with Will Ramsey "and whoever else you think you will need and build a cabin with a fireplace." Chapman specified that the cabin should be battened with planks to make it weather-proof. This was never done, though Huff did plaster the interior log walls with old newspapers to try to seal out drafts.

The transition went smoothly. Adams said that on May 10, he gave Jack Huff his records and the balance of funds, and Huff invited him to stay for dinner that night. Smoky Jack stayed on the mountain to continue his supply runs, until Adams became concerned that his dog was being overworked.

Later that summer, according to *Smoky Jack*, Chapman visited Gatlinburg and told Adams that the committee regretted its decision. There may have been tension between Jack Huff and the Champion Fibre Company, though relations were better by 1930, when the president of Champion built a lodge at Indian Gap and hired Huff to run it.

Huff decided that Adams' half-finished cabin was not up to his standards, and he eventually tore it down.[18] Nor was he satisfied with the first cabin he built, because the timbers rotted quickly on the damp ground. Huff tore it down in the 1940s, after he had built two lodges and the dining hall.

Adams was disheartened to lose his dream job, but if he held any bitterness, he did not vent it in his books. After the association denied his request to be reinstated, Andy Huff employed Adams to lead hikes for guests at the Mountain View Hotel. From the tips he received as a guide, Adams donated $200 to the national park fund.

One token of Adams' disappointment: He stopped calling his dog Smoky Jack and went back to using his registered name, Cumberland Jack of Edelweiss, which was appropriate since they eventually settled in the Cumberland Mountains.

Adams credited Andy Huff with driving the development of the lodge. In closing his 1966 book, he wrote:

> Jack Huff, financed by members of his family, built LeConte Lodge, much as it exists today, from my beginnings. Before Herrick and Myrtle Brown took over the lodge in 1960, Jack and Pauline Huff offered it back to me, and I was approved by the Park authorities. But my doctors laughed at the idea.
>
> From then till now, there have been few years in which I have not climbed Mt. LeConte and enjoyed the hospitality tendered me by Jack and Pauline Huff and later by Herrick and Myrtle Brown, the present operators. But most of all, I have enjoyed visiting again the dark forest of spruce and balsams, hearing the call of the veery and the winter wren, seeing again the delicate beauty of sand myrtle blossoms, and the red splendor of sunrises and sunsets from Myrtle Point and Clifftop.

Unlike Adams, the Huff family had the resources to invest in the lodge. In 1929, the Great Smoky Mountains Conservation Association paid Jack Huff's father $30,000 to acquire 1,400 acres in the Sugarlands, Roaring Fork, and Greenbrier tracts.

Adams suffered from spinal arthritis as well as chronic sickness but continued

---

18. Huff evidently made Adams' cabin available for picnickers. "Trail Up Le Conte Will Be Policed," *Knoxville Journal*, May 15, 1926.

to climb Le Conte as long as he was able. At age 62, he logged his 500th climb. On July 13, 1975, he climbed the Alum Cave Trail to mark the 50th anniversaries of his first paying guests, which he regarded as the birthday of the lodge. His last trip was No. 523. Guide Will Ramsey once told Adams' father, "That son of yours has the 'mountain-est' legs I have ever seen on an outsider. He can out-walk every one of us who have been born and raised in these mountains."[19]

Adams settled in the Alpine community in the Cumberland Mountains, near an old Presbyterian school where his father had served as pastor from 1926 to 1935. In 1930, he married a lady from back home in Illinois, Maxine Day (1901–1997), they built a floral nursery and landscaping business called Alpine Garden, and he became a weaver. In the 1940s he worked as superintendent of fire prevention for the Atomic Energy Commission in Oak Ridge.

When Adams was a sickly boy, doctors didn't expect him to live past 40, but hiking in the pure mountain air was good for his health. He was 58 in 1959 when the Huffs offered to sell the lodge back to him, 74 the last time he climbed Le Conte, and 83 when he died February 2, 1985. A 1971 newspaper story described him as "Thoreau Reborn." Henry Thoreau's *Walden* and a Bible were the only books Adams kept in his cabin.

In the 1970s, Adams endorsed efforts to close the lodge because of the deteriorating facilities and environmental toll. In a 1975 hearing with the park service, he said, "I think LeConte Lodge ought to be closed. I'm sorry I ever started it."[20]

His place in history was summed up by researcher Lindsay Lanois: "Without the impassioned involvement of Paul Adams, the LeConte Lodge would not have been created as a showpiece for the potential national park."[21]

Paul and Maxine, married for 55 years, are buried in Old Pleasant Hill Cemetery in Cumberland County, Tennessee. They had no children, though Jack (who died at age 15 in 1930) was a sire for several registered puppies sold in Knoxville.

---

19. Paul J. Adams, *Smoky Jack*, edited by Anne Bridges and Ken Wise (Knoxville: University of Tennessee Press, 2016).
20. David Witherspoon, *Song of the Winter Wren* (Bloomington: Xlibris, 2001), p. 243.
21. Lindsay Lanois, *The LeConte Lodge, a Lens for the Evolution and Development of the Great Smoky Mountains National Park* (Clemson: Clemson University, 2014).

2

A Man, His Mountain and His Mom

With all due respects to the pioneer work of Paul Adams, Jack Huff is the father figure of LeConte Lodge. He built the dining hall, the original cabins, and some furnishings that are still used today. He and Pauline were married at Myrtle Point and raised two children on the mountaintop (see Chapter 7). In fact, Jack could even be considered the father of the Newfound Gap highway (see Chapter 3) and of snow-skiing in the Southeast.

But his greatest fame is not as a father, but as a son.

In 1928, when Jack was 25 and his mother Martha Whaley Huff was stricken with cancer, he put shoulder straps on a straight-back chair, sat his Mama in it, hoisted the contraption like a backpack, and carried her to the mountaintop so she might see his pride and joy—and behold the majesty of the sunset and sunrise from Le Conte.

The tale has been retold so many times that it has taken on a biblical patina. It is at the heart of the genesis story of LeConte Lodge.

Carl Estel "Jack" Huff was the first of five children born to Andrew Jackson Huff, a lumberman who built Gatlinburg's premier hotel, and Martha Whaley Huff, who was raised in Greenbrier Cove.

When the Great Smoky Mountains Conservation Association was looking to replace Paul Adams as steward of its camp on Mount Le Conte, officials asked Andy Huff if one of his sons might be interested. Jack had climbed the mountain to celebrate his high school graduation—a trip he described as "a life-changing experience"—and he saw grand possibilities.

He called Le Conte "my mountain" in a sweet letter to his fiancé's family, writing: "There's not another girl in the world that I'd ask to live on my mountain with me."[1]

His mom said in a 1929 interview: "When Jack was a boy, he never seemed to particularly care for the mountains, until he once went to the top. And he's been going ever since."[2]

The nameless outpost Huff inherited from Paul Adams in May 1926 had a crude

---

1. Pauline Huff obituary, *Knoxville News-Sentinel*, Aug. 26, 1996.
2. Tuesday, August 14, was a muggy day in Knoxville, with a high of 90 degrees. Jack Bryan, "Mrs. Huff Scaled Peak on Her Son's Back," *Knoxville News-Sentinel*, Aug. 11, 1929.

log cabin with a canvas roof. The trails were rough paths that required guides and were not yet ready for supply horses, much less casual hikers. The landlord (Champion Fibre Company) would soon be selling its land to the federal government. It didn't look like a place with a 100-year future.

To his advantage, Jack had a strong will and a strong back—he once lugged a 150-pound iron stove to the mountaintop. He had influential friends, a devoted clientele, and a raconteur's knack for marketing. He knew how to work a sawmill, a loom, and a mule.

Andy Huff sent a mountaineer named Will Ramsey to help Jack build the original cabin. Disdaining Adams' shack, they built a bunkhouse four times bigger, with a dirt floor, a plank roof covered with tar-paper, bunk beds for 32 guests, three unglazed windows, and a fireplace. The name "LeConte Lodge" was painted on a sign hung over the front door, at eye level. The height of the door was only four feet, six inches. Huff was five feet, 11 inches, so he had to stoop to enter.

In his first season, Huff counted 3,500 overnight guests, an average of about 17 per night. Guests typically slept in their hiking clothes and brought and cooked their own food, as the family-style dining had to wait until he built the dining hall in 1939.

In 1928, the year his mom visited, the 32-bed lodge averaged 24 guests per night.

The *News-Sentinel* reported August 20, 1928:

> Jack Huff has become the "inn-keeper" on the peak, maintaining the cabins and the canteen there for visitors. When he told his mother about the things he saw, she could only guess what they might be like.
>
> He determined his mother should go to the top and see for herself. He took a hickory chair, put a footrest on it, and fastened straps to it that went around his shoulders.
>
> Last Tuesday, seating his mother in the chair, he hoisted her on his back and carried her the entire distance of the mile-high mountain. The trip took 5½ hours. Sunday, Mrs. Huff was brought back in the same manner.[3]

In a 1929 interview, Jack's mom described the ride up as "just as comfortable as sitting in the best chair at home."

Pauline Huff filled in some of the details in a 1975 interview with award-winning reporter Dot Jackson of the *Charlotte Observer*. "Jack's mother had cancer, and the one thing she wanted was to go up the mountain," Pauline said. "So Jack went into training. He ran, and he stopped smoking. He had a little chair made with a rack to rest her feet. He put her in it, she didn't weigh more than 90 pounds, I guess, and he put it up on his back, and up they went, up the Rainbow Falls Trail. They were staying in a tent, and it turned cloudy and rainy. He went back up and built her a log cabin, but she never was able to come back. That was the house I came to as a bride."[4]

Pauline may have been mistaken about Mama Huff staying in a tent, since the

---

3. "JACK HUFF 'PACKS' MOTHER UP LECONTE," *Knoxville News-Sentinel*, Aug. 20, 1928.
4. Dot Jackson, "In A Hiker's Paradise, A Tempest Is Brewing," *Charlotte Observer*, Oct. 19, 1975. Dorothea Jackson Robertson (1932–2016) was named the National Conservation Writer of the Year. She authored *The Catawba River* (with Frye Gaillard, 1983), *Keowee* (with Mike Hembree, 1995), and her novel, *Refuge*, 2006.

bunkhouse was available. Or perhaps Jack gave his mom private quarters in Paul Adams' original cabin, which had a canvas roof.

In 1929, *News-Sentinel* reporter Jack Bryan reprised the story and described Huff:

> Jack Huff is not the strapping Hercules you might expect him to be. He is in appearance slender, but with long, wiry muscles, such as gave the Indian strength and endurance.
>
> Except, of course, for the logs and rocks, readily obtainable, all the material for the cabins, including hardwood flooring for the newer one, was carried up the mountains on Jack's back. His heaviest load was a cook oven which weighed 150 pounds. He does not remember having gone up or down without a burden of at least some 50 pounds.
>
> When Jack Huff first climbed LeConte nearly 18 years ago there were no trails and he spent the night under a lean-to. Now besides the most frequented trail by Rainbow Falls, there are no less than eight other routes up the mountain.
>
> Always with a load on his back, Jack makes the trip up in about two hours, though he probably could do it in about an hour and a half unburdened if he wished. Most hikers find about three hours the most comfortable time practical.[5]

The saga was picked up by a couple of newspapermen with national audiences: Westbrook Pegler of the *Chicago Tribune* (a syndicated columnist who won a Pulitzer Prize in 1941) and Leo Hershfield of the *New York Times* (who became a courtroom sketch artist for NBC-TV). They must have heard the story second-hand, because they both referred to Jack as George Huff.

In 1940, another future Pulitzer winner, syndicated columnist Ernie Pyle, hiked up to LeConte Lodge and got the story straight from Jack. Here is Pyle's account:

The Roving Reporter

LECONTE LODGE, Great Smokies Park—Jack Huff is a mountain man. All of his 30-odd years have been spent here in the Smokies. And for 17 of those years, he has been the entrepreneur at the top of Mt. Le Conte.[6]

He owns the LeConte Lodge. Seven months of the year, he feeds and beds and maybe entertains the hikers and horsemen who come up the trail.

Jack Huff was just out of high school when he first came to the top of Mt. Le Conte, and he had visions of building a mountain-top tent camp for hiking vacationers. That was long before there was any thought of a National Park, and before there was even a horse trail up here. Everything that came up had to come on men's backs.

Today, three pack horses arrive every afternoon loaded with supplies, and the lodge consists of a whole row of cabins and two small log lodges, and a big house for the Huffs' own living quarters. And Jack is still building.

Jack Huff seems timid at first, but he really enjoys talking to people if he likes them. They say he can size up a new arrival in 10 seconds. If the new arrival is a heel, Jack Huff is polite but his conversation becomes a minimum.

Few vacationers can out-think this product of the Smokies. He listens nightly to the radio news; he absorbs scores of passionate orations on world affairs from his guests before the big fireplace; he reads the papers and magazines.

He is a man of many abilities, too. He builds his own cabins; he has a flair for architecture;

---

5. Jack Bryan, "Mrs. Huff Scaled Peak on Her Son's Back," *Knoxville News-Sentinel*, Aug. 11, 1929. Bryan (1903–1980) was a reporter for the *Knoxville News-Sentinel* and the *Memphis Press-Scimitar* before becoming information officer for the U.S. Department of Housing and Urban Development. He was an acquaintance of Huff who helped publicize the lodge.

6. "Seventeen years" probably refers to the time since Huff first climbed Le Conte. If he had been working up there for 17 years, he would have preceded Paul Adams.

construction is his hobby. And he weaves. On the big loom in the dining room, he has woven all the lovely curtains for the lodge windows.

He got his weaving, among other things, from the Pi Phi Settlement School down in Gatlinburg. That is a school founded 28 years ago by the college sorority, to bring a better education to the mountaineers. Pretty Pi Phis come from all over to teach there.

A girl named Pauline Whaling came down from the north, to teach the mountaineers. She was out of Monmouth College in Illinois, and Northwestern University.

But whether she taught, or got taught, I can't quite decide. For she married Jack Huff, and came to the mountain with him. And when their little boy was born, he came to the mountain too—a husky, tow-headed example of a good life.

For seven years, Pauline Whaling has been on the mountain, working with her own hands, helping run things. She is beautiful in her heavy boots and leather jacket.

She leaps around the terraces of the lodge like a gazelle. She was up at 4 this morning to see Jack off on an early trip down the mountain. She herself has hiked the tough eight-mile Newfound Gap trail in two hours flat. She is bountifully happy. "Up here is peace," she says.

A mountaineer's strength is in his heart, and not necessarily in a big body. Jack Huff weighs only 150 pounds, and stands sort of folded up with his hands in his pockets. But his walking feats are astounding.

He has walked 15,000 miles up and down this mountainside![7] He kept count of his round trips until three years ago, and at that time they had passed 1,000. It is seven miles each way, and exactly a mile gained in altitude.

He has often made two round trips in one day, packing great loads up the trail on his back. There are some mighty men in these mountains. Listen to this story:

Andy Huff is Jack's father. He owns the big Mountain View Hotel down in Gatlinburg. He has lived down there for 40 years, but he has never seen his son's lodge up here, although it's only two hours by horseback. "I just haven't got time to go," says Andy Huff.

But Jack's mother saw Le Conte Lodge before she died. She made one trip. Just one. That trip sounds like a legend, but it's true. She came up on her son's back!

It was 14 years ago. Mrs. Huff was a semi-invalid. She wanted to see the sunset from the peak before she died.

So Jack made a light wooden chair. He put arms on it for her, and a board rest for her feet. He put her in it; then lifted her onto his shoulders. Mrs. Huff weighed 90 pounds. In her lap she carried a kitten.

Jack Huff, packing his mother on his back, made those seven miles to the top of Mt. Le Conte in exactly five hours. He stopped only a few times, and that was for his mother to rest, rather than him. "She's the only person who ever came up the mountain backwards," he says. They still talk about it with awe around Gatlinburg.

Mrs. Huff stayed a week on the mountain, in a tent. But it rained all the time. She never saw the sunset. Finally, the dampness became too much for her. One afternoon, Jack wrapped her in a raincoat, put her into her chair, and packed her back down the mountain. Soon after that he started building a log cabin for her, so she would have a drier place to stay the next time. But she didn't live to see it.

That old cabin is the original house of today's Le Conte Lodge. Jack would like to keep it, for sentiment. But he says it isn't built right, and soon it will have to come down.[8]

---

7. Huff's lifetime hiking mileage was probably close to 30,000 miles by 1959—enough to lap the globe. Pauline hiked at least 1,500 miles, equivalent to a round trip to her mom's home in Chicago. In a 1955 Associated Press interview, Jack said his heart was no longer as strong as it used to be, and by then he was getting most of his miles on the golf course. Hal Boyle, "Carrying of Mother Won Respect for Huff," *Knoxville News-Sentinel*, July 14, 1955.

8. Ernie Pyle, "The Roving Reporter," Scripps-Howard Newspaper Syndicate, Oct. 24, 1940.

Worthy of a Bluegrass Ballad

Ernie Pyle's account implies the trip was in 1926, and a display at the lodge says 1929, but the original newspaper account firmly dates the trip to August 14–19, 1928, with Mama Huff spending five rainy nights on the mountain. It was a muggy 90-degree day when they hit the trail, but the Smokies were about to be soaked by the remnants of a hurricane that struck Fort Pierce, Florida, on August 8.

You can see the hickory chair today at the Museum of East Tennessee History in Knoxville. And you ought to hear the story as told in a bluegrass ballad, "The Legend of Jack Huff," recorded by Jimbo Whaley, who is the great-great nephew of Mrs. Huff. (Scan the QR code to listen.)

Jimbo never knew his great-great aunt but has known the story all his life. His song begins with Mama Huff sharing grim news—her doctor says she is terminally ill and her days are numbered: "Might be a month, could be today." After she tells her oldest son not to weep for her, she pleads: "Before I go, just take me there."

Jack Huff turned this chair into a backpack. The chair is now displayed in the Museum of East Tennessee History in Knoxville (Huff family photo, courtesy Cookie Bowling).

The chorus will resonate with anyone who has stood atop Le Conte:

> To feel the cool breeze from the north, blowing 'cross my face.
> Place my feet upon the ground where no one's left a trace.
> High above the pain and sorrow, up where the eagles fly,
> I want to see the sunrise from the mountain ... before I die.[9]

Scan to play

"The Legend of Jack Huff"

The song portrays Jack Huff as "young and not too strong" but fiercely determined to fulfill his mom's dreams.

Huff liked to take photographs and home movies of his adventures. In the case of his mom's trip, the only surviving photographic documentation is a 1929 Knoxville newspaper clipping, which shows him dressed in low-cut boots, shorts, a tank top, and no hat. She is sitting straight, wearing a long coat over a dress.

---

9. Jimbo Whaley, "The Legend of Jack Huff," Pine Mountain Railroad.

Jack told the newspaper in 1929 that he had climbed Le Conte 451 times. Customarily, he hiked up Mill Creek, the forerunner to the Rainbow Falls Trail. This path was about four miles, shorter and steeper than the modern six-mile route described in Whaley's song. The only alternatives in 1928 were Bear Pen Hollow, which is even shorter but perilously steep, or Trillium Gap, which would have been a hike of nearly nine miles from Cherokee Orchard before the Roaring Fork Motor Trail opened in the 1960s.

Was Mama Huff on her deathbed? No doubt she was too feeble for such a hike, but she lived another five years. According to a *Knoxville News-Sentinel*'s 1929 story, she actually cooked meals for her son's crew at the lodge:

> Mrs. Andy Huff is probably the only person who has actually ridden up Mt. Le Conte, the king peak of the Smokies. And if the wishes of many mountain lovers that no automobile roads be built to the peak are regarded, it will probably be many a day before anyone else can make the same boast.
>
> For Jack Huff, her son, on whose back she made the otherwise arduous trip, is not proposing a pick-a-back taxi service for all who are unable to travel on their own legs. Perhaps the trip, which was made just a year ago, was inspired by the memory that Jack and his helpers had of meals their mother cooked. For during her five days on LeConte, Mrs. Huff banqueted the boys with home cooking.[10]

Jack was willing to be a taxi for his mom, but not for his guests. Later that same summer, Dr. H.H. Price, a former football player at Iowa State University, tripped over a stump near the lodge and complained that he was unable to hike down. "We couldn't find his injuries," Huff said, "but I gathered nine men and we packed him three miles down the mountain and brought him to the hotel on horseback. He was given a stimulant and seemed to be all right again. He refused to pay us for carrying him down—and he weighed 180 pounds." Huff took Price to court, and Squire Isaac Maples ordered Price to pay Huff $30.[11]

By the time Martha Whaley Huff died at age 56 in 1933, Jack had built the two oldest cabins that stand today on the LeConte Lodge campus.

The cabin names have evolved over the years. Huff called his original bunkhouse Cabin 1. Today, Cabin 1 refers to the three-bedroom lodge Jack built in 1934 for his honeymoon, Cabin 2 is a renovated version of a two-bedroom lodge he built around 1928, and Cabin 3 is the three-bedroom East Lodge built by Jim Huff in 1984. Cabins 1 and 2 sit on opposite sides of the central staircase. Cabins 4–9 are the single-room cabins on the next terrace, and Cabin 10 is tucked away on the hillside. Cabin 1 is commonly called "the old lodge," even though Cabin 2 ("the new lodge") was built first.

Two cabins are known as "honeymoon cabins." Obviously, this includes Cabin 1, but there is also a small lodge east of the kitchen that old-timers call "the honeymoon cabin." It is supposed that Jack Huff may have reserved this cabin for newlyweds to give them some privacy. It's now used for crew housing.

---

10. Jack Bryan, "Mrs. Huff Scaled Peak on Her Son's Back," *Knoxville News-Sentinel*, Aug. 11, 1929.
11. "Get Money for 'Taxi' on Mt. LeConte," *Knoxville News-Sentinel*, Sept. 15, 1929. Squire Maples (1868–1951) was a descendant of Davy Crockett who served for 43 years with the Sevier County courts.

Jack Huff's original cabin, built in 1926, was "open year-round," according to early park guidebooks (photograph by Jim Thompson, courtesy Thompson Photo Products).

Roots of the Lodge

It is not known how Huff derived the name LeConte Lodge. His family took a California vacation when he was a boy, so it is possible he had visited the LeConte Memorial Lodge, the 1904 visitor center in Yosemite National Park.

The first published mentions of "LeConte Lodge" were a 1926 story in a trade magazine, *The Hotel Monthly* and a 1927 map drawn by H.P Ijams for the Knoxville Chamber of Commerce. The name debuted in the local press in 1926, when the *Knoxville Journal* reprinted the *Hotel Monthly* story.

In the 1930s, guests often referred to the lodge as "Jack Huff's place," "Camp LeConte," or "The House That Jack Built," a nod to a popular nursery rhyme. A 1930 story in the *Asheville Citizen-Times* called the lodge "Jack's Place."

Huff may have had second thoughts about the name, because "LeConte Lodge" was not mentioned in 1935 Knoxville newspaper stories that appear to be press releases he submitted. In the same era, there were two LeConte Hotels in Knoxville, as well as the Hotel LeConte in Greenbrier Cove.[12]

---

12. "Where Is LeConte Hotel? Two Have Taken That Name," *Knoxville News-Sentinel*, Nov. 9, 1929. The Bijou Theatre at 803 South Gay Street in Knoxville occupies the site of the LeConte Hotel, previously named Knox and Lamar. A block away, at 202 West Church Avenue, now the site of the Residence Inn, a boarding house was also known as LeConte Hotel. Greenbrier's Hotel LeConte (1926–33) was the first property

The *Hotel Monthly*, a national trade magazine published in Chicago, typically reviewed swank resorts and carried advertisements for industrial-size refrigerators and white waiters' jackets. Editor John Willy, 66, was an avid hiker and an acquaintance of Orpheus Schantz, who had been Paul Adams' first overnight guest in 1925. In previous issues, Willy[13] reviewed several national park lodges out West, though none of them were quite as remote as LeConte.

Schantz and Will Ramsey guided Willy up the old Rainbow Falls Trail, a steep and rocky four-mile scramble up what is now known as Le Conte Creek. Willy was accustomed to luxurious accommodations, yet he was generous in his "review" of the lodge:

> We reached the "cabin" or LeConte Lodge, as the sign over the door reads, about four o'clock in the afternoon, and after a short rest, started for Main Point[14] to get the grand view. Here was indeed a panorama to please the glad eye. From our vantage point, we had a birds-eye view of approximately two thousand square miles of mountain,

This 1938 logbook records the 10th visit by Orpheus Schantz, who was Paul Adams' first customer back in 1925. The early guest-lists were quite metropolitan, as this page represents Chicago, Pittsburgh, Cleveland, and greater Boston (photograph by Tom Layton).

forest, and landscape view. We could see far into North Carolina. Here were range after range of mountains, as many as seven in one direction. Far off we could see the French Broad River and the Tennessee River. It was a clear day and even the Blue Ridge could be

---

acquired in 1928 through the $5 million Laura Spellman Rockefeller memorial gift that was so vital to the establishment of the park. "Le Conte Hotel Bought for Great Smoky Park," *The Tennessean* (Nashville), May 22, 1928. The 36-bed hotel operated under a temporary permit until 1933.

13. John Willy (1859–1934) should not be confused with John North Willys (1873–1935), a pioneer automaker and father of the Willys Jeep. Willys' company built the Falcon-Knight car that Horace Kephart drove across the Smokies in 1930 (Chapter 3).

14. Cliff Top was known as Main Point or Main Top in the early days of the lodge. From the viewshed Willy describes, it sounds like he also went to Myrtle Point.

seen. In one direction was the Cherokee Indian Reservation. We could see Guyot Mountain, Klingman's Dome, the Chimneys, and many other landmarks. The guide pointed out the route of the proposed new highway to connect Gatlinburg with Bryson City, through Newfound Gap or Indian Gap.

LeConte Lodge deserves a chapter by itself. A bulletin on the trail near the top read "Register at the Great Smoky Conservation Camp." This means the place where the Champion Fibre Company, which owns the mountain, has established a camp for creature comfort of those who reach the top of the hill. They opened it a year ago in a very crude way, and this year have elaborated on the accommodations. Jack Huff, son of A.J. Huff of the Mountain View Hotel in Gatlinburg, built the present cabin and manages it. One of our party christened it "The House That Jack Built." The cabin is twenty-four feet wide by thirty-four feet long; the beds at the door end, the fireplace and lounge at the far end. The construction is entirely of balsam wood, the tree trunks laid lengthwise, and the chinks filled with moss from which grows ferns and oxalis flowers, all the way up to the roof, making a very attractive picture. Inside, the walls are covered with matrices from the *Knoxville Journal*. The roof is of boards covered with tar paper and gravel, waterproof. The floor is of hard dry clay. The fireplace is built of rocks. At one side of it there is stacked several cords of firewood. The fireplace end of the room is bordered with board seats, and a chair-back seat extends across the room in front of the fire.

Ramsey, the guide, spent two months on the mountain helping Jack build the cabin. Jack said that the next improvement will be providing necessary lavatory and sanitary accommodations, which now are of the crudest kind.

The stores are kept in homemade cabinets attached to trees. The register is on a board

Jack Huff built a "crow's nest" in a spindly fir tree that overlooked the campus (photograph by Jim Thompson, courtesy Thompson Photo Products).

desk nailed to a tree. Near the cabin door there is a large balsam tree, on top of which Jack has built a crow's-nest lookout. There is a ladder reaching to the first branches, and then it is a climb up to the crow's-nest to get the view.

The beds are on a board floor covered with a thick layer of balsam branches. We watched the guide make our bed. Over the balsam branches he put three blankets, and two more blankets on top of these folded back for covers; a folded blanket for pillow; extra blanket if needed, we were advised. There is a separate set of blankets for each guest. The fire was kept going all night; the door and all windows open, rain or shine—fine ventilation! There was a pleasant smell of balsam. It was a building without glass and without lavatory facilities. The door was three feet wide by four feet six inches high, with a big window over it. The sleeping accommodations are for 32. Guests do not undress, but lie down in their clothes, four abreast when the cabin is taxed to capacity. The manager said that at one time this season he has had as many as 61 persons sleeping in this cabin. They had come without advance notice, and most of them had to sleep on the floor or on benches.

It is something unusual in hotel accommodations, men and women sleeping in the same room, as democratic as if there was no such thing as caste in this mountain world. And there is not, on top of LeConte, where "Jack is as good as his master," for the time being, and roughing it, every one respects his neighbor, and makes the best of the situation.

The *Hotel Monthly* reviews typically included architectural drawings, so Willy sketched a floor plan of Huff's cabin. The interior would have been dark, with only three small unglazed windows high in the eaves.

Herrick Brown, 13, stayed in the original cabin in October 1927 (decades before he bought the business from the Huffs). He slept under two Boy Scout blankets and had to get up twice during the night to stoke the fire. "Sleeping bags were unknown," he wrote in his diary.

From 1933 through 1949, Jack Huff built the heart of the modern campus, including the dining hall and most of the guest cabins. Herrick Brown opened the office and recreation room in 1971, and

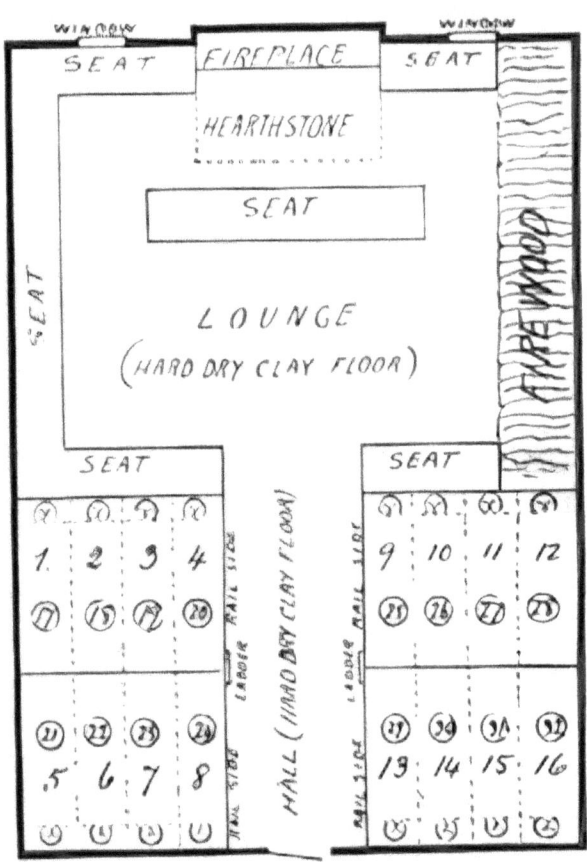

The floor plan for Jack Huff's original cabin was sketched by John Willy, editor of *Hotel Monthly* (1926). Bunks are numbered, and top bunks are circled.

Jack Huff (center, leaning on the bunkbed) in his original cabin in the 1920s. Note that the floor was dirt, the bottom bunks were on the ground, and the walls were plastered with old newspapers to help keep out the draft. To the right of the ladder on the top bunk is Carlos Campbell, author of *Birth of a National Park*. On the bottom bunk, to the right of the post, is Dutch Roth. Campbell and Roth were leaders in the movement to form the national park (photo by Jim Thompson, courtesy Thompson Photo Products).

Jack's nephew Jim Huff, Jr., added the East Lodge in 1984, on the same site where Jack Huff built his first cabin in 1926. Jack left the lodge in 1949 to run the family hotel in Gatlinburg, but the public side of the lodge[15] was essentially finished in his lifetime.

Going Sissy?

With his roots in the hospitality business in Gatlinburg, Jack worked hard to turn the lodge into a comfortable destination.

Newspaper accounts in the 1930s—probably press releases from Huff—said the lodge offered "anything a modern resort hotel has to offer," with amenities including hot baths, free telephone service, and specially prepared meals. The baths were "installed in a special building" but the newspapers did not describe the facilities nor how they worked. Guests nowadays are no longer offered baths, though they can freshen up with a tin pail of hot water from a spigot outside the kitchen.

The *Knoxville Journal* commented: "In a year or two you won't know the old place—it's 'going sissy.'"

The original construction seems to have been mostly spontaneous, with few plans other than what Huff had in his mind. As newspaperman Ernie Pyle noted in 1940, Huff had a flair for architecture.

Here is a timeline of the progress:

---

15. Construction for storage facilities and staff housing has been ongoing. The newest building is the Ashberry, which houses employees. The food shed was also built in the early 2000s, and the single-room cabins were renovated in 2024.

- 1929: Huff said he had accommodations for up to 100 guests, including campsites as well as his 32-bed cabin. Guests were generally expected to bring and cook their own food.
- 1930: The guest list spanned the globe, with visitors coming from Germany, Japan, England, Scotland, Canada, South America, and Africa. In the 1960s, one guest leafed through a 1933 logbook and found entries from New Delhi, India; Alborg, Denmark; Ljubljana, Slovenia; Zurich, Switzerland; and Frankfurt, Germany. Many of the international guests came through tours organized by Schantz, who had been Paul Adams' first customer. Appropriately, Huff offered a "European plan," with nightly rates of $2 for a bed, or $3.50 including three meals.
- 1931: The *Knoxville Journal* described the lodge as a commissary, "where the hiker can buy food, hire blankets, and cook his meals."
- 1932: The heights of Le Conte weathered the depths of the Great Depression, as Huff had plenty of natural resources—timber and stone—to work with. Huff built a stone terrace that remains today as the footing for the oldest cabins on campus. With puncheon planks instead of dirt floors in the newer cabins, it was time to upgrade the beds, so Huff hauled up wire-spring mattresses to replace the original balsam-bough bedding. Brightly colored Hudson Bay blankets began to replace the original olive-drab blankets, which were army surplus from World War I.
- 1933: Even before the national park was authorized, park-service architects approved blueprints drawn by Knoxville architect Charles Barber for the three-bedroom cabin now known as the Old Lodge (which Huff called Cabin 3). This was his first project with hewn timbers, which made for a more weathertight construction than the previous log cabins.
- 1934: Jack completed Cabin 3, which became known as "the Honeymoon Cabin," after he and Pauline Whaling were married (see Chapter 7) at Myrtle Point at sunrise on Sunday, April 29, during the ninth season of public accommodations on the mountaintop. Cabin 2 (now known as the New Cabin) eventually became home to Jack, Pauline, and their son Philip, though they moved to the three-bedroom Cabin 3 by the time daughter Cookie was born in 1944.
- 1935: Huff strung telephone lines down Mill Creek to connect the lodge to the Southern Bell network. Daily weather reports from the mountaintop became a popular feature in the Knoxville newspapers.
- 1936: The park's original master plan envisioned a substantial campus on Mount Le Conte, including dozens of cabins and campsites, plus a picnic area, a large lodge, and a ranger station. By this time, Huff had built four six-bed cabins on a terrace above Cabins 2 and 3, furnished with bunks relocated from the original cabin. Jack's nephew, Jim Huff, used the site of the original cabin to build the East Lodge in 1984.
- 1939: The dining hall opened. "Comfortable accommodations are afforded for 40 people," the *Knoxville Journal* reported. "Those who patronized LeConte Lodge in its early days, when balsam bough beds were used,

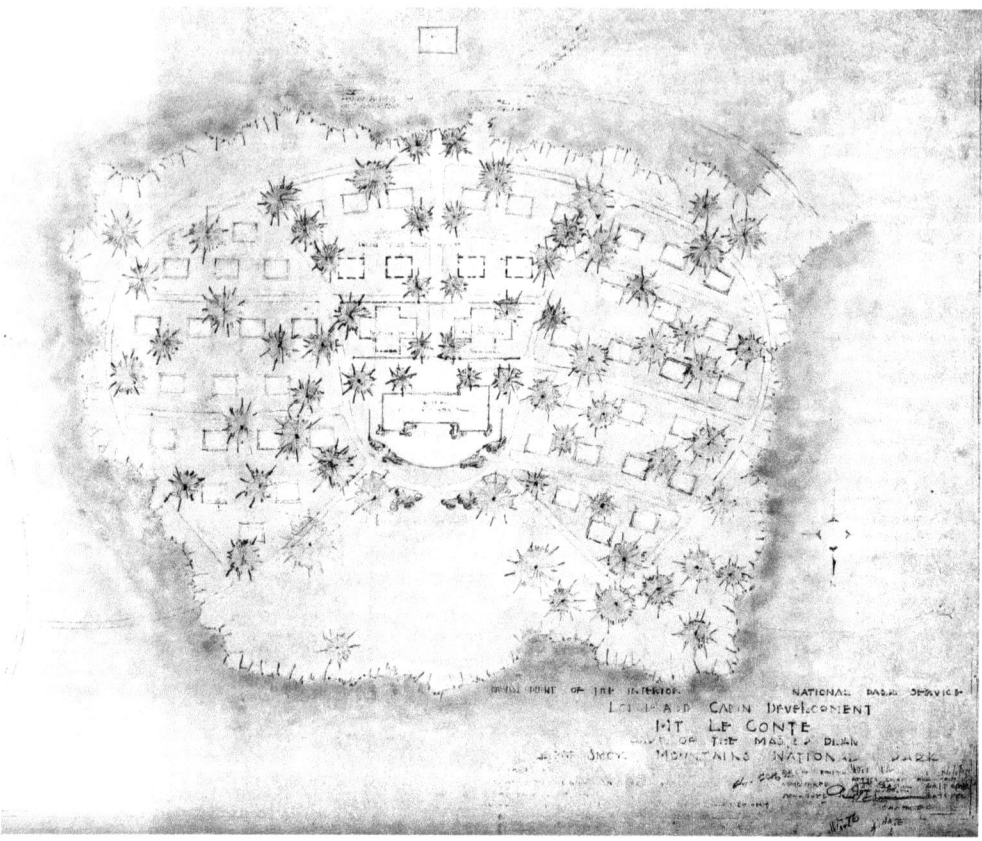

The park's 1933 master plan envisioned a large campus at LeConte Lodge, with dozens of small cabins or campsites arrayed around a central lodge (Great Smoky Mountains National Park Archives).

would scarcely recognize the place now. Warmly heated cabins and tents, equipped with beds with springs, mattresses, and Hudson Bay blankets just as comfortable as those found in the best hotels, are a far cry from the crude accommodations more than 10 years ago."[16]

Detroit columnist Russell McFarland, 52, visited the lodge in 1939 and wrote a feature story headlined "A Northerner Goes 'Up South.'" He described LeConte Lodge as a "hospice for climbers who come from far parts of the world, and for the local boys and girls who like to sweetheart there." He called Jack Huff's lodge "an accessory to his father's caravansary in the valley." After lamenting the rotten logs in the original cabin, McFarland praised Huff's newer construction, including the stonework on the terraced hillsides and the modern kitchen. After McFarland signed in and ordered supper, he climbed up to Cliff Top, "where there was nothing but Heaven above us."

- 1940: Huff added six new tent cabins in addition to lodges he had previously

---

16. "LeConte-Top Inn Highest in the East," *Knoxville Journal*, Aug. 27, 1939.

built. Some of these had triple bunk beds. McFarland described these cabins as half-tents and half-huts. Some of these originally had log walls and tent roofs, according to Huff's daughter Cookie Bowling. Later the cabin frames were wrapped in canvas, followed by board-and-batten siding, and cedar shingles were added to the roofs. Porches were added decades later—many of them are not aligned with the cabin doors.

- 1941: Park officials asked Huff to open a lunch stand for day hikers and to install a water pump at the picnic grounds, near the Boulevard Trail well above the spring.

Huff and his son Philip channeled Basin Spring to improve the flow of water and then worked with park officials to install a water system propelled by a ram pump, an ingenious device that turns gravity against itself. Huff stored water in a concrete cistern behind Cabins 8 and 9. In the 1960s, Herrick Brown built a wood-stave tank that held 10,000 gallons of water.

The ram pump usually is sufficient to power the water system early in the year when the spring is flowing strongly, but motorized pumps are needed as the flow tapers off in the summer and fall. The lodge uses 500,000 gallons of water per season, so the spring is absolutely vital.

In the early years, most of the guest traffic was on weekends, and walk-ups could usually get a room on weekdays. "People didn't know about the lodge," Jack's daughter Cookie Bowling said in a 2021 interview.

After four seasons, LeConte Lodge was attracting

Jack Huff in 1933 at the door of his second cabin, now known as the New Cabin. Jack's "Honeymoon Cottage" is under construction in the background. The sign over the door affirms the "LeConte" spelling. This 1928 cabin was rebuilt in the 1980s, using hewn timbers and the original rafters (Huff family photo, courtesy Cookie Bowling).

Aerial view of the campus in 1936, when Jack and Pauline Huff were new parents. Jack's original cabin is in the foreground. On the left are his 1928 and 1934 cabins. On the right is a temporary mess hall that was replaced in 1939 by the current kitchen and dining room (photograph by Dutch Roth, from the Albert "Dutch" Roth Photograph Collection, University of Tennessee Libraries).

Jack Huff built this loom in 1938 from timber harvested on the mountain. Huff's mother taught him to spin yarn, and he learned to weave in high school. Huff used this loom to weave curtains for the 20 windows in his cabins. Most rooms at the lodge are dark, but Huff set up the loom in a well-lit corner of the dining room (photograph by Dutch Roth, from the Albert "Dutch" Roth Photograph Collection, University of Tennessee Libraries)

The single-room cabins (this is Cabin 5) were originally sheathed with canvas and tarpaper, and the porches were added later (Huff family photo, courtesy Cookie Bowling).

more and more hikers who had delusions of grandeur but may not have been well prepared for such a strenuous expedition. In an effort to manage expectations and maybe drum up some overnight business, Huff wrote this letter in 1930 to the *Knoxville Journal*:

> The purpose of this letter is to correct two wrong ideas or impressions which many people seem to have.
> In the first place, many people are being sent to one-day trips to Mt. LeConte, being told that the trail is only four miles each way. It is true that the trail is only four miles and one-tenth from Cherokee Orchard to LeConte Lodge, near the top, but there are no views to be had from the cabins, and it requires another two-and-one-half miles of hiking to go to Myrtle Point and Main Top, the two points where the superb views are to be had. It would really be better to not send visitors up Mt. LeConte unless they have time to go to both lookout points.
> The average visitor cannot climb LeConte and take the time and energy necessary to take in Myrtle Point and get back to the orchard the same day. This being the case, everyone who is sent up Mt. LeConte should be urged to go up one day, spend the night on top, get up early to see the sunrise from Myrtle Point, then go back to camp for breakfast, later go out to Main Top and then make a leisurely trip down the mountain—possibly by another trail. If the visitors reach LeConte Lodge in time they will find it interesting to go to Main Top and watch the sun set.
> This would make the trip well worthwhile for anyone, but a one-day trip will probably prove a keen disappointment for most people.
> The other point on which there seems to be a lack of proper understanding is that the charge for using the camp facilities at LeConte Lodge. The fee, which a few people have claimed is too high, is a dollar and a half per person.[17] This includes use of a cabin (which I built at my own expense), blankets, cooking utensils (and washing them), wood, and keeping

---

17. Huff's daily charges were the same as the LeConte Hotel in Greenbrier at the foot of the mountain.

the camp clean, etc. To keep this camp going and in good order, I have to employ an average of three men the year round; sometimes I have eight or ten at work.

If there was no such camp on LeConte, it would be necessary for all who spend the night on LeConte to carry a tent, blankets, cooking utensils, and an ax to cut wood with. This being the case, of course, it is out of the question. If that condition prevailed, with numerous camp fires being built around over the top, the whole mountain would be burned off.

After considering the great expense I have in keeping the camp up, and what it saves to those who use it, you can readily see that my charge of one dollar and a half is really very reasonable.

A trip to the summit of Mt. LeConte, with sufficient time to really see some of the distinctive features, will be a genuine treat to anyone. It will give them the best impression they can get of the Smokies.[18]

As World War II dawned, Huff registered with the Selective Service at age 38 in 1941. He was never drafted and was able to keep the lodge open during the war. On Father's Day in 1944, he bought an advertisement in the *Knoxville Journal* to promote the lodge as a peaceful summer destination.

With the end of the war in 1945, the park service began reviewing its concession contracts. The lodge reported an annual income of $6,790.[19]

The 1949 season marked the end of an era. First, the park service asked for competitive bids on its concession contracts. The *Knoxville News-Sentinel* put it like this: "Uncle Sam Today Tacked a 'For Lease' Sign

Fathers Day 1944 advertisement.

---

18. Jack Huff, "For a Trip to Mt. LeConte," *Knoxville Journal*, Nov. 28, 1930.
19. Top earnings were reported by the proprietors of the general stores in Smokemont: George Beck with $16,856 and Jehu Conner (1889–1985) with $10,712.

on Mt. LeConte Lodge." Huff submitted a bid but was prepared to lose the contract, and he announced that any new concessionaire would have to pay him $40,000 for his investment in the facilities.

Two weeks later, on December 14, Huff's father died at age 70, and the family needed Jack, 46, to stay in Gatlinburg to manage the Mountain View Hotel.

There were no competing bids for the lodge, so the park renewed Huff's contract. Pauline Huff agreed to manage the lodge (with hired help) while Jack took care of business down in Gatlinburg. In the 1950s, the lodge did not open until May, to ease the burden on Pauline and her children.

Pauline continued to manage the lodge through the 1959 season. "For ten years, she ran the camp by herself," Cookie Bowling said. "I'm sure Dad gave orders from below."

One night in 1950, a bear got into the kitchen. "Mama cranked that phone up, called Dad, and said, 'What am I going to do?' He said, 'Run it out,' and hung up. She beat a flashlight against a metal tray to make enough noise to get the bear out the door."

With Jack Huff away, construction came to a halt in the 1950s. Yet the lodge was growing in popularity, to the point that, in 1953, the Huffs and the park agreed on an expansion plan to accommodate up to 84 guests per night. The proposal included a new two-story building with a 70-seat dining hall and kitchen on the first floor and a recreation room on the second floor. The existing dining hall would have been converted into staff quarters. A pair of three-bedroom cabins would have been added, plus at least a dozen new one-room cabins.

Construction of the new building began in 1968, under the management of

The Mountain View Hotel, which began as a bunkhouse for loggers, became the heart of Gatlinburg, visited by the Roosevelts and Fords. It also served as a temporary headquarters for the national park (photograph by Dutch Roth, from the Albert "Dutch" Roth Photograph Collection, University of Tennessee Libraries).

Herrick Brown. The new building included the lodge's first flush toilets.[20] Under the restrictions of the 1964 Wilderness Act, additional bunks were not needed, the existing dining room was sufficient, and the upper floor was repurposed as an office and recreation room.

In 1959, as Pauline turned 54, the Huffs decided it was time to sell their interest in the lodge. They received bids from some of their most frequent guests: Adams, 58; John Adler, 39, a doctor in Rockwood, Tennessee; and Brown, 47. They worked out a $37,500 deal with Brown, according to crew member David Witherspoon, whose book reported that the park service disapproved of the financing arrangements and preferred a cash transaction.

Brown had known Huff since 1927, when he visited the lodge as a Boy Scout. Brown wrote a school report about the trip, saying: "This got the mountain in my blood and it wouldn't go away." Decades later, when he retyped the report as a keepsake for his children, Brown wrote an addendum: "Mr. Jack Huff still greets me in October, even though 10 days later than the 1927 date—the payments on the lodge are due Oct. 31!"

The park's inventory in 1959 itemized what the Huffs had built. It listed two multi-room lodges, the dining hall (with attached kitchen and manager's quarters), seven single-room cabins for guests, three one-room cabins for employees, two pit toilets, a woodshed, and a log barn for pack animals. Tap water was piped to the multi-room cabins. At the time, there were three trails open to horses, as well as a public campsite and picnic ground southeast of the lodge, which the concessionaire was expected to maintain. The manager's quarters were expanded in 1986.

"A mom and pop operation"

In understanding the relationship between the lodge and the park, it's important to remember that the lodge came first. Paul Adams and Jack Huff originally operated their camps as tenants of Champion Fibre Company and as agents for the Great Smoky Mountains Conservation Association, which was raising funds to acquire park land on the Tennessee side of the Smokies. The lodge was nine years old in 1934, when Congress officially authorized the development of the national park.

Champion Fibre Company (1893–2023) was a paper mill in Canton, North Carolina. The company originally welcomed Adams and Huff as custodians, mainly to oversee visitors and prevent forest fires.

Champion never harvested trees on Le Conte but was reluctant to sell its investment. Brown said in a 1980s interview that if not for the park, the forests on Mount Le Conte would have been logged before World War II "and gone out of here as newsprint."

The Great Smoky Mountains Conservation Association went through several rounds of negotiations and court hearings with Champion Fibre before closing a deal in 1931 to purchase 39,549 acres on and around Mount Le Conte for $1

---

20. "LeConte Lodge Is Going Modern," *Knoxville News-Sentinel*, Nov. 14, 1968.

million. That's essentially $25 per acre—comparable to the going rate for the entire park ($12,664,462 for 507,654 acres).[21] Through a series of legal steps, the association transferred ownership to the state of Tennessee, which relayed the deeds to the National Park Service.

By the time the Great Smoky Mountains National Park was established, the National Park Service owned several tourist lodges, such as the iconic Old Faithful Inn at Yellowstone and the Phantom Ranch nestled deep in the Grand Canyon. Several other western parks featured privately-owned lodges—often built by railroads and operated under concession contracts—including Zion Lodge in Utah, Many Glacier Hotel in Montana, and the Ahwanhee Hotel Yosemite in California.

LeConte Lodge followed the latter examples, and a verbal agreement between Huff and park authorities established the concessionaire relationship that still guides lodge operations. The Huff family has maintained a strong influence, as the proprietors have been Jack Huff, 1926–1959, Herrick Brown, 1960–1975, a partnership headed by Jim Huff, Jr. (Jack's nephew), 1976–1988, and Le Conte Ltd. (led by William Stokely III and IV) since 1989.[22] In 2024, the Stokelys surpassed Jack Huff for the longest tenure of management.

Many national park lodges across the nation are managed by large corporations such as Xanterra, Delaware North, and Aramark, but LeConte Lodge has always remained "a mom and pop operation," in the words of longtime manager Tim Line.

The lodge acreage is owned by the National Park Service. The concessionaire is responsible for maintaining most of the facilities and has a "possessory interest" in the value of those assets. If the concessionaire were to change, the new operator would be obligated to buy out the interests of the previous operator. In the case of LeConte Lodge, the concessionaire is invested in almost everything man-made except the water and sewer systems, which were installed by the park service.

Before the park was established, Huff received a 10-year contract to build and operate the lodge as a concession under the Great Smoky Mountains Conservation Association. In 1934, when the national park was established, Huff became the Smokies' first concessionaire.

"Real beds and meals," Plus Skis and Toe-Holds

In 1930, Huff was hired to run Balsam Lodge, a roadside inn at Indian Gap built by Reuben Robertson, the president of Champion Fibre Company, Huff's landlord on Le Conte.

Huff planned to operate Balsam Lodge year-round, according to the *Asheville Citizen-Times*: "Since the Tennessee side of the main crest only a few hundred feet north of the lodge is covered with deep snow throughout the winter, Mr. Huff expects to provide the first opportunity for winter sports ever afforded in this

---

21. Carlos Campbell, *Birth of a National Park* (Knoxville: University of Tennessee Press, 1960).
22. Jim Huff, Jr.'s, partners included architect Hugh Ogle (1933–2017) and snow-skiing entrepreneur William Rinearson III (1914–1982).

section. He announced he would build slides for skiing and tobogganing this winter." Indeed, newspaper clippings that winter showed Huff and others skiing.[23]

The newspaper said that Huff would continue to operate "Jack's Place" on Mount Le Conte, with staff at both locations. "At Balsam Lodge, guests are provided with real beds and meals," the story said, implying that the balsam bunks and campfire grub at LeConte Lodge left something to be desired.

Federal authorities had misgivings about the arrangement, since they had evicted so many businesses and residents as they assembled the national park. Arno Cammerer, the future director of the park service, wrote a letter to park superintendent Ross Eakin, cautioning that the Huff/Robertson business at Indian Gap could set a bad precedent:

> I firmly believe that as soon as we have accepted the Champion Fibre Company lands, we ought to tell Jack Huff that the Balsam Lodge operation is not possible for him for another year, and to that extent perhaps it would be well for Mr. Robertson now to give Jack Huff thirty days' notice that he wants his cabin lease himself. That would kind of clear up matters. I do not believe we ought to allow Jack Huff, or anybody for that matter, to secure a "toe-hold" on any new sites for such camping privileges.
>
> The Mount Le Conte establishment of Jack's is an entirely different thing, because he does render a good public service there at the present time. That has been there for a number of years and we can continue it on a year-to-year basis until we find we are administratively up against the necessity of canceling that lease and giving it to somebody else.
>
> All he wanted the last time I talked to him was another year so he would have a chance to break even. If in your judgment after the first year he should be given another year's lease, and perhaps after that still another, that is all right, but we do not want to tie ourselves down with any commitment at the time we actually assume development of the park.

Eakin regarded Huff as an asset to the park and considered hiring him as a warden as soon as Champion sold its acreage. On the 1930 census, Huff listed his occupation not as a lodge operator but as a forest ranger for the Smoky Mountain Park.[24]

Balsam Lodge[25] later became a clubhouse for the Smoky Mountain Ski Club, and in the early 1940s, it was the site of a Ski Carnival, organized by Bill Rinearson, who became co-owner of LeConte Lodge in 1976. Known later as Timber Top Lodge, it burned down in 1958.[26]

Jack and Pauline retired to a home on Holly Ridge overlooking downtown Gatlinburg and the Mountain View Hotel. He served on the Gatlinburg City Council and died at 82 in 1985.

Their son Phillip died in an auto accident in 1986, and Cookie's family still operates Jack Huff's Motor Lodge on the Cherokee Orchard Road at the foot of Mount Le

---

23. "Balsam Lodge in Heart of Smoky Mountains Is Now Opened for Public," *Asheville Citizen-Times*, July 16, 1931.

24. Paul J. Adams, *Smoky Jack*, edited by Anne Bridges and Ken Wise (Knoxville: University of Tennessee Press, 2016).

25. The name Balsam Lodge and the Indian Gap location caused some confusion, as there was also an Indian Gap Hotel (1927–33) on the Tennessee side near what is now the Chimneys picnic area, as well as the 1908 Balsam Mountain Inn (elevation 3,360), a whistle stop on the railroad from Asheville to Atlanta.

26. Southern skiing resumed in 1961 at the Cataloochee Ski Area near Maggie Valley, North Carolina, and in 1962 at Ober Gatlinburg and Appalachian Ski Mountain near Blowing Rock, North Carolina.

Conte. When Pauline died at 90 in 1996, her obituary was headlined "First Lady of the Smoky Mountains."

Two of their great-grandchildren, Cade Huff and Parker Bowling, completed the Tour de Le Conte in July 2020, hiking all six trails in 23 hours, covering 45.7 miles.

3

Almost a Motor Lodge

What if you could drive up Mount Le Conte?

That was more than a rhetorical question in the era when the Great Smoky Mountains National Park was born. The park movement was driven by automobile clubs and the newfound popularity of sightseeing and vacation road trips. Journalist Rollin Lynde Hartt called it "the new and thrilling sport of mountaineering by limousine."

In the fall of 1925, the *New York Times* sent correspondent Frank Bohn to Tennessee to report on the prospects for the new national park. After a daunting quest for the "hotel" on the mountaintop, he reported that the new park would feature "a fine automobile road along this summit."[1]

Bohn did not name his source regarding the road, but it must have been David Chapman or Carlos Campbell, who facilitated his trip on behalf of the Great Smoky Mountains Conservation Association. When he wrote "along this summit," he was likely referring to the state-line crest. In that era, there was not even a road to Newfound Gap.

The national park's 1932 master plan proposed 230 miles of new roads, including a "skyway" traversing the state-line ridge from Newfound Gap across Clingmans Dome and continuing southwest to Silers Bald, Gregory Bald, and Deal's Gap.

The master plan did not include a road to Le Conte. But at the same time, some North Carolinians envisioned the Blue Ridge Parkway running west from Soco Gap along the flanks of Mount Kephart to a southern terminus at Newfound Gap.[2] Had that road been built, it would have at least shortened the hike out the Boulevard ridge to LeConte Lodge.

And what if some bureaucrat had taken the Boulevard literally and tried to bulldoze a spur road along the ridgeline? Imagine Le Conte jammed with tourist traffic, like Clingmans Dome and Cades Cove. If guest cars, construction equipment, and delivery trucks could have accessed Le Conte, who knows what the lodge might have become?[3]

---

1. Frank Bohn, "A New National Park," *New York Times*, Jan. 25, 1926.
2. "Blue Ridge Parkway to Great Smokies Is Opening New Scenic Beauty Vistas," *Knoxville News-Sentinel*, Oct. 2, 1941. Tennessee had proposed the Blue Ridge Parkway to run westward from Grandfather Mountain across Roan Mountain to a terminus in Gatlinburg or Cherokee. The 72-mile Foothills Parkway was approved in 1944 as a consolation prize for Tennessee, yet 80 years later, only 38 miles were complete.
3. Cades Cove might have been lost, too, if the park's original plans had been fulfilled. A dam was proposed across Abrams Creek that would have flooded the cove with a Hetch Hetchy-esque lake 50 feet deep, fringed by hotels and golf courses. "Park Development Plan Revealed," *Asheville Citizen-Times*, Oct. 16, 1932. If you're wondering what a road might have done to Le Conte, consider that annual traffic approaches 800,000 vehicles in Cades Cove and 300,000 at Kuwohi (irma.nps.gov/Stats/Reports/Park/GRSM).

The proposed skyway was never built beyond Clingmans Dome, even though it had some influential boosters, including writer Horace Kephart and Arno Cammerer, future director of the National Park Service.[4]

Hartt rhapsodized in the *Charlotte Observer* in 1925:

> Mountaineering by limousine is still a very tame sport by comparison with what it is destined to become. Last week I motored through the splendid Carolina mountains above Asheville but got no glimpse of the Great Smokies, and even today our car from Knoxville could penetrate no further than Cades Cove. We saw the Great Smokies only from a distance of eight miles. But wait! Once that stupendous chain of mountains becomes the crest of a national park, there will be a highway from summit to summit all along the great divide for 60 miles and more. Hour after hour, you will motor above the clouds, looking down upon a wild chaos of sylvan beauty, and away toward the dim horizon, across range after range whose ethereal blues and purples and soft green melt into an adorable harmony as surprising as it is exquisite.[5]

The Car Went Over the Mountain

If anyone might have driven a car up Le Conte, Jack Huff would have been a good bet. Less than two years after portering his mom up the mountain, he dared to be the first to drive across the roadless mountains between Gatlinburg and North Carolina.

The *Knoxville News-Sentinel* reported on March 30, 1930: "Plenty of motorists have driven far up the so-called Indian Gap state road and some have gone so far as Newfound Gap on the state line, to which point the road has been partially built. But beyond that, no ordinary motorist would dare venture." The distance from Gatlinburg to Smokemont was only 24 miles, but there was no road on the North Carolina side.[6]

Eager to promote a trans-mountain highway to funnel tourists into Gatlinburg, the intrepid[7] Huff borrowed a Plymouth roadster[8] from his father's hotel, rounded up three friends to help clear the route, and drove up to Newfound Gap. He planned to descend via the old Thomas Road, an abandoned Civil War wagon trail that was frequently blocked by erosion, thick undergrowth, logging slash, and trees that had fallen victim to the chestnut blight.

The expedition was in February 1930, during an unusually mild winter. The *Asheville Times* broke the news February 19, 1930, in a dispatch written by none other than Kephart:

---

4. John Parris, "Dream of Road Never Realized," *Asheville Citizen-Times*, Jan. 31, 1982.
5. Rollin Lynde Hartt, "Keen Interest Manifest All Over United States in Great Smokies Park," *Charlotte Observer*, Nov. 1, 1925.
6. "Adventures of a Horse and an Auto," *Knoxville News-Sentinel*, March 30, 1930.
7. Jack Huff was also a passenger on the first plane to land in Gatlinburg, a World War I–vintage Curtis Jenny biplane that landed in 1927 in a rolling pasture behind the original Baptist church. A few sycamore trees had to be cut down to make a runway long enough for the refueled plane to take off. Gatlinburg has no airport, though the Historic Nature Trail is also known as Airport Road, because it was straight enough for emergency landings.
8. "Plymouth First Auto to Cross Indian Trail," *The Tennessean*, May 4, 1930. The Plymouth brand was launched in 1928, and Huff's car had 50,000 miles, many of them on unpaved roads. The 1928 Plymouth roadster listed for $670 and had a 45-hp 4-cylinder engine.

Mr. Huff, accompanied by Fred Cooper, Ray Whaley, and Austin Whaley, all of Gatlinburg, drove his car up the new road Tennessee had built to the top of old Smoky at Newfound Gap.

At that time, from the gap downward on the North Carolina side, there was just plain wilderness except for the rugged old Indian Gap Trail and the wilderness-reclaimed old Thomas Road built by the Cherokee Indians during the War Between the States.

Facing the wilderness, Mr. Huff and his party took a chance. Heading down, they met Dock Connor[9] of upper Lufty who climbed aboard and helped them find a way where no car had been before.[10]

Huff told *The Tennessean* that as they reached the Oconaluftee Valley, they emerged from the woods atop a steep bank cut for a logging railroad. A lumberjack saw their predicament and rounded up enough men and rope to safely lower the car down the embankment. From there they drove down the tracks to the Smokemont logging camp, crossing more than a dozen trestles. They completed the transit in less than five hours.

Chrysler agents in Detroit boasted: "The Plymouth traveled under its own power and once the worst obstacles were removed, performed as surely as if it were on a country road." Understandably, the fenders took a beating.

Huff spent the night in North Carolina before making his roundabout return trip via the valley roads. "When we couldn't find a place to stay, we decided to get in jail for the night," he said. "Do you know—we broke all the laws within reason, and the Asheville police never did arrest us?"[11]

The following day, according to Kephart, Dr. Kelly Bennett and Ray Smith of Bryson City made the trip up the North Carolina side in a Chevy roadster, presumably following Huff's tracks and packing a block and tackle to pull the car up the steepest hills. Imagine the reaction in Gatlinburg if Dr. Bennett arrived before Jack Huff made it back home!

Jack Huff understood the promotional value of a good adventure. In fact, the Knoxville newspaper story "Adventures of a Horse and an Auto" also included the saga of Jack leading the first horse up Le Conte, saddling up for a dramatic photo at Cliff Top (see Chapter 9).

Subsequent reports in *The Tennessean* from Nashville and Detroit-area newspapers credited the trip to Andy Huff, probably because it was his car. In a 1953 interview with *The Tennessean*,[12] Jack Huff verified that he was the driver, and mayor Austin Whaley[13] said he was one of the passengers.

A few months later, Kephart and photographer George Masa drove Huff's route in a Falcon-Knight car to evaluate the feasibility of exploring the Smokies by car. "Keep the automobiles out until the roads are improved," Kephart wrote in the

---

9. D.F. "Dock" Conner (1855–1948) was a farmer who had driven livestock across the Indian Gap. His son Charlie Conner was the namesake for Charlies Bunion. Upper Lufty was a settlement on the Oconaluftee River, upstream from the Champion logging camp at Smokemont.
10. "Adventure in the High Smokies," *Asheville Citizen*, Saturday, July 26, 1958 (reprinting the *Asheville Times* story of Feb. 19, 1930).
11. "Adventures of a Horse and An Auto," *Knoxville News-Sentinel*, March 30, 1930. Kephart's account in the Asheville paper said Huff returned via Bryson City and Maryville, rather than via Asheville.
12. H.B. Teeter, "Gatlinburg Eyes The Future," *The Tennessean* (Nashville), June 28, 1953.
13. Austin "Dick" Whaley (1910–1994) was the first mayor of Gatlinburg, and his wife Martha Cole Whaley (1910–2018) became the town's oldest resident.

Asheville Times on June 16, 1930. En route, Kephart learned a lesson from the logging railroads—back the car down to every other switchback, to avoid tight turns.

Huff's stunt served its purpose: Later in 1930, North Carolina graded the road up to Indian Gap, and by the end of the decade, the highway was routed through Newfound Gap, which was cut down to 5,046 feet, compared to Indian Gap at 5,272. By the summer of 1930, traffic was climbing the North Carolina side of the Smokies.[14]

Promoters of horseless carriages liked to test them against the nation's signature peaks. A Stanley Steamer conquered New Hampshire's Mount Washington in 1899 and a Locomobile chugged up Colorado's Pikes Peak in 1901. Mount Mitchell was accessible via turnpike, billed as "the World's Greatest Scenic Trip," when the national park commissioners drove up in 1924.

By the 1920s, cars had gone higher than Le Conte. In a 1903 cross-country race from San Francisco to New York City, a Packard set an altitude record by crossing a two-mile-high pass in the Rockies. In 1919, an army convoy of World War I trucks drove cross-country from Washington to San Francisco, a 62-day, 3,251-mile junket that crossed California's Donner Pass, nearly 500 feet higher than Le Conte. Colonel Dwight Eisenhower was on the trip and gained a vision for the interstate highway system which he established as president in 1956.

A Model T Ford completed the inaugural Pikes Peak Hill Climb in 1916. But the Model T was engineered for the masses rather than the massif.[15] The granddaddy of the pony-car had a puny 20-horsepower engine that was prone to stalling on hills, for lack of a fuel pump.

There is a legend that Henry Ford once visited the Cloudland Hotel on Roan Mountain, Tennessee's sixth highest summit. The Cloudland was accessible by wagon roads, but if Ford actually visited, it is unlikely that he arrived by car. That inn closed in 1910 (just after the 1908 debut of the Model T), and it was 1915 before Ford began his famous road trips.

In the Smokies, Model Ts made it at least as far as the Sugarlands settlement, where Earnest Ogle owned 13.[16] In North Carolina, Dr. F.J. Clemenger made headlines in 1915 by driving a V-8 King automobile up Bald Mountain (3,020 feet, near Chimney Rock).[17] Virginia's Skyland Lodge (elevation 3,680), now on the Skyline Drive, was an off-road destination for decades until a steamer arrived in 1907.

When Ford and his "Vagabond" friends—inventor Thomas Edison, tiremaker Harvey Firestone, and naturalist John Burroughs—vacationed in the southern Appalachians in 1918, they rode in a fleet of Packard roadsters whose V-12 engines outmuscled the Model T. The Vagabonds avoided the Smokies and took the route of least resistance from Bristol to Asheville, generally following the French Broad River valley and avoiding the high ridges.

The Vagabonds had an unforgettable stop at the Lee family farm west of

---

14. Maude Minish Sutton, "Along Indian Gap Trail into the Smokies," *Charlotte Observer*, July 6, 1930.
15. The most famous mountain climb by a Model T was a 1911 promotional stunt in Scotland, where a Ford dealer challenged his son to drive up Ben Nevis, the highest mountain in the British Isles (4,413 feet). With his allowance at stake, the boy made it to the top, though the trip took several days.
16. Bonnie Tom Robinson, "Only Our Southern Highlands Could Have Produced Such Colorful Characters as Earnest and Lucinda Ogle," *Knoxville News-Sentinel*, July 28, 1940.
17. "First Automobile Climbs Bald Mountain," *Asheville Citizen*, Sept. 4, 1915.

Jonesborough, where Ford playfully volunteered to help an eight-year-old boy sawing wood. "Do you know you're sawing with Henry Ford, who made these cars?" the tycoon teased. The boy retorted, "Do you know you're sawing with Robert E. Lee?" Years later, during the Depression, one of Ford's associates remembered the quick-witted Robert Ernest Lee and gave him a job.[18]

Henry and Clara Ford rode in chauffeured Lincoln sedans when they visited Gatlinburg in October 1926. At the Mountain View Hotel, Andy Huff showed them photos of the Smokies, and Carlos Campbell guided them up to an overlook to see Mount Le Conte, which was snow-white with hoar-frost. Mrs. Ford mentioned that she once hiked down into the Grand Canyon, so Campbell invited her to climb Le Conte. "Oh, I would like to," she said. "Next time."

When the Fords stopped by Wiley Oakley's antique shop, Wiley promised to name his next baby for them. Clara Oakley[19] was born in 1927, and her daddy called her "Mrs. Henry Ford Oakley."[20]

Long before the national park was born, conservationists expressed concerns about road construction and motor traffic spoiling the Smokies. "There is a growing opposition to girdling such peaks as Mount LeConte with automobile roads,"

Henry Ford's "Vagabonds" convoy met "Robert E. Lee" in 1918 in the foothills of Tennessee. Note the difference between the Model T (center) and the Packards (right) (from the Collections of The Henry Ford).

---

18. George Kelly, "When Henry Ford Was in These Parts," *Johnson City Press*, May 22, 1956. Bob Lee (1910–1992) worked for two years at the Ford Plant in Dearborn, Michigan, and came home to manage the Thom McAn shoe store in Johnson City, Tenn.

19. Warner Ogden, "Roamin Man," *The Tennessean* (Nashville), June 9, 1946. Sadly, Clara lived only five months and died two days before Christmas, 1927.

20. "Henry Ford Has Knox Escort to Le Conte," *Knoxville News-Sentinel*, Oct. 27, 1926; W.W. Ayres, "Henry Ford Pays a Flying Visit to Smoky Mountains," *Knoxville Journal*, Oct. 28, 1926. The Fords visited Gatlinburg because Clara Bryant Ford was interested in the Pi Beta Phi Settlement School. Disconcerted by media attention, Henry Ford truncated the visit (skipping a luncheon at the Mountain View Hotel).

according to a 1926 issue of the *Explosives Engineer*, a bulletin written for excavators and miners.[21]

Two co-founders of the Wilderness Society brought the skyway to an impasse. Bob Marshall, a forester from New York, decried the road as an "invasion of the primitive," foreshadowing the 1970s wilderness debate that almost doomed LeConte Lodge (see Chapter 4). Knoxville attorney Harvey Broome persuaded National Park Director Horace Albright to conserve the ridgeline east of Newfound Gap, precluding any parkway along the North Carolina border.

The skyway from Newfound Gap to Clingmans Dome was paved in time for visits by the Roosevelts. President Roosevelt's 1936 motorcade went from Knoxville to Asheville via Indian Gap and stopped for a picnic at Clingmans Dome, where the spread included fried chicken, caviar sandwiches, lobster salad, and chocolate eclairs.

In 1937, Eleanor Roosevelt and her companion Lorena Hickok stayed with the Huffs at the Mountain View Hotel in Gatlinburg, dined on trout and country ham at Willie Myers' Ekaneetlee Lodge in Cades Cove, and visited Clingmans Dome and the Cherokee Indian Reservation. The highway through Newfound Gap was open when the Roosevelts returned September 2, 1940, to dedicate the national park.

As FDR spoke, the German blitzkrieg of Great Britain was imminent.[22] The president saluted the fortitude of mountaineers as he prepared the nation for world war: "The old frontier that put the hard fibre in the American spirit and the long muscles on the American back, lives and will live in these untamed mountains to give to the future generations a sense of the land from which their forefathers hewed their homes."[23]

The road across Newfound Gap was constructed as state highways—Route 71 in Tennessee and 107 in North Carolina—and was subsequently rebuilt to national park standards. In 1951, the trans-mountain road was designated as U.S. 441,[24] and in 1959 the Blue Ridge Parkway connected Soco Gap and Oconaluftee.

After Fred Behrend from Elizabethton, Tennessee, visited the lodge in 1963, he recalled his first visit back in 1933:

> Gatlinburg was then a sleepy place. There was only a narrow blacktop main street. The only outstanding hotel was the Mountain View Hotel, which belonged to the Huff family.
> The highway from Gatlinburg to Newfound Gap was under construction and rough. The scenery was stupendous with steep ridges and gigantic coniferous trees at higher levels.
> From Newfound Gap I hiked for eight miles along the Boulevard, a foot trail which had just been completed to Mt. LeConte.

---

21. Theodore Marvin, "A National Park in Eastern America's Highlands," *The Explosives Engineer*, Nov. 1926.
22. The bombing of London began September 7, 1940, and air raids of England continued for 57 days.
23. The president's honor guard at Newfound Gap included a 20-year-old soldier named John Adler (1920–2022), who served with the 10th Mountain Division in World War II, became a doctor in Rockwood, Tennessee, logged more than 100 hikes to Mount Le Conte, and made a bid to buy the lodge when the Huffs retired.
24. "U.S. 441 Extended into WNC Area," *Asheville Citizen-Times*, Nov. 2, 1951. Highway 441 extends from Miami to the coal-mining town of Rocky Top, Tennessee. In the 1950s, it was promoted to tourists from Chicago and Detroit as the "Dixie Highway."

Jack Huff, now operator of Mountain View Hotel[25] and Jack Huff's Court in Gatlinburg, was the only person at the lodge, then just an open shelter. I had been caught in thunderstorms and the temperature was cool. The hot coffee Huff brewed was very welcome.

There has been no change in the 30 years in the approach to the top of Mt. LeConte and the lodge. The trails are still the same, although improved by the Park Service.[26]

Backpacking Was the Only Way

Far above the road-building frenzy, LeConte Lodge remained accessible only the old-fashioned way—by foot or by horseback. No wonder that Smokies explorer Paul Fink titled his book *Backpacking Was the Only Way.*

Energized by FDR's New Deal in the 1930s, the Civilian Conservation Corps built six trails accessing Le Conte: Rainbow Falls, Bullhead, and Trillium Gap from Cherokee Orchard; Alum Cave Bluff and the Appalachian Trail/Boulevard Trail from the Newfound Gap highway; and Brushy Mountain from Greenbrier Cove to a junction with Trillium Gap.

There are also two steep trails on the North Carolina side which access the Boulevard via the AT. That gives Le Conte hikers a choice of eight maintained trails.

More than 20 off-trail routes have been explored. Jenny Bennett (1953–2015) explored all 12 creeks that flow from the mountain. Paul Dinwiddie's 750 ascents included 25 routes, 19 of them bushwhacks. A map in the 1998 book *A Natural History of Mount Le Conte*[27] shows three additional routes that are no longer maintained trails—Bear Pen Hollow, Huggins Hell, and Roaring Fork.

Back in 1933, the original guide to the national park recommended two trails to the lodge, Rainbow Falls and the Boulevard.

Adams described the pre–CCC paths as lightly traveled and poorly marked. He told of hikers climbing trees to get oriented and scout their route. Gene Dearing left this comment in a 1922 logbook: "It is truly God's playground, but I think the devil himself had a hand in the trail up here."

If you wanted to climb Le Conte in the days before the CCC blazed the way, you would have been wise to hire a guide such as Wiley Oakley, Will Ramsey, or Alex Cole. According to Knoxville columnist Bert Vincent, Oakley told his guests, "'Jis pay me whatever you want.' Five dollars would have been pretty good pay. But if there were half a dozen or more in the crowd, they'd slip Wiley $1, likely $1.50 each. Sometimes he'd make $15." Compare that to $12 per week that CCC workers were earning.[28]

---

25. The Mountain View Hotel was a stately inn that was a familiar gateway to Gatlinburg, facing west at the fork of the roads to Sevierville and Newport (now U.S. 441 and 321). Andy Huff opened the inn in 1916 and rebuilt it in 1932, but it closed in 1986 after Jack Huff's death. Jim Huff, Jr. (grandson of Andy Huff and nephew of Jack) proposed a $30 million renovation that would have preserved the historic main building as the front of a 326-room Marriott convention center, similar to the 1984 renovations at Asheville's Grove Park Inn. However, the proposal fell through, and the old inn was torn down and replaced by an amusement park called Fun Mountain.

26. Fred W. Behrend, "Mt. LeConte is Well-Known Attraction," *Elizabethton Star*, July 7, 1963.

27. Kenneth Wise and Ron Peterson, *A Natural History of Mount Le Conte* (Knoxville: University of Tennessee Press, 1998).

28. "Bridle Trails Planned for Park," *Chattanooga News*, Aug. 12, 1932.

3. Almost a Motor Lodge

The Smoky Mountain Hiking Club, organized during a 1924 hike to Mount Le Conte, was instrumental in scouting and planning the park trails.[29]

Trail construction was a priority for Ross Eakin as soon as he was appointed superintendent in 1931, three years before the park was officially authorized. Eakin assigned engineer Robert P. White and landscape architect Roswell Ludgate to prepare trail plans, so the nascent park was shovel-ready when the CCC was chartered in 1933.

The park was appropriated $509,000 in 1932 to build the Appalachian Trail northbound from Newfound Gap, plus the Boulevard Trail and another 13 miles of trails on the North Carolina side. The park eventually had 18 CCC camps, each employing more than 100 men. The Kephart Prong Camp (Company 411) was responsible for building the highway on the North Carolina side of Newfound Gap.

Most early Le Conte hikers followed the Rainbow Falls route from Cherokee Orchard or Bear Pen Hollow from the old Indian Gap Road. "The top of this peak is not in the least inaccessible," the *Knoxville Journal & Tribune* reported in 1922. "Many parties of boys and girls have ascended the rough paths or blazed a new trail through the brush and undergrowth for the pleasure of camping above the clouds and viewing a perfect sunrise before it reached mankind in the valley."[30]

Paul Fink climbed Bear Pen Hollow with Walter Diehl[31] on September 24, 1916. Fink described the journey:

> For several years Walter had been visiting the Great Smokies in company with the Bain brothers[32] and others from Knoxville and had been singing to me praises of their beauty and their wild ruggedness. All this was at a time when one could seldom find a single person who had even so much as heard of those mountains, much less visited them.
>
> His stories had whetted to a keen edge my craving to see for myself what was there. He agreed to take me on a personally conducted tour to Le Conte, a peak even more unknown than the mountain range itself. So the night of September 21, 1916, found us in his room in Knoxville sorting out our gear and making up our packs. He, the more experienced, was using a duffle bag and pack harness, while I still depend on the old Army issue knapsack, with blanket in a waterproof roll on top.
>
> No motor roads penetrated the Smokies that early, and if they had, we had no car to ride over them. Easiest access was by rail, so we rode the K&A[33] Railroad to Walland and then the Little River Railroad to Elkmont. This road had been built by the Little River Lumber Company, that for more than twenty years had been cutting timber on the northwestern slopes of the Smokies. It entered the mountains along the twisting, tumbling Little River, up a canyon so constricted that often the road had to be blown out of the faces of cliffs dropping sheer to the water's edge.
>
> Shouldering our packs at Elkmont, we followed first an old trail built by the U.S. Forest

---

29. The club's trail committee included Marshall Wilson, Lucien Green, F.J. Shulley, Dutch Roth, and Harvey Broome. The nomenclature committee (which researched and documented names) included Paul Fink, Hodge Mathes, Robert L. Maxon, Brockway Crouch, and Jim Thompson. "Naming the Smoky Mountains—A Matter of 300 Years," *The Tennessean* (Nashville), June 19, 1932.
30. "Mountain Inspector Is Here for Go at Mount Le Conte to Credit It on U.S. Geodetic Survey," *Knoxville Journal & Tribune*, June 11, 1922.
31. Walter S. Diehl (1893–1976) became a navy captain in World War I and an aeronautical engineer. The navy has a fleet replenishment tanker named in his honor.
32. The Bain brothers were descendants of Davy Crockett. Their father, Samuel Bain, was a botany professor at the University of Tennessee.
33. K&A was the Knoxville and Augusta Railroad, an ambitious name for a route that made it no further south than Maryville.

Service to the Huskey Gap, on Sugarland Mountain. Here I had my first glimpse of Bull Head, with the massive bulk of Le Conte behind it. A few minutes' look, to get an idea of its immensity, and down the side of the mountain we went, dropping to the West Prong of the Little Pigeon River.

The only trail of which we had heard was the rudimentary one up Bear Pen Hollow, leaving the river and turning left up a little hollow a few hundred yards above Cole Branch. For the first eight or nine hundred feet—altitude—the grade was easy and the going good, but after leaving the top spring of the little brook the sides of the ravine closed in and grew much steeper. Thirty degree slopes were the usual thing, and forty-five degree ones were common. There were occasional blazes, and at times a faintly marked footway, and there was little trouble following it. That is, there was little trouble finding it. Following it was something else entirely. The man who blazed that trail was much more concerned about finding the shortest way to the top, rather than the easiest way of getting there.

When we finally clambered out of the ravine to the crest of the ridge we had our first view of the Cliff Top of Le Conte. The top of the ridge was a real knife edge, a bare few feet wide, choked with bushes and with precipitous slopes on either side. A native had told us that just about here a new and better trail turned off to the right, its beginning marked by a spruce tree decorated with many tin tobacco tags tacked onto the bark. This trail, as he phrased it, "surrounded the top," saving considerable climbing and rough going.

The trail swung around to the North side of the Cliff Top, where a lone ascent was feasible, passing through thick balsam and up moss covered ledges to the open top, this covered with waist-high rhododendron to the very brink of the cliffs. At the edge of the timber, Walter searched a moment, then showed me, carved perpendicularly on a balsam tree, the legend, "W.S. Diehl, '14, '15." While he was adding "16" to the list of dates, I registered on a tree close by. Pushing through low hanging balsam boughs, we stepped into the open. There, suddenly as a picture flashed on the screen, was a scene so grand it almost took my breath.

Beyond the cliff-rimmed gorge of Huggins Hell at our feet, and stretching away into the distance as far as one might see, were peaks innumerable, with sharp, high ridges and deep ravines everywhere. The air was clear, far more so than usual, and we could easily distinguish many details of the landscape ordinarily invisible. Far beneath us, in the valley of the river, were the Chimney Tops, that only a few hours before had towered twelve hundred feet above our camp. Now they were a mere minor detail of the scene. Faint as a whisper, hardly to be distinguished from the sighing of the breeze in the balsams, came up the sounds of the stream three thousand feet below. It was easy to realize why all this had been called the roughest and wildest region east of the Rockies, for it would be hard to conceive a timbered country more rugged. Every ridge was like the edge of a gigantic saw. Cliffs were rare, as is usually the case in mountains as old as these. Where they did occur, they were almost masked by a lush curtain of bushes.

Only the urge to push on to the High Top dragged us away from the rugged majesty of the scene. The mountain top between the two peaks is a hundred yards wide, mantled with as dense a stand of balsam as one might hope to find. A storm a few years before had leveled many trees here. The fallen trunks and jutting branches formed a veritable *cheval-de-frise*, made more difficult by a rampant new growth sprung up among the fallen timber. A short, fruitless struggle with this showed we could not hope to push through in the time available and reluctantly we returned to the Cliff Top for a long last look before starting down off the mountain. Later we were told that other than being able to say that we had reached the highest point on the mountains, there was little to be gained, for the High Top was so densely timbered there was no good lookout.[34]

---

34. Paul Fink, *Backpacking Was the Only Way* (Johnson City: Research Advisory Council, East Tennessee State University, 1975).

(From left) Pioneer hikers Paul Fink, Myron Avery, and Walter Diehl. Fink and Avery are wearing tumplines over their heads, which helped support their backpacks by taking some of the load off their shoulders. Diehl led Fink on his 1916 climb of Le Conte. Avery was chairman of the Appalachian Trail Conference from 1931 through 1952. When the ATC met in Gatlinburg in 1931, he hiked 170 miles from Mount Oglethorpe in Georgia and stopped at LeConte Lodge (Great Smoky Mountains National Park Archives).

Bear Pen was also the route that Jack and Pauline Huff scaled for their 1934 wedding at Myrtle Point. Who knows why the bridal party chose such an arduous route instead of the brand-new bridle trail out the Boulevard?

Bear Pen is not maintained as an official park trail, but adventurers occasionally bushwhack up the old 2.4-mile route.[35] The path is accessed from U.S. 441 at a pullout just above the road's distinctive loop, and it connects with the Alum Cave Trail at the Hallelujah Turn, on the ridgeline west of Cliff Top. The route passes the wreckage of a 2016 plane crash.

Rainbow Falls Trail

Rainbow Falls was the general route followed by the national parks commission in 1924. John Willy, editor of the trade magazine the *Hotel Monthly*, wrote this account after he hiked up in 1926 with guide Orpheus Schantz:

> Our ambition was to reach the top of LeConte Mountain, one of the highest peaks in the park, and reached only by foot trail. (There is a new trail being made for horses that will be open next season.)
>
> We climbed this hill, a party of five, including Mr. Schantz and the guide, William Mitchell Ramsey, who had been four years in the mountains with a surveying party. The summit is eight miles from Gatlinburg by foot and will be ten miles by horse trail. About half the distance of the foot trail can be made by motor, which we did, to the Cherokee Orchard.
>
> Mr. Schantz was in his element climbing this trail, and we took a longer time than usual in making the ascent because of interest in the tree and plant life so abundant every foot of the way. First we drank at the old mill, then followed the trail for a mile to Rainbow Falls, where the water tumbles in a single fall of 81 feet; this waterfall was pictured in the *National Geographic* Magazine for July 1926, as one of the most beautiful in America. It was indeed a beautiful sight, the right bank a thicket of rhododendron in bloom; all around the virgin forest, some of the trees growing when Columbus discovered America. The trail followed the creek to within three-fourths of a mile of the summit. It was a music of waterfall all the way. There were many rather difficult sections to negotiate, but we got through after crossing and recrossing on stepping stones, climbing steep places with the aid of tree roots, and finding a way over jumbled boulders. It is a refreshing trail, in that it is shady all the way, no scenery except trees until you reach the summit.
>
> As we traveled, Mr. Schantz called particular attention to the trees. There are sugar and other maples, locust, chestnut,[36] hemlock, several kinds of oak, black walnut, poplar (tulip), buckeye, yellow birch, hickory, basswood, cherry, ash, magnolia, cucumber, and many other kinds. There were vines of many kinds in luxuriant growth; wild grapes, rhododendrons, white in the lower altitude, purple near the top of the mountain, dwarf Carolina rhododendron on the top; laurel; holly. There were acres and acres of ferns, galax, patches of tiger lilies, wild hydrangea, mountain orchids, mountain oxalis, and on top of the mountain, above the balsams, was a heavy growth of sand myrtle.[37]

---

35. Jordan Lacy, who explored Bear Pen Hollow in 2022, describes the route as one and a half miles with 2,700 feet of climbing from U.S. 441 to West Point, plus another 0.4 miles on the ridgeline to the Alum Cave Bluff Trail.

36. Before the national park was born, about one-third of the trees in the Smokies were chestnuts. These forests were wiped out by a parasitic fungus that was accidentally introduced in America about 1904. The American Chestnut Foundation in Meadowview, Virginia (140 miles northeast of Le Conte), is working to develop a blight-resistant chestnut.

37. John Willy, "The Great Smoky Mountains National Park," *Hotel Monthly*, Sept. 1926.

3. Almost a Motor Lodge

The original Rainbow Falls path rock-hopped along Mill Creek and gained 900 feet per mile over 4.1 miles—shorter, steeper, and wetter than any of today's trails. More than a dozen streams in the Smokies were called Mill Creek, so the park renamed this one Le Conte Creek and named the trail for Rainbow Falls.

Oakley said he and attorney Reuben Cates established the original trail, and he credited Cates with naming the waterfall.[38] The 1932 nomenclature committee called it LeConte Trail.

In 1929, newspaperman Leo Hershfield visited the Mountain View Hotel in Gatlinburg and climbed Le Conte on a dare from "the tavern keeper's comely daughter (whose long familiarity with the mountain having bred something akin to disdain for its heights)." He started late in the day, declined to take a guide, and trudged alone up the Mill Creek route. After two exhausting hours, he met some downbound hikers who told him he was nowhere near the halfway point. As the sun set and dusk fell, the drama rose in Herschfield's account in the *Chattanooga Times*. With no idea how much farther he had to go, he felt lost and realized that a cry for help would be in vain:

> Panic reared its ugly head when the trail was lost as the half-light of the trail grew dimmer with the approach of night; where the path was ankle-deep cold mire, the earthy condensation of the mists that so often shroud the summit. Then what a feeling of desolation when one's hail was not answered, but which desperation was changed to a glow of triumph when, far off, was seen a faint gleam of light. "Excelsior!" It was the lodge maintained by the tavern keeper's son. No lost traveler in the Alps could have been happier at the sight of a St. Bernard with a cask of spirits stowed under his dewlap than was this bedraggled climber at the sight of Huff's lodge with its huge open fire, the welcome food, the heavy blankets and the sweet-smelling balsam bunks.[39]

In the valley below Rainbow Falls, modern hikers generally follow the route of the 1924 national parks commission. In 1932, switchbacks were built to carry the trail around and above the waterfall and cliffs (where the 1924 group had to scale a leaning tree) and then up across Rocky Spur, which eased the grade to 580 feet per mile and also opened up some views. As a result, the mileage from Cherokee Orchard to the lodge increased from 4.1 to 6.6. The longer trail was designed to accommodate pack horses, who carried supplies to the lodge for more than 50 years. Laura Thornborough, writing in the *Knoxville Journal*, called the new route "a well-graded lady-like trail."

Thornborough interviewed landscape architect Roswell Ludgate about his design: "The LeConte trail, after it leaves the falls, will climb the mountain by a series of switchbacks to avoid the 45-degree grade encountered on some sections of the old trail. After recrossing LeConte Creek about 1,000 feet above the top of the falls, the trail will start for the top of Rocky Spur, coming out at an elevation of about 5,000 feet. It will then swing over to the far side of Rocky Spur and in so doing will

---

38. J.A. Dunn, "Seen and Heard," *Knoxville Journal*, Feb. 13, 1928. It's uncommon to see a rainbow at the falls. General Reuben Cates (1867–1925) was the prosecutor in Knox County.
39. "An Idyll of the Great Smokies," by Leo Hershfield, *Chattanooga Daily Times*, Sept. 2, 1934. The tavern keeper's comely daughter would have been one of Jack Huff's younger sisters, Stella or Mattie. Herschfield (1904–1979) became a cartoonist who sketched courtroom scenes for the *New York Times* and NBC-TV, including the assassination trials of Jack Ruby and James Earl Ray.

give a panorama of about 180 degrees. Two far-reaching panoramas from different points on Rocky Spur can be obtained from the new trail. No longer will it be necessary to climb to the high peaks on Mt. LeConte before one can get a view."[40]

Rainbow and Trillium are the only trails on Le Conte that remain open to horses. There is no longer a stable at the lodge—only a hitching post on the Trillium Gap Trail—so horseback riders must make day trips rather than staying overnight.

Historically, most lodge guests have arrived on foot rather than on horseback. In 1961, Herrick Brown counted 2,170 overnight guests plus 2,000 day-hikers—and only 106 rode horses. Saddle traffic has diminished in recent years. "It wasn't a good place to ride," said Myrtle Brown. "There was nowhere to get off to rest. You had to keep going up."

One Le Conte pilgrim who took advantage of the saddle trips was Gracie McNicol, a retired nurse from Maryville who had to stop hiking up Le Conte after she suffered a stroke at age 76 in 1967. Gracie made her last 89 ascents by horse, including her 244th and final trip on her 92nd birthday in 1983. Her biographer wrote of Gracie's milestone 200th trip: "No other climbers other than lodge personnel were known to have attained it."[41] Even when she rode up, Gracie preferred to hike down, as walking downhill felt safer than riding. She usually stayed two nights on her visits.

The Rainbow Falls Trail was renovated in 2018 by Trails Forever, a partnership between the national park and Friends of the Smokies.

Rainbow Falls rarely freezes into a solid column. John Northrup photographed this "hourglass formation" during a polar vortex in 2014. Dutch Roth captured a similar scene in 1958 (courtesy John Northrup).

---

40. "Climbing Le Conte Just an Afternoon Walk," by Laura Thornborough, *Knoxville Journal*, Dec. 4, 1932.

41. Gracie and author Emilie Ervin Powell were evidently unaware of Ron Valentine, who had made hundreds of climbs by that time. Gracie's total stood as the record for women until Margaret Stevenson logged #245 in 1986, on her way to #718 in 1997.

Boulevard Trail

As soon as the northbound Appalachian Trail reached Mount Kephart,[42] it made sense to build the mile-high Boulevard Trail along the ridgeline to Anakeesta Knob, Myrtle Point and Le Conte. By 1934, the AT was completed as a Class A[43] bridle trail—suitable for horses—all the way from Newfound Gap to Davenport Gap at the northeastern corner of the park. Jack Huff occasionally used the Boulevard as a supply route, with mules dragging loaded sleds along the path to the lodge.

From Newfound Gap, hikers follow the Appalachian Trail northbound for 2.7 miles and then turn left onto the Boulevard Trail. Just beyond the junction is a half-mile spur trail over Mount Kephart (6,217 feet) to "the Jumpoff," a clifftop with dramatic views of the Porter Creek gorge.

The 1932 park nomenclature committee noted that "Boulevard" was an ironic name because the route was much more rugged than maps suggested. The northbound Appalachian Trail climbs 1,000 feet from Newfound Gap, and after a refreshingly level mile-high stretch, the Boulevard makes another 1,000-foot climb (crossing the scar of a 1993 landslide) as it approaches High Top, the 6,593-foot summit of Le Conte. The spur trail to Myrtle Point was hacked out by Paul Adams' crew in 1924 for the national parks commissioners. In 1933, the CCC added a hitching post at the junction, so that horseback riders could walk out to Myrtle Point.

The viewshed from Myrtle Point on a crystal-clear day encompasses the highest peaks in five states: Kentucky (Black Mountain, 92 miles northeast), Virginia (Mount Rogers, 126 miles east-northeast), North Carolina (Mount Mitchell, 66 miles east), Georgia (Brasstown Bald, 58 miles southwest) and, of course, Tennessee (Kuwohi, seven miles southwest).

In 1933, a Nashville newspaper reporter named Betty Burns and two Knoxville men, Lamar Matthews and former University of Tennessee football player Squiz Green, rode bicycles up the AT and Boulevard. "We took the new 8½-mile bridle path from the Indian Gap Highway on the border of Tennessee and North Carolina," she wrote. "The trail is about five or six feet in width and is excellent for horseback riding or hiking, but the steep slopes and none-to-gentle grades of rock and mud do not make bicycling particularly inviting." The route she describes followed the Appalachian Trail northbound from Indian Gap. At that time, there was no highway across Newfound Gap.[44]

Arriving at the lodge, she had "a cup of the worst coffee I have ever drunk and a few beans. Our bill for this small quantity of food amounted to 95 cents." The riders were careful on the way up but had to hurry through a storm on the way down: "Our

---

42. Mount Kephart was formerly known as Mount Collins but was renamed in memory of Horace Kephart (1862–1931), a leader in the national park movement. The current Mount Collins, three miles along the Appalachian Trail northeast from Clingmans Dome, is named in memory of Robert Collins, a North Carolina mountaineer who was a guide for Arnold Guyot.
43. Class A trails were required to be 6 feet wide with a grade of no more than 15 percent. "Smoky Trails Work Goes On," by Laura Thornborough, *Knoxville Journal*, Jan. 22, 1933.
44. "Nashville Girl with First Bicyclists to Conquer Famous Mount LeConte," by Betty Burns, *Nashville Banner*, June 23, 1933.

brakes began to squeak and steam, our tires were almost flat, but on we rode, escaping a dash into 'Death's Valley' only by the grace of God."

If they were the first to do it, they were also the last to do it legally. A week later, park authorities decreed that anyone riding bikes or motorcycles on the trails was subject to arrest.[45]

Trillium Gap Trail

As the lodge became a destination, other trails took shape. The lower Trillium Gap Trail was envisioned by Huff as the Roaring Fork Lead, and there has been some speculation that when he carried his mom to the lodge in 1928, he actually used Trillium rather than Rainbow.

Trillium was built by a Sevier County road crew in 1926, starting in Cherokee Orchard. Paul Adams, co-founder of the lodge, worked on this project in lieu of paying road taxes. His crew built a horse trail to Grassy Gap (elevation 4,700) and continued on up to an impassable section they called the Bluffs. From there, they turned left and roughed out a footpath along the ridgeline toward High Top, which Adams called East Peak. The CCC later blasted a route across the Bluffs to extend the trail up to the lodge.

Grassy Gap was renamed as Trillium Gap in May 1930 by Horace Albright, the second director of the National Park Service, after he rode a horse up to the gap. Since then, trout lilies and spring beauties have replaced trillium as the dominant groundcover.[46] Albright spent the night at "Jack's Place" and wrote a letter from there to Joseph Nisbet LeConte, whose family was the namesake for the mountain. "Little Joe" had succeeded John Muir in 1915 as president of the Sierra Club.

After the Roaring Fork Motor Trail opened in the 1960s, the Trillium Gap Trail gained a half-mile connector from the Grotto Falls parking lot. Tourists flock to Grotto Falls, where water from the Basin Spring pours over a ledge and the trail ducks behind the waterfall. Trillium Gap is the route used by the llamas who carry supplies to the lodge, usually making three trips per week.

Trailhead signs say Le Conte is 6.7 miles from the Roaring Fork trailhead. However, mileage signs in the Smokies are not definitive. For example, the sign at Trillium Gap says 3.6 miles up to Le Conte and 2.8 down to the trailhead, which would add up to 6.4. The lower end of Trillium to Cherokee Orchard adds an additional 2.4 miles, so the route options from the orchard are 8.8 miles via Trillium, 6.6 via Rainbow, and 7.1 via Bullhead. Margaret Stevenson referred to the lower Trillium connector as the "bridle trail," because it was used by horses before the road was extended up from Cherokee Orchard.

From the Roaring Fork Road, the climb to the lodge averages 490 feet per mile, which is a comparable grade to the Alum Cave Bluff route.

As the trail arrives at the lodge, the Basin Spring is on the left and the ram

---

45. "Alpha & Omega," *Knoxville Journal*, June 19, 1933.
46. "Albright Gets Thrill from LeConte Trip," by John T. Moutoux, *Knoxville News-Sentinel*, May 22, 1930.

On his 55th birthday in 2013, Terry Tinnell became the first to reach LeConte Lodge in a wheelchair (courtesy High on LeConte, blog of LeConte Lodge).

pump is downstream to the right. Also near the top of the trail is a hitching post for horses. Trillium was renovated by the Trails Forever program in 2020.

Terry Tinnell chose Trillium in 2013 when he climbed Le Conte in a modified wheelchair. Tinnell heard about the lodge one Christmas when his family discussed the most beautiful places they had ever visited. His brother-in-law, Jim Myers, mentioned Mount Le Conte, and Tinnell decided he wanted to visit—despite being in a wheelchair because of inflammation in his spinal cord. Lodge officials advised against the trip.

"Our motto was FFA," Tinnell said. "If you choose the right friends, family and attitude, you can climb any mountain." He entered the lottery and got a reservation for his 55th birthday in 2013. With the help of 14 strong friends and a service dog named Cocoa, the ascent took 7.5 hours and went according to plan. On his descent a rock bumped him off a ledge, and he had to grab a tree limb to avoid a disastrous fall.

Now, if someone asks the guy in the wheelchair what's the most beautiful place he's ever been, he can answer, "Of course, it's Mount Le Conte."[47]

Trillium was also the route the Rev. Rufus Morgan chose for his 93rd birthday hike in 1978. Morgan was almost blind and hiked with a hand on a friend's shoulder.[48]

---

47. "Mount Le Conte—to the Top," by Josh Pate, *Ability* magazine, 2013.
48. "Morgan's 93 and Still Climbing," by Helen Arthur, *Charlotte Observer*, Oct. 17, 1978.

Bullhead Trail

The CCC built the Bullhead Trail in 1933. Bullhead Mountain had burned in 1926, leaving scorched hillsides similar to those seen after the Gatlinburg wildfire of 2016. With the trees gone, rhododendrons and laurels were the first plants to colonize the hillside. As they grew to head-height, they eclipsed the views, so the CCC built the Bullhead Pulpit as a lookout platform. In 1997, former CCC corpsman Harry Jett wrote a letter to park superintendent Karen Wade documenting the history of that work.

The Bullhead pulpit was built as an overlook by CCC workers in 1933 (courtesy Stephen Jett).

> On May 17, 1933, at the age of 22, I joined the Civilian Conservation Corps, enlisting at Fort Oglethorpe, Georgia. About two hundred of us were shipped to Gatlinburg, Tennessee, where we established Camp H.A. Morgan,[49] Co. No. 1458. We were divided into several crews, and I was assigned to a trail building crew of which George Preston was the foreman and Tillery Whaley was the sub-foreman.
>
> Under the supervision of Mr. Preston and Mr. Whaley we began building the Bull Head Mountain Trail. We worked on this all summer, but after Labor Day we were sent to Mt. LeConte where we stayed for six weeks working on the higher part of the Rainbow Falls Trail. We lived in an old log house that was torn down several years ago. After six weeks on LeConte we went back to Bull Head Mountain. Barbee Hazelwood and I were assigned to clearing the brush, mostly laurel and rhododendron, from the trail ahead of the graders. When spring came we were so far ahead of the rest of the crew, we decided to build something that would enable us to see over the rhododendron into the valley below. We quit cutting brush and began gathering stones, and with these stones we built the platform and scratched a large flat stone "Bull Head Lookout." Many years later my son and I came off LeConte via the Bull Head Trail. The stone platform was still there but the stone with the name on it was gone.

---

49. Harcourt Morgan (1867–1950) was president of the University of Tennessee and chairman of the Tennessee Valley Authority. Camp 1458 was in Sugarlands.

In Jett's lifetime, trees overtook the hillside, and there was no longer an open view from the lookout, so the perch became known as the Bullhead pulpit. Then the new-growth forest was wiped out in the 2016 wildfire, and it once again became a lookout. The Bullhead Lookout is one of several "pulpits" on Le Conte. Two more are outcroppings on the Alum Cave Bluff Trail.

Early white settlers called Le Conte "Bullhead" because of the silhouette of the ridgeline when viewed from the west. The trail approaches the top of Bullhead Mountain (4,282 feet) and then flanks Balsam Point (5,818) and West Point (6,344) before joining with the Rainbow Falls Trail for a final push up to the lodge, which some weary hikers describe as the hardest half-mile in the Smokies.

Bullhead is the longest route on Le Conte, climbing nearly 4,000 feet over 7.1 miles, including the initial approach on the Old Sugarlands Trail. Yet Daniel Bice chose it as his route in 2019 when he climbed on a prosthetic leg, having lost his lower right leg because of blood clots. If you feel like your backpack is overloaded, consider that Bice had to pack a spare leg.

In the 1980s, Gracie McNicol said Bullhead was the best trail for wildflowers. Her friend Anita Crabtree documented 1,097 varieties.

Veteran hiker Scott Anderson calls Bullhead "100 percent my favorite trail on Le Conte. It is unmatched for unique, sparse beauty and massive open views, and best of all it is the second least-populated trail on the mountain." Anderson is a five-time completer of the Tour de Le Conte—which challenges hikers to complete all six trails in 24 hours.

Alum Cave Bluff Trail

As the shortest route to the lodge, with a convenient trailhead on the Newfound Gap Highway 11 miles south of Gatlinburg, Alum Cave Bluff is the busiest trail on Mount Le Conte. On a Saturday morning in October 2021, Kathryn Brunk counted the traffic as she came down from the lodge—she met 990 hikers in three hours. That's about one hiker per 10 yards.

On Ed Wright's 1,000th hike in 1997, he met 350 hikers on Alum. Wright welcomed company and used Alum for all but 50 of his 1,310 ascents. When he ascended the other routes (Rainbow 26 times, Bullhead 19, and Trillium five) it was usually a detour dictated by weather or trail conditions. His journals show that he descended Boulevard just once, and there is no record that he ever set foot on the Brushy Mountain Trail. Wright estimated that he met more than 120,000 people in 26 years of hiking Le Conte.

The sign at the trailhead[50] says 5.0 miles to Mt. LeConte, and another sign at Alum Cave says 2.7 to go. Five miles is the distance to the junction with the Rainbow Falls Trail. The actual mileage is 5.1 to the lodge, 5.5 to the summit, and 6.2 to Myrtle Point. The finishing stretch is mostly flat, after you round what is called the

---

50. The Alum trailhead is known as Grassy Patch, because it was a clearing in the forest 100 years ago when Davis Bracken occupied a cabin built by Champion Fibre Company.

"Hallelujah Turn" just west of Cliff Top. In the forest east of the turn (to the right as you hike up) is the site of the national park commission's 1924 camp. The Alum Cave Trail was not carved out until 1935, so when the commissioners descended the south side of the mountain, they had to bushwhack down to the cave.

The Alum Cave Bluff Trail was routed through Arch Rock on a suggestion from Wiley Oakley.[51] Before the rock steps were built, hikers in the 1930s had to climb a series of three ladders as they passed through Arch Rock.[52]

On rainy days, Oakley used to guide fishermen to the arch, where they could stay dry under the overhanging rock while catching trout from pools, which were later washed away by storms. The trail follows Styx Branch for about a half mile after it turns away from Alum Cave Creek.

Styx Branch is a curious name that must have come from someone familiar with the River Styx in Greek mythology or Dante's Inferno. It drains an impenetrable chasm called Huggins Hell, just as the River Styx bounded the realm of the dead. In mountain parlance, an inescapable rhododendron thicket is known as a "hell,"[53] and legend says that this one was named in memory of a mountaineer named Huggins who disappeared in there.[54]

Winter hiking through ice-encrusted Arch Rock was treacherous until this ladder was installed, as shown here in 1936 (photograph by Dutch Roth, from the Albert "Dutch" Roth Photograph Collection, University of Tennessee Libraries).

51. "Trail to Mt. LeConte by Alum Cave Relocated to Go Through Arch Rock," by Laura Thornborough, *Knoxville Journal*, Dec. 3, 1933.
52. "A Northerner Goes 'Up South,'" by Russell McFarland, *Knoxville News-Sentinel*, Aug. 27, 1939.
53. Decades later, crew member David Witherspoon described the undergrowth in Huggins Hell as "too dense to permit movement but too steep to prevent it." *Song of the Winter Wren*, p. 30.
54. Paul Fink was the first to record the name Huggins Hell.

From a distance, the ridges encircling Huggins Hell reminded some mountaineers of a volcanic crater, which would have added another dimension of hell. In 1925, Paul Adams explored this possibility. Looking for evidence of brimstone along the top of the ridge, he stepped on a loose rim stone and tumbled 200 feet down a steep and rocky washout. Miraculously, he was not badly injured, and his faithful dog Smoky Jack scrambled down to rescue him. Realizing that climbing out would be impossible, Adams made an emergency camp and bushwhacked downstream until he emerged the next day on the old alum miners' trail, proving the hard way that Huggins Hell was not a crater.

When friends realized Adams was missing, they organized a search, and early editions of Knoxville newspapers reported that the famous Smokies pioneer was lost in Huggins Hell. Adams' father, a pastor, heard the news at a train station in Memphis. "Father later confessed that he had given some thought to my funeral arrangements," Adams wrote in his book, *Smoky Jack*.

Before the trail was routed through Arch Rock, some adventurous hikers followed a knife-edged cliff called Duck Hawk Ridge, popularly known as Hole-in-the-Rock Ridge, because it has two keyholes visible from Inspiration Point, two miles up from the trailhead.

Duck Hawk once was a gut check for Smoky Mountains Hiking Club members but has been off limits since 1997 for the protection of nesting falcons and reckless hikers. Farther up in the vicinity of Trout Branch, the original path headed directly up the mountainside and crested near the location of the current backcountry shelter, bypassing some of the unforgettable cliffs and ledges just below Cliff Top.

In 1975, a blasting crew led by Barney Ogle worked to level out the cliffside trail near the top. Lodge crewman David Witherspoon remembers how one blast startled Blackie, the lodge workhorse: "How to explain to him? It's only people dynamiting the earth to

Paul Dinwiddie on Duck Hawk Ridge, which once was part of the Alum Cave route. Hikers are no longer allowed on the knife-edge ridge (courtesy Edwin C. Jones).

walk over it."[55] Wright nicknamed the cliffside section as "Betty Jean's Stairway to Heaven," a tribute to Sister Betty Jean Barnett, a Catholic nun who made 217 ascents.

Wright also named "Paul's Nose," a rocky profile on Cliff Top visible from Gracie's Pulpit that reminded him of Paul Dinwiddie, and "Shirley's Rock," a favorite rest stop for Shirley Henry on her 173 climbs. Just above the upper steps is a small promontory that Dinwiddie called "Lu's Pulpit," in memory of Ernest LuAllen, who suffered a fatal heart attack at Arch Rock in 1992 while descending from his 141st climb.

The steep southern face of Le Conte makes the Alum Cave Trail susceptible to washouts. The trail was closed in 1993 by a landslide near Arch Rock and in 1995 because of damage from Hurricane Opal. Florida businessman Richard Haiman[56] donated $65,000 to rebuild the trail, a gift which was matched by the Friends of the Smokies.[57] Haiman climbed Le Conte three times in 1997 as he battled terminal cancer, and after he died at age 59, he left $1 million to endow projects in the park, including the 2016 renovation of Alum, which included rebuilding the steps through Arch Rock.

Wright missed Alum while it was closed, but his joy at the reopening was short-lived. "Alum Cave Bluff Trail is just as hard as any of the other trails to Mt. LeConte," he wrote. "You just finish it sooner."

Gracie's Pulpit is a natural rock outcropping a quarter-mile beyond the cave that became a favorite halfway point for Gracie McNicol, who climbed Le Conte 244 times. She was always glad to get past the dusty cave, which she described as a "dirty place" in her book *Gracie and the Mountain*.[58]

Gracie didn't own a car and took the bus from Maryville (where she lived in a cramped 29-foot trailer) to the park. Trailways stopped at the Alum Cave and Newfound Gap trailheads. When Gracie walked down Boulevard, she had to be prompt to catch the 2:30 p.m. bus stop at Newfound Gap.

From Gracie's Pulpit, the entire southern face of Mount Le Conte is visible, from Balsam Point on the left to Myrtle Point on the right. The lodge is on the opposite side of the ridgeline, so her destination was not visible from her pulpit.

The crest of the trail became known as the "horse gate," because for many years a wooden rod was hung across the trail to keep horses at the lodge from wandering out onto the dangerous ledges beyond. Jack Huff's daughter, Cookie Bowling, remembered when a horse fell off the ledge and miraculously survived.

The average grade on Alum is comparable to Trillium, gaining 500 feet per mile. Several trail runners who have completed this ascent in under one hour. As of 2024, the fastest known times were 46 minutes up by Stan Wullschleger and 26 minutes

---

55. *Song of the Winter Wren*, p. 46.
56. Richard Haiman (1938–1997) was co-owner of the Budget Rent-a-Car operations in Florida. Tom Brosch (1940–2022), owner of the Happy Hiker store in Gatlinburg, helped administer Haiman's fund.
57. Trails Forever is a partnership of the Great Smoky Mountains National Park and the non-profit Friends of the Smokies. Created in 2012 and backed by a $6 million endowment, the partnership provides a full-time trail-building crew. Trails Forever renovated Alum in 2015–16, Rainbow Falls in 2017–18, Trillium Gap in 2019–2020, and Ramsey Cascades 2022–24. FriendsoftheSmokies.org/TrailsForever.
58. *Gracie and the Mountain: Growing Young Hiking Mount Le Conte*, by Emilie Ervin Powell, 1981, The Overmountain Press, Johnson City, Tennessee.

down by John Northrup. Northrup made seven round trips in one day in 2012, and Wullschleger made six laps in 2007. At age 66 in 1991, Wright made three round trips in less than 12 hours.

Even before the modern trail was established, there was traffic along the lower Alum route, which was roughed out for the national parks commission in 1924. LeRoy Jeffries, an officer with the American Association of Mountaineering Clubs and the American Alpine Club, descended Alum July 6, 1926, after overnighting in Huff's cabin. "The scene from LeConte looking toward Clingmans Dome is not excelled by any I have ever seen here or abroad," he said in an interview with the *Knoxville Journal*. "Though LeConte lacks the altitude of the western peaks, it easily excels them in scenic beauty."

Conservationist Edward Abbey[59] wrote this description of the Alum Cave trailhead in December 1973: "An inch of virgin snow all over the ground—I am the first to walk this trail today. I cross the West Prong of the Little Pigeon River on a wooden footbridge, pausing in the middle of the bridge to admire the view upstream. It looks like a scene invented by Eliot Porter[60]: granite-like boulders lodged in the torrent and sheathed in ribbed, rippled layers of ice; spillways and plunge pools, the roil and rush and roar of the complicated waters; giant hemlocks leaning over the stream, fresh snow clinging to their bark; the stones and pebbles of the creek bed gleaming through the flawless clarity of the water; and over all, illuminating the scene and blending with its shadows, the soft gray light of the humid mountain air, filtered by cloud and by the random reticulation of the commingled tree branches and pine needles overhead."

Brushy Mountain Trail

On the north side of Mount Le Conte, the Porters Creek Trail from Greenbrier Cove leads to the Brushy Mountain Trail, which joins the summit network at Trillium Gap and provides a sixth route to Le Conte. The 4,991-foot summit of Brushy Mountain is a heath bald reached by a half-mile spur trail that offers a dramatic silhouette view of Mount Le Conte.

At 9.1 miles, this is the longest route to the lodge.[61] The trail passes the "Fitified Spring," which percolated after a 1916 earthquake created a natural siphon but has now run dry. Also along the way are the Smoky Mountain Hiking Club cabin, built in 1934 from poplar and chestnut logs salvaged from old cabins, and the ruins of the Messer Barn, a cantilever design that collapsed in 2023. The clubhouse was designed by Knoxville architect Charles Barber, an avid hiker who designed the national park headquarters and drew blueprints for Jack Huff when he built the "Old Lodge" on Le Conte.

---

59. Edward Abbey (1927–1989) was a national park ranger who became an environmental activist and author.
60. Eliot Porter (1901–1990) was a nature photographer, described by Ansel Adams as "master of nature's color."
61. The Hotel LeConte in Greenbrier advertised in 1926 that this was the "shortest route to the top of Mt. LeConte," perhaps because some of the approach trails along Porter Creek were driveable. *Knoxville News-Sentinel*, June 13, 1926.

Greenbrier was a substantial settlement with a thousand people living in eight coves, plus a hotel in an old schoolhouse. A century ago, Greenbrier's population outnumbered Gatlinburg, which counted 75 residents in 1930 and 1,300 in 1940.

Even before the park was established, Greenbrier Cove was already threaded with rough roads and paths. In 1925, four men rode horses from the Hotel LeConte up Brushy Ridge past Trillium Gap and reached within a mile of the Le Conte summit.[62] In 1926, Lucinda Hudson of Knoxville rode a horse up the same route. "The feat of reaching the top of Mount LeConte has always been by rather arduous mountain climbing, but by going a new trail it is now possible to make most of the journey by horseback," according to the *Knoxville News-Sentinel*.

The CCC established Camp 1460 in Greenbrier and named it Camp David Chapman in honor of the vice-chairman of the Great Smoky Mountains Conservation Association. It was located about two miles up the Greenbrier Road, where Rhododendron Creek joins the Little Pigeon River.

Because Porters Creek is so isolated from other trailheads, the Brushy Mountain Trail has become a popular finish line for the Tour de Le Conte, which involves hiking all six trails in 24 hours.

The CCC had 22 camps in the Smokies, employing 4,000 men who built the original trails by 1934. Lodge logbooks from 1937 show hikers using all six trails. After 1935, the CCC focused more on building roadside facilities, until the corps was disbanded at the start of World War II.

The Tour de Le Conte

Mike Povia and Lee Lewis were co-workers at the Happy Hiker store in Gatlinburg in the 1990s when a trail map of Mount Le Conte caught their eye. "We looked at the six trails that go up Le Conte," Lewis told Morgan Simmons of the *Knoxville News-Sentinel*. "Why not hike them all, but try to do it in less than a day?" They decided to chase the dream, even though neither Lewis, 33, nor Povia, 51, had ever hiked more than 20 miles in a day.

On November 8, 1992, they set foot on the Alum Cave Bluff Trail at 4:45 a.m., reached the lodge at 6:58, gulped coffee to ward off the 26-degree chill, and headed down the Boulevard at dawn. At Newfound Gap, they climbed into the back of a pickup truck and a friend shuttled them around to the Grotto Falls trailhead. They headed up Trillium Gap and reached the lodge at 2:29 p.m. and headed down Rainbow Falls. Night was falling as they reached Cherokee Orchard, but they still had miles to go. They headed up Bullhead, reached the lodge for the third time at 10:45 p.m., and headed down to Trillium Gap to finish on the Brushy Mountain Trail. Their 43-mile jaunt ended at 3:14 a.m., with more than an hour to spare.

Thus was born the Tour de Le Conte, also known as the 24 Hours of Le Conte, puns adapted from the names of famous French races.

---

62. "Knoxville Men Use First Horses on LeConte," *Knoxville Journal*, July 25, 1926. The riders were White Tallant and J.A. Snyder of Knoxville, Ray Owenby of Sevierville, and Mack Whaley of Greenbrier Cove.

3. Almost a Motor Lodge

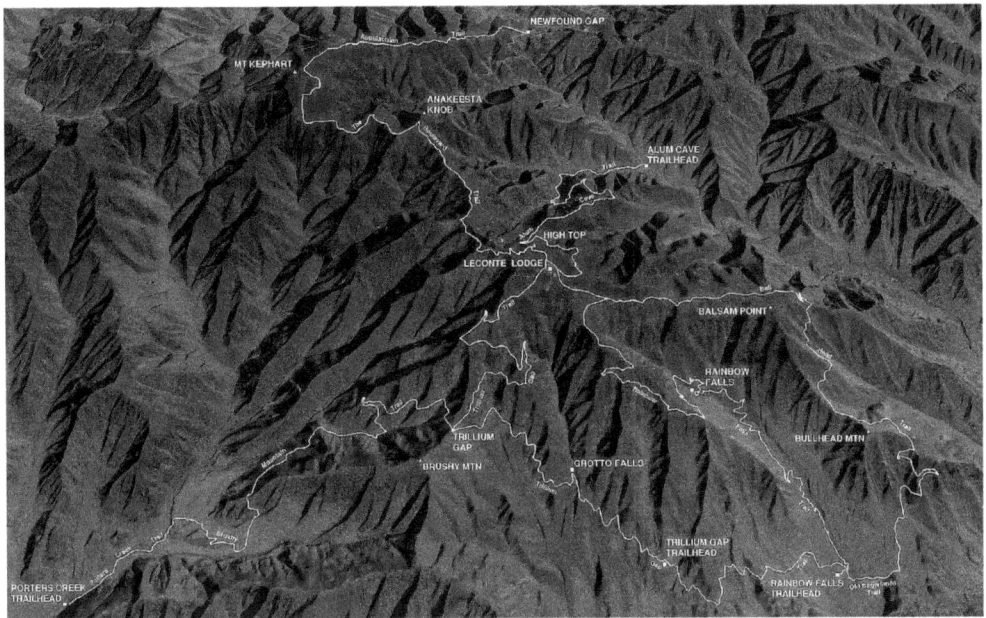

This is the course run by brothers Anthony and Elias Groft on November 27, 2020, when they completed the fastest Tour de Le Conte, 45.3 miles in 8:03:38. Starting at Cherokee Orchard, they went up Rainbow in 1:24, down Trillium in 1:36, up Bullhead in 1:27, down Alum in 0:45, up AT/Boulevard in 1:50, and down Brushy Mountain in 1:22 to finish in Greenbrier Cove (map by Anthony Groft).

Since then, dozens of individuals, ages 15 to 68, have completed the tour. John Northrup, the manager of LeConte Lodge, has done it four times. Brothers Elias and Anthony Groft set the speed record in November 2017 when they finished in 8:03:38. At a walking pace, the tour requires miles and miles of nighttime hiking. Completers are listed at lecontest.com/lecontest-tour.

The tour doesn't have written rules, but there is a consensus that completion should include the entirety of all six trails, including the lower stretch of Trillium Gap that Lewis and Povia bypassed. Otherwise, the trails can be done in any order. It is permissible to use shuttles between the trailheads. Some have pre-positioned bicycles at Newfound Gap so they can coast down to the Alum trailhead and complete the tour "unsupported."

An extreme version of the Tour de Le Conte is the Le Conte Star, which involves going up and down all six trails. As of 2023, only two men had completed it in 24 hours: Anthony Groft, 88.3 miles in 23:20 in 2023, and Zachary Andrews, 78.2 miles in 23:38 in 2020.

Traffic at the Trailheads

Guests hiking to LeConte Lodge have learned to arrive early at their chosen trailhead, before the parking lots overflow with casual tourists attracted by the names of Alum Cave, Rainbow Falls, and Grotto Falls. (Never mind that Alum is not a cave. One afternoon in 1996, Margaret Stevenson met an upbound hiker who was carrying a flashlight to explore the "cave.") If the sign said Dusty Cliff, maybe the Alum Trail wouldn't be as overcrowded.

Zach Andrews hiked 78 miles on Mount Le Conte in 2020, going up and down all six trails in 24 hours. Zach has the summit elevation tattooed over his heart (courtesy Zach Andrews).

Many tourists go no farther than Arch Rock, which is not a cave, either, but simulates the dark and damp experience of walking through a mountain. (Meanwhile, their cars occupy parking spaces, blocking out lodge hikers.)

The national park has been dealing with escalating traffic, just like the lodge. In 2021, the park counted 14.1 million guests, the most ever, though traffic slacked off to 12.9 million in 2022. The only national park units with more visitors in 2023 were the Blue Ridge Parkway, 16.7 million, and the Golden Gate National Recreation Area, 14.9 million.

The Smokies see about five million vehicles per year, including a million crossing Newfound Gap, many of them passing through on the way to the pavilions in Pigeon Forge or the casino in Cherokee. However, plenty of visitors stop along the way, and the parking spaces are limited: 141 at Newfound Gap, 69 at Alum Cave, 48 at Cherokee Orchard and 17 at Grotto Falls. Near the Alum Cave trailhead, it was not uncommon to see a half-mile line of cars parked along the shoulders of U.S. 441.

As park officials struggled to bridge the gap between relentless traffic and limited federal funding, they instituted a parking fee, called "Park It Forward." The plan was designed as a fund-raiser, though it might also be a deterrent to casual parking. In theory, increased funds could be used to improve traffic flow, but park officials say there is little room in the wilderness for additional parking, nor do they plan to offer reserved parking.

For safety purposes, authorities want to eliminate dangerous roadside parking, so they erected split-rail fences and boulders along roadsides near the trailheads. Lodge manager John Northrup worked to coordinate a shuttle system so guests could park in Gatlinburg rather than at the trailheads.

One fringe benefit of the parking pass was that it redirected hiker traffic onto trails other than Alum, where the parking lot is notorious for filling up by dawn.

Parking passes in the Smokies cost $40 per year, $15 per week, or $5 per day. More than a dozen national parks charge more for an annual pass, including $80 at Grand Canyon and Yellowstone and $70 at Yosemite and Rocky Mountain.

Some Tennesseans contend that the federal government guaranteed "free access" to the Smokies when the park was formed in the 1930s. Indeed, when the Newfound Gap Highway and the Little River Road were deeded to the national park, the state included a clause forbidding tolls on those roads.

Parking fees are not unprecedented in the Smokies. In 1932, when Cherokee Orchard was still privately owned, hikers who drove from Gatlinburg to the Rainbow Falls trailhead had to pay 50 cents for parking. That's the equivalent of $8 today. In 2021, the park instituted a $14 parking fee to manage overcrowding at the Laurel Falls trailhead.

4

Extinction?

Almost Lost in the Wilderness

Across the hundred years of its existence, LeConte Lodge has been threatened by fire, buried in snow, and lashed by storms. Yet nothing has threatened the existence of the lodge more than a few pieces of paper signed by President Lyndon Johnson.

The 1964 Wilderness Act changed the face of the national park system and ushered in a new dynamic in relation to how parks should shield their most precious holdings from overuse and abuse. Under the Wilderness Act, the park service recommended in the 1970s that Le Conte Lodge be removed, so that the mountaintop could return to its natural state.

Battle lines soon were drawn between environmental activists who favored dismantling the cabins and lodge advocates who portrayed it as a beloved doorstep to the very wilderness the parks were designed to celebrate.

As early as the 1950s, park officials debated whether lodging in the wilderness was appropriate. As the park service prepared for a nationwide renovation program called Mission 66, Superintendent Edward Hummel proposed closing LeConte Lodge but was overruled by his regional director, who called the lodge "a reasonable exception to the general policy."

As President Johnson signed the Wilderness Act in a Rose Garden ceremony September 3, 1964, he declared: "This is a very happy and historic occasion for all who love the great American outdoors, and needless to say, that includes me. The bills that I am signing this morning are in the highest tradition of our heritage as conservators as well as users of America's bountiful natural endowments."

The act defined wilderness as "an area where the earth and its community of life are untrammeled by man, where man himself is a visitor who does not remain." An area of wilderness was further defined as an area of undeveloped federal land retaining its primeval character and influence, without permanent improvements or human habitation, which is protected and managed so as to preserve its natural conditions.

The bill's language obviously was open to interpretation, but it encouraged individuals and organizations who sought to keep and expand the "wild" in the parks.

The act was supported—indeed, celebrated—by numerous environmental and conservation groups. Harvey Broome, a Knoxville attorney and frequent Le Conte

4. Extinction?

President Lyndon Johnson signs the Wilderness Act September 3, 1964, in the White House Rose Garden. Le Conte hiker Harvey Broome (co-founder of the Wilderness Society) is pictured on the left, behind the podium. On the right, leaning in, is Secretary of the Interior Stewart Udall. Speaking with the president are (from left) Margaret Murie, "Grandmother of the Conservation Movement," and Alice Zahniser, whose late husband Howard wrote the first draft of the Wilderness Act. Mr. Zahniser adapted the defining phrase from conservationist Polly Dyer: "A wilderness, in contrast with those areas where man and his own works dominate the landscape, is hereby recognized as an area where the earth and its community of life are untrammeled by man, where man himself is a visitor who does not remain" (courtesy LBJ Library).

hiker, was a co-founder of the Wilderness Society and a key promoter of the act. He was present when Johnson signed the bill into law. No doubt he had the Smokies on his mind when he defined wilderness as "bits of eternity, which have a preciousness beyond all accounting."

Much of the focus of the bill centered on huge swaths of land in remote areas, such as the Wrangell-St. Elias Wilderness in Alaska, now a 13 million-acre national park. But much smaller parts of the park system also were impacted, and that eventually brought the force of the Wilderness Act to the high ridges of the Smokies.

In 1974, the National Park Service proposed that 390,500 acres in the Smokies—about three-quarters of the park—be considered wilderness. In a December 1974 letter to Congress supporting the proposal, President Gerald Ford wrote that the park boasted "an impressive array of unspoiled forests."

The proposal eliminated a 400-acre corridor that would have protected the lodge. But the revised proposal presumed that the lodge would close in 1977.

Even before the Wilderness Act, park officials expressed concern about the environmental impact of the lodge operations. Jack Huff and Herrick Brown operated a sawmill to produce lumber for construction and maintenance projects, and the cabins were heated by wood-burning stoves.

In the late 1950s, Superintendent Fred Overly wrote a letter to Pauline Huff, permitting the lodge crews to "remove any trees adjacent to the buildings at LeConte Lodge in order to prevent damage to the buildings." The sawmill that Jack Huff used to build the lodge had been silenced since 1950, when he left the lodge to manage the family hotel in Gatlinburg. Herrick Brown resumed sawmill operations in 1960, but after the Wilderness Act became law, he was no longer allowed to cut trees, harvest firewood, or mill lumber.

Parts of the facility were in disrepair, and the landscape was less than pristine. An inspection by Chief Ranger Lee Sneddon in April 1968 led to a critical report about the lodge:

> The accumulation of years of litter has resulted in a less than tolerable situation. Cans, broken toilet stools, bed springs, radio antenna, metal sinks, iron scrap, tarpaper, aluminum roofing scrap (barn area), old stoves (one at barn and other in lodge area), scrap lumber, old shingles and other miscellaneous debris, are scattered throughout the brier and timber, mainly downhill from the lodge area.

This did not fit anybody's definition of "wilderness."

Sneddon also noted that dragging logs (for use as firewood or construction) had damaged the trails. He recommended numerous changes, including the removal of a small building, cleaning of the powerhouse and pump shelter "to cut down the fire hazard" and the addition of an incinerator for waste disposal.

There was no hint, however, in the early years after the passage of the Wilderness Act that the lodge might be a target for removal. In fact, the park's 1964 master plan included a "rustic lodge similar to LeConte Lodge" in the vicinity of Spence Field.[1] "It appears that the visitor demand for the back-country, chalet-type experience may exceed the ability of the LeConte Lodge concession to satisfy it," superintendent Keith Neilson wrote in 1970. "Perhaps some thought should be given to providing a second back-country, chalet-type concession here."

In August 1974, the U.S. Public Health Service conducted an environmental health survey at the lodge and found numerous problems, including poor lighting and septic tank drain issues. The report even nit-picked non-wilderness issues such as "soup bowls … badly pitted."

"Civilizing the best fresh water in the world"

The water from Basin Spring appears pristine, but the park mandated in 1976 that the lodge chlorinate its drinking water. Winter caretaker David Witherspoon called it a "bureaucratic chlorinator … civilizing the best fresh water in the world."

The park service was concerned about water safety after a 1975 incident at Crater

---

1. "New Road Over Smokies Urged," *Knoxville News-Sentinel*, Aug. 12, 1964. Spence Field (el. 4,920) is on the Appalachian Trail 16 miles west of Clingmans Dome and features two springs at 4,800 feet. It is more than four miles off-road.

Herrick Brown (in the light-colored pants, his back to the camera) and crew sawing lumber in 1973. When the blade hit a knot, the sawmill sometimes would launch the lumber overhead. Brown worried that the Occupational Safety and Health Administration might shut down the sawmill, but the Wilderness Act got it first (photo courtesy LeConte Lodge).

Lake in Oregon, when 500 people became ill after drinking water was contaminated by a sewage leak. That's not a threat at the lodge, where the septic drain field is well downhill from the spring. Any risk of contamination would be far downstream in Roaring Fork.

From the 1920s, lodge guests had used crude pit toilets. When Brown was building the office in 1968, he plumbed the basement for flush toilets, anticipating that the park would install a septic system. The entire project flew in the face of the wilderness concept, as a heavy backhoe had to be airlifted to the lodge, piece by piece, using Marine Corps helicopters. Then the septic system failed because the thin mountain-top soil could not handle the drainage. The new flush toilets were unusable for several years, though they have been open to overnight guests for the last four decades.

The signing of the Wilderness Act did not prompt immediate federal action. There were studies to do, meetings to hold, legislators to convince, and voices to raise.

Environmental activist Edward Abbey, a prominent critic of park development in other states, jumped into the controversy in his 1970 book, *Appalachian Wilderness: The Great Smoky Mountains*. Noting the numbers of visitors flooding the park, Abbey offered an abrupt solution:

> Keep cars out of the parks. Cars and all other forms of motorized locomotion. The national parks should be for people, not for machines. Let the machines find their own national parks and keep out of ours.[2]

---

2. The Blue Ridge Parkway, an embodiment of Abbey's "park for cars," is the only national park unit that attracts more visitors than the Smokies. In 2022, the Parkway counted 16.7 million guests, compared to 13.3 million in the Smokies.

> Set a man on foot at the entrance to the park, at any entrance, with no means to proceed except by his own energy and inclination, and he faces a vista as wild and immense as that which confronted Hernando de Soto, William Bartram or Daniel Boone.[3] What was an excursion becomes an adventure.

At the same time, there was a similar debate out west in Yosemite National Park, where there are six back-country lodges along a 51-mile trail called the High Sierra Loop. Photographer Ansel Adams once advocated purging all development from Yosemite Valley, but his perspective changed in the 1970s, when he opened the Ansel Adams Gallery in Yosemite Village.

"Any attempt to reduce Yosemite Valley to a wilderness area would be futile—socially and politically—and would be a real disservice to the people at large," he said. "The maximum appropriate number of people should see Yosemite and should experience the incredible quality. To shut it off from the world would be somewhat similar to closing St. Paul's Cathedral for the sake of architecture!"[4]

The possibility of closing LeConte Lodge reached key Smokies individuals by the summer of 1974. Discussions were underlined by the fact that manager Herrick Brown, 61, was considering retirement. If there was a "good" time to consider closing the lodge, this might be it.

The threat to the lodge prompted a quick response from the board of directors of the Great Smoky Mountains Conservation Association, which released a statement August 13, 1974:

> If Le Conte Lodge were to be closed—perish the thought—it would mean that a large portion of the present patrons would be denied the rare privilege of getting that "mountain-top experience." Those who would climb this grand old mountain anyway would have to resort to the more strenuous one-day trips, thus missing the thrill of the ever-changing sunsets and sunrises. Or, they would have to carry bedding and cooking equipment for an overnight trip.

Two days later, Carlos Campbell, the association's secretary and a force in the early development of the park, wrote a letter to Washington urging that the lodge be saved. Among other comments, Campbell stressed that closing the lodge would be a case of "the Wilderness idea ... being carried too far."

Park service director Ronald Walker responded to Campbell by letter: "The removal of man-made structures does not remove opportunity for a wilderness experience," he wrote. "As you know, camping equipment is available now, made of lightweight materials which do not create undue burdens for people who are capable of hiking into the back-country."

Meanwhile, wilderness advocates rallied to the cause. The Smoky Mountains Hiking Club Conservation Committee called for dismantling the lodge and removing shelters along the Appalachian Trail inside the park. The club's statement said:

---

3. De Soto (1500–1542) was a Spanish conquistador who explored the southern Appalachians in 1540 in a quest for gold. Bartram (1739–1823) explored the Cherokee nation and climbed Jore Mountain (probably Wayah Bald, south of the Smokies). Boone (1734–1820) bypassed the Smokies on his westward trips via Cumberland Gap.

4. *Yosemite & Sequoia: A Century of California National Parks*, edited by Richard Orsi, Alfred Runte, and Marlene Smith-Baranzini, University of California Press, 1993.

The A.T. shelters and the Mt. Le Conte Lodge are good examples of the slow-spreading damage which developments of this kind can cause in the area in which they are located. They have become littered, eroded and threadbare from heavy use and abuse. With approximately 10,000 people staying overnight at the lodge and the trail shelter on Mt. Le Conte each year, is it any wonder that the area is so littered, overused and trammeled that it is depressing to go there and see the gross injustice which has been done to the top of a beautiful mountain? When the lodge was established, no one realized the damage it would eventually bring to the mountain. It has been a friend to many people. It has served a purpose but it has outlived its usefulness. It must now be removed before it completely destroys the beauty of the mountain which motivated its beginning.

Each side considered its view righteous. Either the lodge was a haven and symbol for those who loved the mountain, or it was a blight on the landscape of one of the Smokies' finest summits.

Two patron saints of the lodge—Paul Adams and Pauline Huff—reacted very differently to its plight.

Adams wrote Knoxville columnist Carson Brewer in support of the wilderness plan and expressed regret that he had founded the camp: "Little did I realize when I started the camp there that I would live to see the destruction that has come to the top of that most beautiful mountain. Each year now, as I climb it once or twice, I see more and more destruction of nature which has gone on since my last hike up it. I remember the top of Mt. Le Conte when it was absolute wilderness, and very few trails. In fact, there was not a trail there at all, except for bear trails occasionally, when I first visited the top in 1918."

In the same article, Pauline Huff envisioned a future for the lodge built by her husband, Jack. "Everybody can't back-pack," she wrote. "Neither can everyone hike to Le Conte to spend the night. Some people can't walk trails at all. So it seems to me there is a need in the Smokies for wilderness areas, for trail shelters, for LeConte Lodge, where hikers can stay overnight and for motor trails where people who must ride can be in the forest, too."[5]

In 1974, park superintendent Vincent Ellis asked the Browns what should become of the lodge. They agreed it should be closed and reclaimed by the wilderness. Their lease was about to expire, but they agreed to a three-year renewal while the matter was resolved.

In an interview with Carson Brewer of the *Knoxville News-Sentinel*, Brown said that operating the lodge had gotten harder, because it was challenging to attract and keep top-quality employees. Brown had labored for years to build the office, and during that time he had deferred maintenance on the campus.[6]

In 1975, two dozen environmental groups formed the Great Smoky Mountains Park Wilderness Advocates to foster an emphasis on wilderness management in the park and specifically to support removal of the lodge.

As news about the threat to the lodge spread across the country, waves of letters arrived in the mailboxes of legislators, park officials, and newspaper offices supporting or opposing the closing.

---

5. Carson Brewer, "This Is Your Community," *Knoxville News-Sentinel*, Aug. 4, 1974.
6. Carson Brewer, "How Lodge Closing Proposal Came About," *Knoxville News-Sentinel*, Aug. 4, 1974.

Leon Dure III, a University of Georgia professor, wrote to Nathaniel Reed, the assistant secretary of the interior, in October 1974:

> I imagine that there are some good features in this Wilderness Proposal for the GSMNP, for certainly this Park bears an enormous amount of traffic of all kinds; but those who wish to destroy the lodge and the shelters expose in themselves an incredible degree of elitism and selfishness in my opinion. The clientele of LeConte Lodge should never be equated with the hordes that descend upon Gatlinburg or Cherokee or that overland U.S. Rt. 441 that crosses the Great Smoky ridge line. The people that make up the lodge's clientele generally have two things in common—a love of the lodge, its setting and the wilderness experience it affords, and the fact that they are mostly middle-aged or older!
>
> To destroy the lodge in response to pressure from a small group of self-appointed spokesmen for nature lovers is not in keeping with the overall fine reputation of the National Park Service. There must be a middle ground where extremes are not resorted to, to satisfy extremists.

Gracie McNicol's hiking career spanned from the tenure of Pauline Huff to Tim Line. In the 1970s, she said, "It's not like the old days, but things seem to run smoother and more clockwise now than ever."[7] Gracie defended the lodge at a public hearing in 1979, saying that at age 87, she had climbed Le Conte 215 times. "If you keep hiking, you keep well," she said.

In the spring of 1975, as the lodge marked its 50th anniversary, the National Parks & Conservation Association voiced its support for closing the lodge in a letter to the park office. A few days later, Roger Miller, the park's acting superintendent, responded to the group by noting that closing the lodge "is still our goal."

In July 1975, superintendent Boyd Evison, in a letter to Carlos Campbell, offered a broader explanation of the park service's decision to close the lodge:

> When LeConte Lodge is closed, I believe we can manage use of that area by hikers as well as we can manage that of any other backcountry area. The unsanitary and unsafe conditions exist there essentially be*cause* the lodge is there—and all efforts at making its use of the area safe and sanitary have failed. I sympathize with those who feel an attachment to the lodge, and with those who *can* get to it—and sleep in it—but who *can't* get to the site (or a similar one) can sleep in a tent. But I suspect the numbers of such people are even smaller than those of people who can't even get to, and sleep in, the lodge. And I don't think we should build a road in there for those people (which would be the next step in the rationale for keeping the lodge). There is *no* other wilderness area even remotely comparable to the one of which LeConte Lodge and all of its problems are now imposed.

A park statement supporting the closing of the lodge included these reasons: the physical condition of the buildings, garbage and sanitation disposal problems, fire hazards, and the difficulties associated with resupplying the lodge.

By December of 1975, however, there was movement in the National Park Service office against the idea of removing the lodge. "I feel we have unjustly used the establishment of wilderness to justify removal of Le Conte," wrote park service director Gary Everhardt. "In testifying for wilderness in a number of areas before the House recently we accepted more permanent and substantial improvements and facilities than Le Conte. Can we not accept the continuation of Le Conte as

---

7. *Song of the Winter Wren*, p. 14.

a traditional and historical use within the Great Smoky Mountains National Park wilderness?"

In a memorandum dated January 20, 1976, park service director J.L. Norwood revealed that the future of the lodge was being reconsidered. "The decision to phase out the lodge has been controversial," the memorandum stated. "The prevailing interpretation of our actions seems to be that we are phasing out the lodge so the land can be included in the wilderness proposal for the park. This, of course, is not our primary motivation. LeConte Lodge has special significance to the 8,000 people who stay overnight each year. Their opposition to closing the lodge after the 1977 season is understandable. The lodge has provided a traditional service that antedates the park's establishment."

The park service decided to extend the deadline through 1979. "One alternative," Norwood wrote, "is to continue the present operation providing we can reverse past degradation, assure adequate safety and sanitation, and minimize harmful impact on the area. In the event the LeConte Lodge operation is continued, I will recommend a change in the wilderness proposal to include an enclave containing the lodge area."

The back and forth continued. Frances Scheidt, a resident of Knoxville, Tennessee, wrote the park to support the removal of the lodge. "It would be a blessing for my grandchildren to be spared a Disneyland-type distraction up there, and I see that as a real possibility sometime in the future if that whole mountain top is not included in Wilderness," she wrote.

Jim Huff, Jr., and his partners bought the lodge in 1976 from Herrick Brown, who stayed on the staff to assist in the transition. Huff's team encouraged guests to lobby on behalf of the lodge, which irritated park authorities. "Please furnish us with a copy of the letter that you send to guests of LeConte Lodge, after their visit, encouraging them to write me, other Interior officials, and members of Congress," park superintendent Boyd Evison wrote to Huff in August 1977. "If possible, I'd also like to have copies of the letters posted at the lodge, as samples of correspondence supporting its continued operation."

By September 1977, the park reported that Huff's team had made several changes to lessen its impact on the wilderness. To reduce the laundry load, the lodge experimented with sheet-bags—so that each guest used only one sheet. Firewood was no longer being used for heating or cooking, the number of nightly guests was limited to 40, and food service for day hikers was discontinued. The cabins have 67 beds and the dining room seats 60, but under national park guidelines, the lodge no longer operates at full capacity.

Several scholarly studies kept lodge operations under scrutiny.

A 1976 study led by Rosemary Nichols of Duke University analyzed the ecological impact of the lodge on its immediate area and the surrounding mountain landscape. Among the findings: Garbage in and around the lodge was responsible for repeated issues with bears, several of whom would return almost on cue. The amount of bare rock exposed in heavily trodden areas around the lodge constituted what the study called "an extreme on the impact gradient."

When Nichols published her 1977 report, *The Ecological Effect of LeConte Lodge*, she estimated that day hikers outnumbered overnight guests 3 to 1. The annual trail traffic on the mountaintop was estimated at 28,000 to 32,000 visitor days. Excluding winter, that's an average of about 120 visitors daily.

A follow-up to the Nichols study was led by Susan Power Bratton and Paul L. Whittaker in 1977. It concentrated on the impact of visitation on the mountain. The study concluded that removal of the lodge would lead to "substantial but not complete recovery" of vegetation in the lodge area and that much of the lodge area would continue to be impacted by day hikers. The study considered the impact of the possible closure of the popular but congested Alum Cave Bluff Trail and concluded that vegetation in the trail corridor would show significant recovery but that traffic—and resulting damage—likely would increase on the mountain's other trails.

By January 1978, after the completion of various studies, the park had come to terms with the idea that the lodge could remain in the wilderness setting. In a memorandum to the park's assistant superintendent, Superintendent Evison wrote that "we can expect LeConte Lodge to go on operating as long as it is 'acceptable' in terms of environmental impacts and human health and safety. Rosemary's and Susan's studies indicate that the lodge is only one of several factors in the degradation of the environment on Mount LeConte; so we will try to devise methods of overall reduction of those impacts." As part of the compromise to save the lodge, the park proposed limiting day hikers and closing the 12-bed backcountry shelter, though those measures were not implemented.[8]

Tim Line, the long-time manager of the lodge, supported the changes on the mountain. "I was pro-lodge because I needed a job," he said. "But the changes were good. They helped the environment and reduced the amount of stress on the trails. It's a national park, and you have to protect it. If the lodge had to go, so be it."

Seth Orme was the winter caretaker at the lodge from 2017 through 2020. His solitary winters gave him lots of time to think through the lodge's place in the wilderness. He wrote of how he reconciled the lodge's intrusion on the wilderness:

> I used to really dislike mountaintop establishments. Why in God's name do we find the highest, most beautiful, and most biologically sensitive areas just to build something on them? Over time, this sentiment has changed. By finding a balance between access and preservation, we develop opportunities for people to know a place while still preserving the landscape as a whole. If we created these national parks and just made them inaccessible—people would fall out of love with the place.
>
> One of the reasons we have this national park is because of this lodge. If there wasn't access for those who would eventually make the final decisions about another national park—they wouldn't have understood the real value in the landscape they saw on paper. You have to know a place to truly value it.

By 1980, the lodge seemed safe. Significant changes had been made. Llamas replaced horses for delivery trips up and down the mountain, minimizing the wear on the trail. Bulk supplies were being airlifted by helicopter. Woodcutting on the mountaintop ceased.

And the lodge lived for its centennial.

---

8. "Le Conte Lodge Expected to Stay, but with Fewer Accommodations," by Carson Brewer, *Knoxville News-Sentinel*, April 28, 1978.

National Register of Historic Places?

The National Register of Historic Places was authorized by the National Park Service in 1966, just two years after the Wilderness Act became law. Some wanted to register the lodge as a way to preserve it.

As ancient as the lodge looked, none of the buildings were old enough to qualify for the National Register in the 1970s. The standards include age (a minimum of 50 years), architectural integrity, and historical significance. There's no denying the historical significance of the 1924 Le Conte camp—essentially the birthplace of the national park—but nothing remains of the original structures. The site might qualify for a historical marker, but not for mandatory preservation.

Jim Huff, Jr., who operated the lodge 1976–1988, was familiar with the National Register. In 1987 he arranged to have his grandfather's 65-year-old Mountain View Hotel registered as a historical landmark. Huff planned a $34 million renovation that would have transformed the hotel into a Marriott convention center similar to the 1984 renovation of the Grove Park Inn in Asheville.[9] Yet the deal fell through, and the iconic hotel was razed and replaced by an amusement park. Obviously, the National Register does not offer ironclad protection.

In 1983, the park awarded Jim Huff, Jr., an unprecedented 15-year lease. He announced plans for a complete renovation of the lodge facilities built by his uncle Jack. The $300,000 project included the new three-bedroom East Lodge, designed by Gatlinburg architect Hugh Ogle, the deck on the office, and new windows, roofs, and porches on existing cabins. One guest cabin east of the kitchen was converted into staff housing. Terms of the lease called for the park to receive three-quarters of a percent of the lodge's gross receipts. At the same time, the park renovated the water system with two 7,000-gallon tanks, a new ram pump, and flush toilets.[10]

The lodge dining room will be 86 years old in 2025, but it has undergone some renovations and expansions which compromise its architectural integrity. The same is true for the Old Cabin, opened in 1934 and substantially rebuilt in the 1970s, as well as the row of one-room cabins built in the 1940s. Even the iconic central staircase has been renovated with cut stones airlifted to the mountain.

Also, the National Park Service has its own standards for preservation of historic structures, and in 1983 in the context of the Wilderness Act, the park classified the lodge as "non-historic buildings."

Even if the buildings are not original, much of the furniture is, including sturdy bunk beds and dining-room chairs built by Jack Huff. There has been some discussion that those items might qualify for the national register.

Other park locations have been approved for the National Register, including the 68-year-old Mayna Treanor Avent cabin in 1994, the 63-year-old Clingmans Dome tower in 2012, the 51-year-old Look Rock Tower in 2017, the 73-year-old Fontana Dam in 2017, and the 80-year-old Mount Cammerer lookout in 2019. Historic

---

9. "$30 Million Renewal Planned for Historic Mountain View Hotel," *Knoxville News-Sentinel*, Feb. 15, 1987.

10. "Facelift Planned at LeConte Lodge After Operators Sign Long Lease," by Carson Brewer, *Knoxville News-Sentinel*, May 21, 1983.

districts were declared for Cades Cove in 1945, Roaring Fork in 1976, Oconaluftee in 1982, Elkmont in 1994, and Cataloochee in 2022. Scattered throughout the Smokies, several additional homesteads and churches are on the national register.

The 1903 LeConte Memorial Lodge in Yosemite National Park was registered in 1987 as a National Historic Landmark. The structure remains, but the name was lost in 2016 because of Joseph LeConte's association with slavery. It's now known as the Yosemite Conservation Heritage Center.

5

Storms of the Century

Weekend weather forecasts for April 1, 1987, predicted one to two inches of snow in Knoxville with possibly higher accumulations in the mountains. Nevertheless, 18 hikers who held coveted reservations at LeConte Lodge headed up the trails. Hiking up in the snow sounded like fun, especially with a warm cabin and supper awaiting. Or maybe they dismissed the forecasts as an April Fool's joke. After all, spring was already budding in the foothills, just two weeks before Easter.

Then the snow came in feet rather than in inches—two feet in Gatlinburg and four feet up at the lodge, where snow drifted to the rooftops. The trails were impassable and the guests were stranded. "We had to get word to all their relatives and bosses that they were going to be there for a while," general manager Tim Line said.

The lodge crew and guests shoveled paths to the dining room and the bathrooms. But hiking down the snow-covered trails would have been dangerous and pointless. "It wouldn't have helped even if they could get down the mountain because the roads were closed," Line said. "On the fifth day it warmed up, and there was a big thaw. We started sending people down. It was a slush-fest."

The crew had plenty of food stockpiled (the annual helicopter airlift had been one week earlier), but serving three meals a day was challenging. Lisa Line baked bread so she could serve grilled-cheese sandwiches.

It wasn't just the guests who got stir-crazy. One evening, the Lines' four-year-old son, Nathan, dashed into the kitchen and broke up a card game shouting: "Mom, Grace is gone! She's disappeared." Grace, the Lines' two-year-old daughter, had been playing on the porch when she dropped a doll into the snow. She stepped off the porch to get it and plunged into a snowdrift that was far over her head. Thankfully, her parents were able to quickly scoop her out.

Epic snows are not unusual on Le Conte, but guests rarely saw them until the lodge season was extended, driven by the demand for reservations and facilitated by the warmer accommodations after propane heat replaced the old wood stoves. In Jack Huff's era, the lodge season customarily ran from Easter to Halloween, though he was glad to open up in winter, and he listed the lodge as "open year-round."

In the 1950s Pauline Huff usually opened on May 1. Herrick Brown pushed the closing date into November in 1968. Since 1993, the lodge has customarily closed the Wednesday before Thanksgiving. The lodge opened March 19 in 2012 and 2018 and March 20 in 2023, treading on the last days of winter.

July and August are the only months when snow has not been recorded at the

Perched on Le Conte's throne, the Old Cabin commanded a regal 100-mile view over the Tennessee Valley, well before the dining hall was built and the Tennessee Valley Authority dammed the French Broad River to form Douglas Lake 5,500 feet below (photograph by Jim Thompson, courtesy Thompson Photo Products).

lodge, and even in those months there have been overnight freezes. In 1961 there was a freeze the night of July 4, plus a 20-degree night on Memorial Day weekend.

The latest flurries recorded at the lodge were June 2, 1956, and the earliest were September 24, 1985. Seven times since 1978, the lodge has had snow on the ground on Mother's Day, including five inches that fell May 6, 2016. Even as late as June 15, 2020, the temperature dipped to 34 and the grounds were covered by an inch of hail. On July 4, 1996, Ed Wright reported a temperature of 49 degrees at the Alum Cave trailhead and 39 at the mountaintop on his 886th ascent.

On March 19, 1936, the *Knoxville News-Sentinel* reported snow six feet deep at the lodge, quoting "an attendant at Jack Huff's cabin." The same storm left drifts 10 feet deep in the North Carolina mountains near Newland, 125 miles northeast of Le Conte. In 1947, snow accumulated five feet deep at Newfound Gap.

More recently, the record snowfall on LeConte came during the "Blizzard of '93," also known as the "Storm of the Century." Rick Morgan, the lodge's winter caretaker, measured snow 63 inches deep, though weathermen off the mountain calculated the official total at 56 inches—the most of any location in the nation.[1]

The lodge was not yet open for the season, yet Morgan was not alone on the

---

1. New Hampshire's Mount Washington is famous for having the nation's most extreme weather, yet its one-day record for snowfall is 49.3 inches. Over the course of a year, Washington overshadows Le Conte with an average of 281 inches and a record of 566 inches (47 feet) during 1969. The Mount Washington Observatory has measured snow in every month, with 1.1 inches in July 1957 and 2.5 in August 1965.

mountain. A hiker named Boyd Rutherford was camped in the back-country shelter near the lodge. As the storm developed on March 12, 1993, National Park rangers radioed Morgan and asked him to check on anyone who might be at the shelter. Morgan found Rutherford well prepared for the weather, with tarps to keep out the snow. Morgan invited him to spend the night at the heated lodge, but Rutherford decided to tough it out.

"Later that night, I heard a faint voice outside," Morgan said. "It was Boyd, and he had decided to come down from the shelter when it got really bad." He was fortunate to make it, considering the white-out conditions. "By morning, the snow piled up so deep that we couldn't go out the door. had to climb out the window. I had snowshoes with me and I remember walking across the tops of the buildings, the snow had drifted so high."[2]

Morgan and Rutherford had plenty of food stockpiled. The one thing they lacked was a camera to capture the scene. "I really had it better than almost everyone else in the eastern part of the state," Morgan said. "I didn't even have to prepare for the blizzard. We already had propane stoves, kerosene heat, the park service radios to communicate, and a battery-operated television. I was happy. I was watching it all on television."

One morning, Morgan heard a raven pecking on the window, and he shared one of his biscuits with the bird. The bird came back every day, begging by clicking a shard of blue glass onto a rock. Morgan kept the blue glass as a memento.

TV told Morgan and Rutherford how fortunate they were. The storm killed more than 300 people from Cuba to Canada. In the foothills of the Smokies, helicopters air-dropped bags of food for stranded residents and tourists.

After several days, Rutherford wanted to check on his fiancée in Sevierville, and he and Morgan hiked down together. "The drifts completely covered Alum Cave Trail," Morgan said. "The trail was just gone." At one point, Morgan slipped off the trail and Rutherford caught him by his collar, preventing what might have been a tragic fall.

The lodge also had snow four feet deep in the early spring of 1960. There was no winter caretaker at that time. Herrick Brown had just acquired the lodge and wanted to check on the conditions, so he hiked up the Rainbow Falls Trail on March 23 (along with Ernest Dickerman and Martin Inman, Jr.). It was the first time any of them had hiked on snowshoes, and the ascent took nine hours. Brown said the icicles on trees tinkled like bells.[3]

Over the course of an average season, the lodge sees eight feet of snow. The annual record is 164 inches (almost 14 feet) in 2010.

Drought is rarely a problem, as the lodge averages 85 inches of rain per year. The Basin Spring has never run dry, though in 1962, an unseasonable spring drought threatened the operation of the lodge.[4] In August 2012, after a 10-day dry spell, the lodge blog reported, "our spring is looking a little sad." The record rainfall for a

---

2. "1993 Blizzard a Cliffhanger for LeConte Lodge Caretaker," WBIR-TV, by Jim Matheny, March 12, 2018.
3. "Le Conte Trek Filled with Music," by Carson Brewer, *Knoxville News-Sentinel*, March 27, 1960.
4. "First Rain in a Month Soaks Knox Area," *Knoxville News-Sentinel*, May 11, 1962.

month was 18 inches in July of 2022, when there were only six dry days in the entire month.

Converting the snow to its liquid equivalent, the lodge averages nearly 100 inches of precipitation per year—twice what Knoxville gets.

Hundreds of miles from the coast, Le Conte is not immune to hurricanes. The most intense was Sandy, which dumped 34 inches of snow at Halloween 2012, two days after making landfall in New Jersey. Fifteen guests checked in during the storm, arriving as late as 11 p.m., and most of them stayed extra days because the trails were impassable.

Hurricane Opal in October 1995 left six inches of snow atop Le Conte and caused landslides that washed out the Alum Cave Bluff Trail. The lodge and the park were closed by Hurricane Florence in September 2018. In 1951, a cloudburst that brought six inches of rain and 70 mph winds caused more than 40 landslides in the Alum Creek watershed, including several that washed out the trail.

Le Conte weather-watchers know the ninth tropical storm of the season often has eyes for the Smokies—Ivan in 2004, Irma in 2017, Ida in 2021, and Ian in 2022. An unnamed hurricane in 1928 put a damper on Jack Huff's piggy-back hike with his mother.

In 1931, park promoter Carlos Campbell asked the U.S. Weather Bureau to establish an official weather station at the lodge. Huff offered to monitor the station, but instead, the station wound up being installed in 1937 on Mount Mitchell. The lodge has kept unofficial weather records since 1978, on charts posted in the office.

Other records are anecdotal. Paul Adams saw two extremes in 1925, with a summer high of 81 degrees and a low of minus 37 Fahrenheit on New Year's Eve. Decades later, after Adams' accounts were forgotten, the lodge boasted that the temperature had never reached 80. Then the last two days of June 2012, the temperature hit 81.4 and 81.5. It was too hot for the llamas to work, so a helicopter was chartered to airlift supplies.

On July 29, 2021, the thermometer hit 79.1, and the lodge was swarmed by White-Striped Black Moths. "They tend to show up on the warmest days of summer, especially when the lower elevations are getting baked," the lodge blog reported. "When the lodge surpassed 80 back in 2012, these little flutterers were everywhere. Yesterday, their population density skyrocketed around the lodge. So the theory still holds true."

The coldest night during the guest season was six degrees on April 10, 1973 (back when the cabins were heated by wood-burning stoves). "Of course, it gets a lot colder in the winter months," Herrick Brown said. "We open April 1 and close in early fall. This six degrees is the coldest we've ever had in our regular season."[5]

Co-owner Bill Rinearson called 1976–77 "the coldest winter in a century."[6] Twice, the thermometer bottomed out at minus 22, and by the end of January, snow accumulated 42 inches deep.

The lodge registered below-zero temperatures every winter until 2021, when

---

5. "Scientists 'Enjoy' Frigid Night on Mt. LeConte, *Knoxville News-Sentinel*, Jan. 2, 1928.
6. *Song of the Winter Wren*, by David Witherspoon, p. 219

the low was 3 degrees on February 2. If that was a token of global warming, the chill returned for Christmas 2022, when the winter caretaker registered minus 22 on December 23. The morning after Halloween 2023, the temperature dipped to 7 degrees, the earliest single-digit reading in lodge records.

The lodge has been struck by lightning several times. On May 10, 1963, 35 youths from the First Baptist Church of Gatlinburg were spending the night, when lightning struck a tree next to a cabin. The *News-Sentinel* reported that Bill Lewis and David Beeler had their shoes blown off by the blast, but they escaped injury. In 1975, lightning struck the kitchen sink as Herrick Brown was on the telephone nearby. In July 2022, a bolt struck near the dining hall and damaged some communications equipment.

The aurora borealis, or northern lights, are rarely visible above the boreal forests of Le Conte. When they do extend this far south, it is usually around the spring or fall equinox. Lodge guests saw them the night before Easter in 1973 and in October 2024. Allyson Virden watched for them each September during the years that she and her husband Chris served as site managers.

On the night before Halloween in 1972, a foraging bear woke up Herrick Brown, and he stepped outside his cabin to witness "the brightest aurora borealis display I've ever seen." He described the lights spanning 90 degrees of the northern horizon.[7]

In August 2017, a solar eclipse crossed four national parks, from the Grand Tetons to the Smokies. The lodge was just outside the path of totality. The lodge blog reported: "Camp gradually became darker, the temperature dropped five degrees, we saw Venus and a few stars out, and then back to normal. The valley was purple and blue for a few seconds and it seemed as though we were looking through a bubble to a different world. The diamond ring was beautiful as it offset the slivered sun."

Living with Nature in All Her Moods

In 1926, Huff sent a notice to the *Knoxville Journal* offering to open his cabin upon request for winter hikers.

In 1928, the lodge hosted a group of scientists who had convened in Nashville for the American Association for the Advancement of Science. They experienced a 68-degree drop in temperature in a span of 18 hours, from 48 in Knoxville to minus 20 at the lodge. The *Knoxville Journal* reported that Brockway Crouch, a Knoxville florist, "looked a minute too long at morning scenery and now he has a frozen ear. Albert 'Dutch' Roth suffered a frozen finger from too much exposure in taking pictures of the snow scenes."[8]

After Herrick Brown took over in 1960, he offered to open the lodge during the winter, usually for fellow members of the Smoky Mountain Hiking Club. On one February night in 1976, as Brown was finishing his tenure, he had a party of 52 camped in the new office.

---

7. *Knoxville News-Sentinel*, Nov. 1, 1972.
8. "Returning Visitors to Le Conte Says Temperature on Peak 20 Below Zero," *Knoxville Journal*, Tuesday, Jan. 3, 1928.

In a 1960 letter to a birdwatcher's column in the *Knoxville Journal*, Brown wrote, "I have winterized one of the smaller cabins so as to be more comfortable on winter overnight trips. Should any of the watchers want to stay there, have them contact me a few days in advance. It doesn't take much excuse to get me up there anyway. The cabin will hold four and we could open another, if necessary. Although the lodge is not officially open, several parties plan to avail themselves of the services this winter."[9]

Brown was careful to make sure that his winter guests were well prepared for severe weather. He knew that winter on the mountain could be dangerous, even for experienced hikers.

At least 23 hikers have died on the slopes of Mount Le Conte, five of those in winter conditions. Eleven suffered heart attacks, and four fell. Most were seasoned hikers and Le Conte veterans. Four of the fatalities were medical professionals, and two were youths. Another eight individuals have died in aircraft crashes around Le Conte (see Chapter 8). There have been two murders and two suicides.

On January 30, 1971, Charles Lindsley was the sweeper behind a group of students from Asheville School as they hiked up the Alum Cave Trail. He slipped on icy rocks and plummeted down the "upper slide," the site of a 1951 landslide at the head of Trout Branch. (Nowadays, safety cables are fastened to the rocks to provide handholds alongside the trail.) His group couldn't find him, so they proceeded up to the lodge, where teacher Jim "Pop" Hollandsworth was able to call the park service for help. A search team used ropes to descend the cliff and found Lindsley's body (with a broken neck) far down the mountainside on a sheet of ice.

Lindsley was a Princeton graduate and a chemical warfare specialist during World War II. Ora Blackmun eulogized him in her book, *A Spire in the Mountains*: "As a nature lover and student, and as a tireless hiker, he has inspired boys to learn to live with nature in all its moods." For more than 40 years, the Carolina Mountain Club held memorial hikes each January. Hollingsworth even made the hike in his mid–80s, climbing the Alum Cave Trail through snow drifts that were chest-deep.

Dr. Lea Callaway, 56, a surgeon and former mayor of Maryville, Tennessee, reserved a cabin to celebrate New Year's Eve in 1965. Climbing the Boulevard Trail with friends and family, he felt short of breath. Doctors in his group stayed with him, while crew member Joe Schlatter hustled up to the lodge to call for help. The phone line was down, so Schlatter cranked up a generator and used the ham radio to alert park rangers. Unfortunately, Callaway passed away of a heart attack before he could be rescued.

In May 2005, Dr. John McCallie Bolinger, 55, from Chattanooga, suffered a heart attack near the top of the Alum Cave Trail. His fellow hikers were able to summon another doctor who was staying at the lodge and called 911. However, they reached an operator in North Carolina who had trouble communicating the exact location to the park service. By the time rangers arrived, Bolinger had passed away, and the next morning his body was carried down on horseback.

Ernest LuAllen, 69, was returning from his 141st climb of Le Conte on New

---

9. "LeConte Lodge Now Available in Winter," by J.B. Owen, *Knoxville Journal*, Dec. 29, 1960.

Year's Day, 1992, when he suffered a fatal heart attack at Arch Rock. He was hiking with LeConte veterans Paul Dinwiddie, Bill Sharp, and Henry Neel. Dinwiddie wrote in his journal: "Lu had acted normal in every way until he suddenly collapsed while talking. I believe that he died instantly." LuAllen was an army veteran of World War II. A promontory 4.1 miles up the Alum Cave Bluff Trail is now known as "Lu's Pulpit."

Albert Brigance was climbing Le Conte to celebrate his 75th birthday when he died September 12, 2007. An Air Force veteran from Oklahoma, he had retired to Tennessee (where he had hiked all the trails in the Smokies) after a career as a renowned educator and author in California.

Philip Davenport, 47, was hiking down Alum Cave Bluff Trail when he suffered a fatal heart attack on July 15, 2017. Davenport, a carpenter from Nashville, had spent the previous night at the lodge with a church group.

Nathan Kirkham helped with several rescues during the four years he worked on the lodge crew. "I only carried the guests part of about 1.5 miles up to the lodge up Trillium and Alum Cave Bluff Trails. I'm no Jack Huff, who can carry his mom up the whole trail in a chair strapped to his back. I remember feeling 10 feet tall, bulletproof and invincible, when one of those guests recovered enough to hike down on her own. I remember feeling incredibly humbled when the other one did not."

The latter case involved a 90-year-old dentist who was climbing with his family but became exhausted a mile below the top of the Alum Cave Trail. The crew got him to the lodge and made arrangements for him to stay an extra day, because storms prevented a rescue flight. The next day, the man felt well enough to eat in the dining room, but he collapsed that night. The lodge is equipped with a battery-powered AED (artificial external defibrillator) and a doctor was on site, but life-saving efforts were in vain.

"I was never prouder of my LeConte Lodge staff than on that difficult night," Kirkham said. "They were wonderful, exceeding even lofty expectations of the guardians of the top of Tennessee. We gave the man the very best possible effort of surviving in a difficult place. Instead of dying in a fall or exposure the night before on the trail, we allowed him to spend his last day in a beautiful place with his family."

Three Boy Scouts lost on Le Conte in March 1957 found haven at the lodge. They were on a hike organized by Troop 94 of Greeneville, Tennessee. The boys were "thinly clad" for a day hike and searchers feared they might not survive a wet, wintry night. But they followed their Scout training, stayed together, and found a shelter.

"We were not very scared," Victor Thorne, 13, said in a newspaper interview. "Our Scout manual said that if lost at night, to stop and not to walk any more. About 10:30 last night, we got up to a cabin on Mount LeConte and stayed there. There were several cabins, and one of them was open, so we went in there and spent the night on the floor. We didn't sleep very well. It started hailing and the wind came up pretty strong about midnight."[10]

After rescuers found them, Victor and Jimmy Grubb, 11, were strong enough to hike down. Mike Harmon, 12, "was a little sick from the ordeal, and was carried

---

10. "Night on Le Conte Hits Rescuers Harder Than Lost Scout Trio," *Knoxville Journal*, March 19, 1957.

down by members of the Morristown rescue squad." The *Nashville Banner* described the boys as "tenderfeet at mountain hiking."

In February 1970, another lost Scout was not so fortunate. Geoffrey Hague, 16, of Morristown, became separated from his troop after a snowball fight. Sixteen inches of snow fell after he disappeared, and it took more than a week for searchers to find his body.

Back in 1938, two early-spring hikers found a decomposed body in a rhododendron thicket along the trail to Cliff Top, within a half-mile of the lodge. Identified as Susanna Ingraham, 58, she had worked as a nurse in Knoxville. Rosa and George Townsend[11] called her their "city friend," and in late summer 1937 they invited her to join them for a hike to LeConte Lodge.

Ingraham once described the summit of Le Conte as "the most beautiful thing I have ever seen—I'd like to stay here always." Unemployed in the fall of 1937, she headed up Le Conte for a star-gazing trip, telling her roommate, "If I don't return in four or five days, give my clothes and personal belongings to whoever you want to." Authorities concluded that she died of exposure.

Guide Wiley Oakley said Ingraham was the first death on LeConte in 25 years. He recalled a man who was caught in a bear trap and only his skeleton was found.

The Coolest Job in Tennessee

During the winter, a caretaker stays at the lodge to maintain the facilities, file weather reports, and post the daily blog at highonleconte.com. Some call this "the coolest job in Tennessee."

Needless to say, it takes a unique soul to work this lonely 100-day assignment. The caretakers usually come down once a week for supplies and volunteers hike up occasionally to give them a day off. David Witherspoon, who came down only once in 12 weeks in the winter of 1975, felt that he lost his social graces during his long hermitage. He lived without a clock all winter. If he needed to know the time, he would dial the time-and-temperature number in Sevierville. "It's paradise," he told the *Knoxville News-Sentinel*.[12]

No hiker services are available in winter, and the water system is turned off and drained. However, it's not unusual for day hikers to visit the lodge even in the depths of winter, replenishing their water from the Basin Spring. In 1991 when Ed Wright set the annual record with 230 climbs, he made 10 climbs in January, 11 in February, and 13 in December.

Herrick Brown hired the first winter caretaker, Jim Gamble, around 1972. "During the winter, people would get stuck up here and break in to save themselves," Brown said in an interview with WBIR-TV. "We had so much trouble, we had to

---

11. George Townsend (1880–1962) was the son of Col. Wilson Bailey Townsend (1854–1936), the timber tycoon who jump-started the national park campaign in 1926 by selling 76,507 acres for less than $4 per acre. The town of Townsend was named for him.

12. "Witherspoon Enjoys Solitude, Nature Atop Mt. Le Conte," by Carson Brewer, *Knoxville News-Sentinel*, Jan. 21, 1977.

5. Storms of the Century

Tim Webb was filling in for the winter caretaker during a 2011 storm that left snowdrifts more than three feet deep (photograph by Marsh Wilkes, courtesy Tim Webb).

keep a man up here in the winter. The first year, he figured he thawed out and dried out 200 people."

Even in the first half-century, the lodge was occasionally occupied during the winter. Paul Adams stayed on the mountaintop in 1925 to work on his cabin, Jack Huff in 1937 to work on the dining room, and Jim Huff, Jr., in 1977 to oversee renovations.

During a cold spell in November 1937, when the dining room was under construction, Jack Huff told a reporter that he expected overnight temperatures to dip to minus 20—the coldest he had seen since 1928. "There are no guests or visitors up here now," Huff said. "We're having a hard job keeping warm. The houses are covered with a sheet of ice, and that helps keep the wind out." The same paper included a tragic story of a family with eight children burning wooden furniture to survive a 22-degree night in Knoxville.

J.P. Krol read dozens of books during five winters as caretaker. "It's hard to imagine a more inspiring place to start a day," he said in a 2014 interview.[13]

Winter caretakers have included Gamble and Scott Gillette, 1971; Gamble and Al Bedinger, 1972; Dick Ketelle and Bedinger, 1973; Dan Kitchen, 1974; Witherspoon, 1975–76; Rusty and Deborah Nail, 1977–1980; Tim and Lisa Line, 1981–83; John and

---

13. "For LeConte Lodge Caretaker, Nothing Tops Winter in Smokies," by Morgan Simmons, *The Tennessean*, March 10, 2004.

Donna Mansfield, 1989–90; Jeff Hostler, 1990–91; Rick Morgan, 1992–93; Bruce Newman, 1994–97; Ron Underwood, 2000–02; Rusty Kirby, 2004–05; Henry Neel, 2005–06; Doug McFalls, 2009–10; Alex Hughes, 2010–11; Krol, 2011–17; Seth Orme, 2017–20; Philip "P-Nut" Clarkson, 2020–22; and Bert "Wildcat" Emerson, 2022–25.

The Mansfields honeymooned at the lodge, hiking up in a soaking rain. "I never wanted to see this place again," Donna Mansfield said. Yet they joined the crew in 1987. "We thought it would be like putting some adventure in our lives," John said.[14]

With the twenty-first-century advent of blogs, wireless access, and digital photography, in 2009 the McFalls launched the daily blog, originally called "Living on Le Conte," a project that was carried forward and refined by site managers Allyson and Chris Virden. The blog has become almost a daily newspaper, found at highonleconte.com/daily-posts.

Weather Extremes and Trends

Precipitation totals are based on calendar years, so snow totals do not represent a full winter season.

Year	High	Low	First Snow	Last Snow	Snow Inches	Rain Inches
2023	77	1	October 15	May 11	55	78
2022	76	-22	October 18	April 10	67	103
2021	79	3	October 29	April 23	46	94
2020	74	-6	December 1	May 10	81	114
2019	77	-5	October 31	April 20	29	103
2018	75	-8	November 2	April 17	70	115
2017	75	-7	October 28	May 6	42	90
2016	75	-7	October 21	May 5	65	52
2015	74	-24	December 18	March 23	37	89
2014	74	-17	October 5	May 10	95	76
2013	73	-5	October 23	May 6	98	99
2012	81	-4	October 24	April 24	71	83
2011	75	-8	October 20	May 11	86	89
2010	74	-8	October 4	March 30	164	78
2009	72	-22	October 17	April 21	96	96
2008	74	-12	October 28	April 29	84	69
2007	75	-8	October 16	March 26	50	53
2006	72	-7	October 24	May 16	85	75
2005	78	-12	October 26	April 14	101	62
2004	73	-8	October 15	April 14	95	100
2003	76	-18	November 24	April 11	154	92
2002	75	-2	November 27	April 13	66	80

---

14. The Mansfields joined the crew in 1987 after spending their honeymoon at the lodge. "Mountaintop Life Couple's Adventure," by Jan Maxwell Avent, *Knoxville News-Sentinel*, Feb. 13, 1989.

6

Tragedy and Thanksgiving

Thanksgiving weekend of 2016 seemed like a good time to climb Mount Le Conte. There was a smoky wildfire across the valley on Chimney Tops, but rangers expected it to burn itself out. So Erin Howard and her friends headed up the Alum Cave Bluff Trail to get the miles she needed for her 100-mile goal in the centennial year of the National Park Service.

"By the time we reached Cliff Top, the smoke rolled in and was so incredibly thick," she said. "We decided not to stick around and started our descent. When we reached the split for Alum or Bullhead, we debated on the safest way down since we had encountered many smoky sections on the way up. We decided to stick to our route and kept hiking down Alum."

"By the time we got home that evening, the fire had spread and we found out that Bullhead was on fire about the same time we would have been heading down. We are all thankful that we kept hiking down Alum. There's no way we could have outrun the fire had we gone Bullhead."

In the hours Erin was on the mountain, gusting winds whipped the Chimney Tops fire out of control, scattering hot embers for miles and sparking the deadliest wildfire in the United States since 1947, taking 14 lives. More than 32 square miles were scorched, and 2,460 buildings were destroyed around Gatlinburg, Pigeon Forge, and the fringes of the park.[1] "It was truly devastating," Howard said, "and we sat and just cried all evening thinking about those who lost their lives."

As the inferno spread over the mountains and torched ridgetop resorts, no one knew how far it reached on the mountaintop. Le Conte Lodge had recently closed for winter, so there were no guests to worry about. Park authorities called Tim Line, who had just completed his 40th season as the lodge manager, advising him to evacuate the winter caretaker, J.P. Krol—just in case. That night, friends with a view of Mount Le Conte told Line that the blaze appeared to be sweeping beyond Bullhead Mountain near the mile-high level. "We were afraid the lodge wouldn't be there in the morning," he said.

Fortunately, the wind shifted, rain intervened, and the inferno burned out more than a mile high on Balsam Point, barely two miles from the lodge. "Two days later, the park service did a flyover and saw that the lodge was fine," Line said.

---

1. Investigators concluded that the fire began with two boys playing with matches on the Chimney Tops Trail. "Sources: Teens Toying with Matches Started Wildfire," *The Tennessean*, Dec. 10, 2016. Arson charges were dropped in 2017.

As hiker Benny Braden basked in this sunset at Cliff Top, smoke was rising from the mountain known as "Chimney Top." It erupted into a wildfire the next day (courtesy Benny Braden).

Dewey Slusher hiked the Bullhead Trail just weeks after the fire and described three miles of utter devastation, with large boulders fractured by the intense heat. "It will not recover in my lifetime, maybe never, at least to any semblance of what it was," he said (photo courtesy Dewey Slusher).

Line said it was a "miracle" that the lodge survived. "Our happiness at saving the lodge was muted by the unbelievable human losses," he said. "It was the saddest event that I ever experienced in a lifetime in the Smokies."

At a backcountry facility such as LeConte Lodge, there is no greater threat than wildfires. In November 2023, under ominous conditions reminiscent of 2016, the lodge canceled the final night of the season because of the risk of fire.

Across the nation, several national park lodges have gone up in smoke. In 2017 lightning sparked a wildfire in Montana's Glacier National Park that gutted the Sperry Chalet. The stone walls survived, and the chalet was rebuilt and reopened in 2020.

The Glacier Point Hotel in California's Yosemite Park burned because of an electrical short in 1969; it was accessible by road but was 28 miles from the nearest fire station. The hotel has been replaced by the Glacier Point overlook, with a majestic view of Half Dome.

The original Grand Canyon Lodge, an architectural treasure on the north rim designed by Gilbert Stanley Underwood, burned in 1932 and was rebuilt in 1937.

In the Smokies, Timber Top Lodge at Indian Gap was destroyed by fire in 1958.

LeConte Lodge has limited fire-fighting resources, with fire extinguishers in each cabin and four hydrants throughout the camp. However, the 14,000-gallon water system was drained down in November 2016, due to the fall dry season and in anticipation of the winter closing. Even with a full tank, there would be no way to defend the lodge against a raging wildfire.

During the 1970s wilderness debate over the future of the lodge, the park mandated a firewall between the kitchen and dining room. David Witherspoon, the winter caretaker, described how carpenters with hand saws "amputated" the kitchen and inserted a concrete-block wall. Manager Herrick Brown told Witherspoon that the firewall requirement was the craziest thing that ever happened to the lodge.

In the decades when the Smokies were logged, forest fires were all too common. During Paul Adams' tenure in 1925, a wildfire east of Le Conte scorched a ridgeline and left the barren knob now known as Charlies Bunion.

In Jack Huff's first year, 1926, another fire reached Balsam Point, the same extent as the 2016 fire 90 years later. As a result, modern scenes along the Bullhead Trail—charred tree trunks being replaced by thick green laurel—are reminiscent of the terrain faced by CCC trail builders in the 1930s. In fact, the stone pulpit on the Bullhead Trail was built as an overlook so hikers could see over the rhododendron that was growing thickly to replace the burned-out forest.

Only You Can Prevent Cabin Fires

A century ago, the Champion Fibre Company hired patrolmen to guard against wildfires on Mount Le Conte and built a rickety lookout tower on Cliff Top. The company saw the presence of the lodge as a practical way to guard against uncontrolled

Champion Fibre Company's fire lookout on Cliff Top in 1924. The hikers are the founders of the Smoky Mountain Hiking Club, which marked its centennial in 2024 (photograph by Jim Thompson, courtesy Thompson Photo Products).

campfires. Paul Adams and Jack Huff were not just innkeepers but were also acting as Smokey Bear.[2]

"We never had a fire on the mountaintop, but we did discover a few down in the valleys," Adams wrote. In the days before two-way radio, if a fire was spotted, one of Adams' workers would have to hike down to Gatlinburg to report it. Smokey Bear would have been proud of Smoky Jack, Adams' dog, who learned to extinguish cigarette butts by burying them in dirt or by stomping on them.

On the occasions when fire has broken out at the lodge, the crew has been able to keep the flames under control.

Jack Huff, raised by a lumberman, took pride in the lodge's fire safety record. Even though the timber cabins were tinderboxes, heated by wood stoves and fireplaces and lit by kerosene lamps, the lodge had no fires until October 11, 1957, when a chimney fire destroyed a crew cabin occupied by Rosie and Birdie Ogle. Asleep when the fire broke out, they were able to escape. The crew saved their personal belongings, but the cabin and furniture were lost. The wind was calm, so no other cabins were involved.

---

2. Smokey Bear is a mascot developed by the U.S. Forest Service in 1944, and his name does not seem to be connected to the Great Smoky Mountains. A black bear cub rescued from a New Mexico wildfire in 1950 became known as Smokey and lived at the National Zoo until 1976.

6. Tragedy and Thanksgiving

Pauline Huff told a newspaper reporter that the fire would not interrupt guest services. "Nothing of the beauty of the mountaintop, as far as the forests, the sunrises, and the sunsets, has been spoiled," she said. "We are sorry, however, that our 31st year with a perfect no-fire record has been broken."[3]

In October 1964, a fire destroyed Cabin 6, which faces the central staircase. In 2011, the survivors of that fire were interviewed by the *Knoxville News-Sentinel*. "Every time I see these photos, I can't believe we're alive," said Ellen Bean.

Ellen and Terri Jolly were zoology students at the University of Tennessee, and because of a storm, they were the only guests who made it up to the lodge that night. The next morning, they lit a fire in the wood stove to take the chill off their cabin and then hiked out to Myrtle Point to see the sunrise. As they returned toward the lodge, they noticed an orange cast to the sky, which they thought might be the alpenglow of the sunrise. Then they reached the lodge and found their cabin aflame. Evidently, a mouse had built a nest next to the rusty chimney flue, and that's where the blaze started. The crew used a fire extinguisher and the water system to fight the fire, and by knocking down a wall they were able to save the bunkbed and the women's backpacks.[4]

Cabin 6 was destroyed, and manager Herrick Brown buried the charred debris and rebuilt the cabin. Eight years later, Brown needed some hardware for a construction project, so he exhumed the remains of the cabin and salvaged some metal parts.

Brown built a wood-staved tank in 1968 that held enough water to operate flush toilets and provided enough pressure for fire hoses.

In November 1975, the last year that wood stoves were used, the winter caretaker, Witherspoon, had to extinguish a fire on the shingles of his cabin, known as The Shack. The blaze started from an overheated chimney flue. As he doused his roof with buckets of spring water, he dreaded the inevitable headlines: "Caretaker Sets Fire to Lodge."

Significantly, the lodge has not had any cabin fires in nearly a half century since 1976, when kerosene heaters replaced the fireplaces and Franklin stoves. Hikers from the 1970s recalled getting a whiff of kerosene fumes when they rounded the Hallelujah Turn at the crest of the Alum Cave Trail. In the 1990s, the lodge switched to propane heaters. Kerosene lamps are still used to light the cabins.

Early crews used wood-burning stoves to cook meals. Hardwoods burned hotter and were the preferred fuel, but since they did not grow near the summit, they had to be cut farther down the mountain and dragged up to the lodge.

A butane stove was installed in the kitchen in the 1960s, though it was not efficient to use as long as the heavy five-gallon tanks had to be brought up two at a time on pack horses. Once helicopters began airlifting 500-gallon tanks each spring, propane replaced kerosene as the fuel for cooking meals and heating the cabins. The lodge uses 30 tanks, which are swapped out during the spring airlift. The tank farm is downhill from the lodge, and the fuel is piped underground to the cabins. The newest propane kitchen stove was airlifted and installed in 2022.

---

3. "LeConte Lodge Has First Fire in 31 Years," *Knoxville News-Sentinel*, Oct. 12, 1957.
4. Morgan Simmons, "A Tale Rekindled," *Knoxville News-Sentinel*, Feb. 20, 2011.

The first solar panel was installed in 2004. Because the lodge is on a north-facing slope, passive solar heat is not practical. Former owner Jim Huff, Jr., said in 2021 that he believes the lodge should be "all green," running completely on solar power.

Guests can get hot water from a spigot outside the kitchen. Jack Huff once hauled up a bathtub, so his children enjoyed warm baths whenever the kitchen had hot water left over.

The crew had hot water available on days that Brown ran his belt-driven sawmill. It was powered by a Lycoming six-cylinder engine salvaged from a 1925 Gardner[5] automobile. Brown rigged up an old water heater as the radiator. "The water was quite hot and also quite black, so no one used this 'free' hot water," Bedinger said. The crew preferred a more conventional water heater that burned wood chips from the sawmill.

The fire hoses also serve secondary purposes, as the crew uses them to flush out the privy toilets at the end of the season.

A Ring of Far

One night in April 1937, Jack Huff spotted an orange glow on the northern horizon that turned out to be a wildfire in the coal-mining town of Whitesburg, Kentucky, 104 miles away—approximately halfway from Le Conte to Cincinnati.

At that time, the *Knoxville Journal* analyzed the viewshed from Mount Le Conte, pointing out that a circle with a 104-mile radius would encompass six states, from Chattanooga to South Carolina.

"I am sure we can see into Virginia and North Carolina from LeConte," Huff said, "but whether we can see Georgia and South Carolina would depend on whether we can see over the mountains." In fact, Georgia's two highest peaks (Brasstown Bald and Rabun Bald) are visible from Myrtle Point. The Blue Ridge in South Carolina is eclipsed by higher mountains in North Carolina, but in October 1980, on a crystal-clear day—antithetical in the Smokies—Margaret Stevenson said she was able to spy the TV tower on Hogback Mountain in Greenville County, South Carolina.[6]

Kuwohi (the peak formerly known as Clingmans Dome) boasts a six-state view, as Caesars Head in South Carolina is within the line of sight from its observation tower.[7]

Huff also pushed the horizons on July 4, 1931, when he launched fireworks from Cliff Top. *The Knoxville News-Sentinel* was deluged with calls from folks asking about flashes of light over the Smokies.[8]

---

5. The lodge sawmill was dismantled in the 1970s. Russell E. Gardner (1866–1938) was a Tennessean who built cars that were popular in the Midwest in the 1920s. Lycoming is now known for airplane engines but began by powering automobiles in 1910.

6. Hogback is the most prominent peak in South Carolina, with a distinctive 459-foot TV tower on the 3,189-foot summit, which Stevenson recognized from the years she lived nearby in Tryon, North Carolina.

7. Despite the "See 7 States" slogan on barn roofs advertising Chattanooga's Rock City, only four states (Alabama, Georgia, Tennessee, and North Carolina) are visible from that promontory. The boast originated with speculation by Civil War sentries posted on Lookout Mountain.

8. "Sky Lights Prove to Be Fireworks," *Knoxville News-Sentinel*, July 5, 1931. This was before the establishment of the park, which outlawed fireworks.

For obvious reasons, fireworks are not allowed in the national park. But lodge guests on July 4 and other holidays are often treated to distant firework shows above towns in the Tennessee Valley.

The most dramatic fireworks ever seen from Le Conte would have been December 7, 1972, when winter caretakers Jim Gamble and Al Bedinger witnessed the lift-off of Apollo 17, the final Apollo mission and the only moon mission launched at night. Mount Le Conte stood high above the clouds that night, and the glowing trail of the Saturn V rocket was visible on the southern horizon. Herrick Brown said that his workers saw the first stage separation "very well."[9] Florida's Cape Canaveral is 500 miles south of Le Conte, and the stage separation was at an altitude of 40 miles.

That's why the south-facing ledge along the trail between High Top and the lodge is known as "Apollo Point."

---

9. "Two See Rocket from Le Conte," *Knoxville News-Sentinel*, Dec. 7, 1972. Cape Canaveral was then known as Cape Kennedy.

7

"Ain't no mountain high enough"

Mid-century visitors who wanted to see a bear at LeConte Lodge were wise to ask the little girl with blonde curls. Cookie Huff was known to Knoxville newspaper readers as the Queen of Le Conte. She knew the bears by name and wasn't afraid of them.

A generation later, little Barbara Brown became the unofficial bear guide, and guests would tip her a dime for hints about where to see them.

Cookie Huff Bowling and Barbara Brown Lindsay are reminders of an era when the lodge managers raised their children atop the mountain: Jack and Pauline Huff with Cookie and her brother Philip; Herrick and Myrtle Brown with Carolyn, Glenn, and Barbara; Tim and Lisa Line with Nathan, Grace and Jacob; and Jim and Billie Huff with Jay, Julie, and Neil. From 1940 into the 1990s, the playful chatter of children was part of the lodge ambiance.

Those children are the fruit of romances that sound like scripts for TV movies. Pauline Whaling came to the Smokies as a missionary teacher from Chicago and eloped to Le Conte with the innkeeper, Jack Huff. Myrtle Graybeal was a coed at the University of Tennessee when she caught the eye of Herrick Brown on a hike to see the flame azaleas on Gregory Bald, 40 miles southwest of Le Conte. Tim Line and John Northrup, the managers of the lodge for the last half-century, met their brides as fellow workers on the lodge crew.

Cue the soundtrack by Diana Ross: "Ain't no mountain high enough—nothing can keep me, keep me from you!"

Pauline and Jack Huff: The Dream Team

Jack Huff's bride might never have entered his world if not for an ominous dream that compelled his parents to work with Northerners to open a school in Gatlinburg.

In 1910, the Pi Beta Phi sorority took on a service project to run a school in an underserved community in Appalachia. They zeroed in on Gatlinburg, a working-class settlement a long way from the bustling prosperity that tourism would eventually bring. But folks in Gatlinburg were reluctant to contribute land or funds for the school.

Andy Huff was a sawmill operator who was becoming a successful hotelier, and his wife Martha was an advocate for public education. After a nightmare where she saw the town's children being swallowed up by a dreadful fog, Martha told Andy that he had to rescue the children, whatever the cost. Andy and a business partner were able to work out an 11th-hour deal to secure land for the school, which was just the second formal school in Sevier County when it opened in 1912. Andy Huff led the fundraising effort by pledging $250.

The Pi Beta Phi Settlement School shaped the Huff's five children: Jack (1903–1985), James (1906–1984), Stella Sue Cox (1908–1990), Mattie Lawson (1910–1983), and Blanche "Boots" Arthur (1913–1997). The boys married teachers; two of the girls became Pi Phis in college; and Stella returned as a teacher. The Pi Beta Phi school emphasized crafts and industriousness, and Jack learned to weave on a loom the school installed in 1915.

Pauline Whaling (1905–1999) was a graduate of Monmouth College and Northwestern University who boarded a bus from Illinois in 1932 to become a teacher in Gatlinburg. Jack Huff courted her and took her on frequent hikes to Mount Le Conte, where he had run LeConte Lodge since 1926. "The 20th time, they took the preacher along," according to a 1980 story in the *Atlanta Journal-Constitution*. By her account in an interview on WBIR-TV's *Heartland* series, they eloped.

The night before their wedding, Jack and Pauline hit the trail at 10 p.m. and hiked overnight to reach Myrtle Point by sunrise.[1] None of their parents attended, and the two witnesses (Ralph Lawson and Jack's sister Mattie) were later married. Whoever wrote the subhead in the *Knoxville Journal*[2]—"Bride and Groom Take Short Hike Before Ceremony"—was oblivious to the strenuous climb up Bear Pen Hollow.

Jack had just finished building what is now called "the Old Cabin," so the newlyweds wouldn't have to hike down for their honeymoon.

Jack and Pauline had two children: Philip (1935–1986) and Cookie (born 1944). Cookie Bowling's family now runs Jack Huff's Motor Lodge, which is across the street from the Pi Beta Phi School, which marked its centennial in 2012.

Pauline loved living at the lodge. In a 1939 story in the *Knoxville Journal* that described her as a Chicago girl, she said, "I wouldn't trade the top of this mountain for the rest of the world." In a 1975 retrospective with Dot Jackson of the *Charlotte Observer*, she said, "I was there 26 years, and oh, it was heaven on earth."[3]

Pauline took pride in a spotless kitchen, in spite of frequent visits by bears. "When the health inspector came up to inspect the lodge, we got an A every time," Cookie said. "The last time they came, they gave Mama a 100."

In a 1983 newspaper interview, Pauline said the mountain was a healthy place for her children. "They never had an infectious disease of any kind. They were well all the time."[4]

---

1. "Jack Huff Picks Mountain for Wedding," *Knoxville News-Sentinel*, April 29, 1934.
2. "WED ON PEAK," *Knoxville Journal*, April 30, 1934.
3. Dot Jackson, "In a Hikers' Paradise, a Tempest Is Brewing," *Charlotte Observer*, Oct. 19, 1975.
4. Carson Brewer, "Baby, It's Cold Outside, but Mountaintop Is Great," *Knoxville News-Sentinel*, Dec. 4, 1983.

WED ON PEAK

Bride and Groom Take Short Hike Before Ceremony.

Jack Huff, picturesque mountain guide, married Miss Pauline Whaling, of Chicago, Sunday morning on Myrtle Point, most noted of the three mountain peaks, in the Great Smoky mountains.

The ceremony was performed by the Rev. William Weaver, pastor of the Gatlinburg Baptist church, after Mr. Huff had escorted the bride on a hike that led through the mountains.

Those who witnessed the wedding were Miss Mattie Huff, sister of the groom and Ralph Lawson, a friend of both the bride and groom.

The bride is the daughter of Mrs. Clara Whaling of Chicago. She has been a teacher in the Pi Beta Phi School at Gatlinburg for two years.

Sunday's ceremony marked the second marriage in the Huff family within a week. Miss Blanche Huff, sister of Jack Huff was married April 22.

Jack and Pauline Huff eloped in 1934 and were married at sunrise at Myrtle Point. The photographer struggled to capture the picturesque scene. Speaking of "picturesque," it's not often that a wedding announcement uses that word to describe the groom. Probably this meant he was a guide to picturesque mountains. The headline writer also underestimated the "short hike." Jack and Pauline hit the trail at 10 p.m. and hiked overnight to reach Myrtle Point by dawn (Huff family photo, courtesy Cookie Bowling).

Cookie Bowling says bears were a reality of her childhood. "I wasn't afraid of them," she said. "I'd run them up the tree." She recalled one bear named Rosie who became so tame that Philip was able to mow grass around her feet.

Philip was a hard worker who kept the lodge grounds neatly mowed with an old-fashioned rotary push-mower and a scythe. "After that," his sister said, "they let it go back to nature. But it looked really good then." Philip also discovered the oldest relic on the mountain, the Walker Stone (see Chapter 11). Philip worked on the lodge crew until he began his 10th-grade year at a military boarding school.

Dorothy Ellen was three months old in 1944 when Pauline carried her to the lodge. Her brother nicknamed her "Cookie" because of her sweet tooth, and *Knoxville News-Sentinel* columnist Bert Vincent christened her in 1952 as the "Queen of Le Conte":

> She has her mother's hair, light and silky. She has mountain eyes of the Huffs. They are round—blacker than the blackberries that grow up there. They dart this way and that, so fast you can hardly catch them. She is shier than a young squirrel, and about as lively. That mountaintop 6,000 feet up from any other children is her home from the time school is out down in Gatlinburg until school starts in the fall.
>
> Up here she has the rocks to play with, and the flowers and birds. She has the stars and the moon to look at nights and blue skies in daytime, and thunderheads and bears and other

Pauline Huff (center) with Philip and Cookie (Huff family photo, courtesy Cookie Bowling).

animals, including tourists, whom Dorothy Ellen looks at and grins at but seldom speaks to. But she spoke to me. She even asked me to come back some time. That's why she's my queen.[5]

Cookie spent her first 15 summers at the lodge. Some years she came down early for school (staying with her extended family) and otherwise she had the advantage that her mom was a teacher.

Though life on the mountain could be lonely, Cookie said she never complained about it. The hardest part was the transition to town life each winter. "Going to church, I was very timid," she said. In hindsight, she says the lodge was a good place to grow up.

Cookie met Bruce Bowling in college, and they were married at the First Methodist Church of Gatlinburg, where her mother was one of the early members. Their last hike up was a family reunion in 2014. "Our last hike took us seven hours," Cookie

---

5. "Strolling with Bert Vincent," June 10, 1951, *Knoxville News-Sentinel*.

said. "That's okay—if you go fast, you don't see the little birds' nests and eggs." Bruce added: "Just be there before they ring the supper bell."

When the Huffs decided to sell the lodge in 1959, they offered the operation to Philip, 23, who was almost the same age his father had been when he started building the lodge in 1926. Instead, Philip decided to go into business in Gatlinburg. He died at age 50 in an auto accident, six months after his father's death.

Jack's brother Jim also married a Pi Beta Phi teacher—Henrietta McCutchan, who came to Gatlinburg from Missouri. She made dozens of hikes up Mount Le Conte, including one on her 88th birthday in 1994.

The third of their children, Jim Huff, Jr., brought the lodge back into family ownership in 1976 when he purchased the concession contract from Herrick Brown. Jim and Billie Huff raised their three children at the lodge, and Neil Huff remembers the mountaintop as a special place to grow up.

Herrick and Myrtle Brown: Off the Road

When Herrick Brown was a boy, his family operated a small hotel with cottages atop Greystone Mountain near Greeneville, Tennessee. "Those were the days when folks simply went and sat out their vacations," he wrote.

Brown was nostalgic for that kind of lifestyle, so he was intrigued in 1959 when he heard that the Huffs were ready to sell LeConte Lodge. As a traveling salesman for an industrial supplier, Brown longed for a job "off the road," so to speak, and the lodge certainly fit that definition—as a place where his clients would come to him.

"I wondered if he knew what he was getting into," his widow Myrtle Brown said in a 2022 interview. "It was hard to convince me, but it was a move we needed to make. He was happy with it, and I think I was more helpful than he thought I would be. It worked out."

The Browns already had two children, Carolyn and Glenn, and the Huffs had demonstrated that raising a family on the mountaintop was reasonable. "What are we going to do with our little daughter in school?" Myrtle wondered. "She had been in the first grade in Knoxville. Herrick said, you don't have to be up there when school is in. For years, I went up the day school was out, and then came down on Labor Day."

Practical challenges aside, the idea of living on the mountaintop was appealing. The Browns shared a love for the mountains and had met on a wildflower hike to Gregory Bald.

They both brought useful life skills to the lodge. Myrtle's grandmother in Laurel Springs, North Carolina, lived in a house without electricity and running water, so she had known since childhood how to "lay a fire" and clean kerosene lamps.

Herrick was a hard worker who understood mechanical systems and equipment. Though he knew little about building a log cabin, he and his crews worked for three years to build the office, which opened in 1971. He also built the laundry on the crew side of the campus.

The Browns' third child, Barbara, was born in 1963, and at age of three she

Myrtle and Herrick Brown took over the lodge in 1960 (Brown family photo collection).

became one of the youngest children to climb the Alum Cave Trail. "I didn't think I could carry her, so I let her come up at her own speed," Myrtle said. When guests brought up children, Barbara and her siblings would play with them, and she also helped the crew with their chores, including stripping beds and cleaning lamps. As Barbara grew up, she had the privilege of greeting guests who arrived on horseback and taking their horses to the stable, which was along the Trillium Gap Trail.

Cliff Top became the children's gym set, and guests sometimes got nervous at the sight of the Brown children playing on the precarious ledges and climbing a tall tree they called "Flat Top." But neither gravity nor bears ever hurt them.

Myrtle said that during the years they ran the lodge, it felt like a second home to her. The Browns, like the Huffs, kept a home off the mountain, and they usually spent their off-seasons traveling. Herrick enjoyed riding iconic trains, including the renowned Blue Train in South Africa and steam excursions with the Southern Railroad. The Browns also visited the Canary Islands and the Alhambra fortress in Spain (where Christopher Columbus was commissioned for his New World explorations). However, lodge responsibilities caused Herrick to miss many of the October hikes he dearly enjoyed, and by the 1970s, he was ready to retire rather than fight the Wilderness Act.

All the Brown children frequently return to climb Le Conte. Glenn Brown became an attorney and retired from the Federal Aviation Administration in Alaska. As a boy, he liked to play on the roof of the woodshed. Later, he learned to use an adz to hew the logs for the office—an assignment that ended when the tool slipped and he cut his ankle. He rode down on a mule to see the doctor.

Carolyn is an accountant in Arizona. As a teenager, she missed her friends in Gatlinburg and made good use of the telephone. Especially in later years, she has come to appreciate her unique childhood on Le Conte. Barbara is a physical therapist living in North Carolina.

Tim and Lisa Line: A Bear-Crashed Wedding

Dr. Felix Line often took his son Tim on hikes to Le Conte, so he was not surprised when Tim wanted to join the lodge crew after through-hiking the Appalachian Trail in 1976.

If Tim's parents had any misgivings, it was whether this was a good career track for someone with a marketing degree from the University of Tennessee. "They put me through five years of college, and then I go to work at LeConte making $14 a day with room and board," Tim said. "The saving grace was I met Lisa the following year, and we ended up staying. It all worked out in the end, but everybody was a little worried for a while."

When it came time to plan a family, Dr. Line, a pediatrician, had no qualms about his grandchildren being raised on a mountaintop. "We asked him if there was any reason we shouldn't do this," Lisa said. "He was used to hiking, and he loved

Above: Eye patches became formal attire at Tim and Lisa Line's wedding, after he was injured chasing a bear. *Opposite:* Lisa showed her artistry—and her sense of humor—by portraying the bears and the lodge on their wedding cake (courtesy Tim Line).

the mountains, too. I think he thought Tim had the greatest job in the world. He was for it. He came up the mountain and gave our kids their checkups and vaccinations."

Tim and Lisa became the site managers for the lodge, and their two older children, Nathan and Grace, grew up at the lodge. After they hired Chris and Allyson Virden as site managers in 2003, the Lines raised their youngest boy Jacob off the mountain, but he grew up to work at the lodge.

Their daughter is named for Gracie McNicol, who made the last of her 244 ascents in 1983, during the Lines' tenure.

The Lines were married in 1979 in Cincinnati, choosing a location near Lisa's home for the sake of the family. Tim will never forget the week before the wedding, because it involved a bear, a plastic surgeon, and a hospital honeymoon.

Shortly before leaving the mountain for the wedding, the Lines and their crew were cleaning the kitchen after supper when somebody shouted that a bear was breaking into Cabin 9, which is adjacent to the forest at the eastern end of the cabin terrace. Tim grabbed a fire extinguisher to scare the bear away. "Just as I got there, the bear left the cabin and went up the trail toward the water tank. I followed him. He turned off the trail into the woods, and I went after him. There was a stump, and I tripped and fell, and my eye hit it. I saw stars."

"I staggered back to camp. When I walked in, my face was all bloody. They thought I had been mauled by the bear. Then my eye started swelling. The next day, my whole face was swollen. I went off the mountain and then realized I was seeing double. My dad knew an eye doctor, and I went to see him and he referred me to a plastic surgeon. There's a little bone that holds up your eye, and I had blown it out."

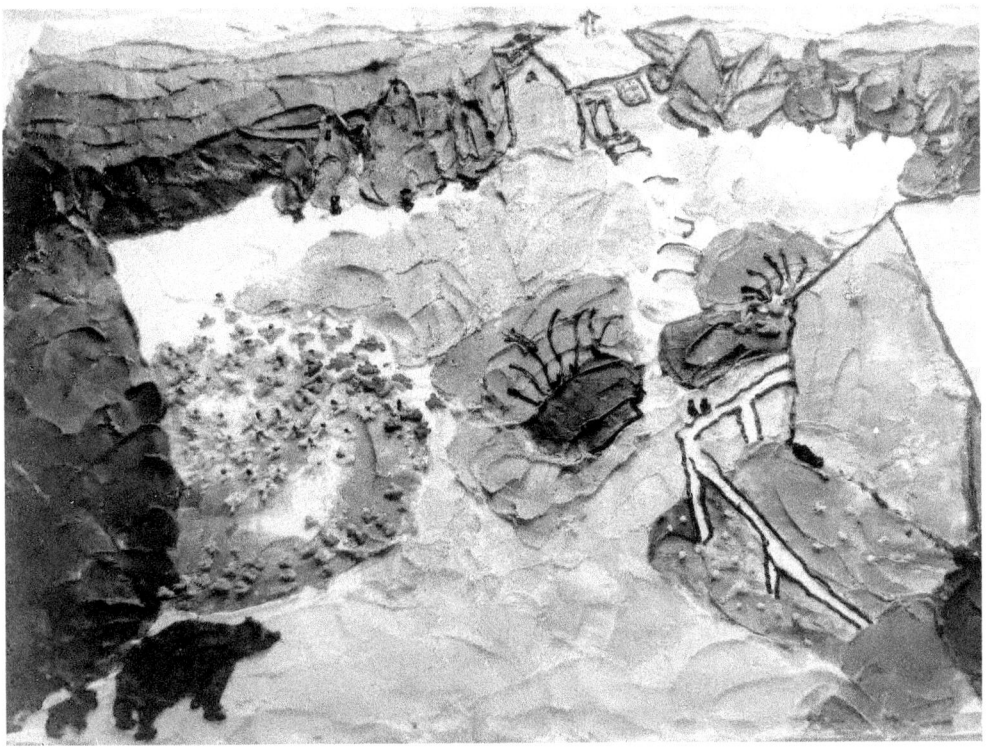

"He said right after the wedding, come back and you're going to have eye surgery. So we went to Cincinnati to get married as scheduled. I got married wearing an eye patch. All the other men in the wedding wore eye patches, too. After the wedding, we came home to Knoxville, I had surgery and I spent my honeymoon at Baptist Hospital."

Lisa had fallen in love with a man and a mountain. "I was a really romantic teenager when I fell in love with Mount Le Conte," she said. "I soon learned that there was both beauty and wilderness, but you better bring your rain jacket."

The Lines bought an old farmhouse (complete with a chicken coop) on their second anniversary in 1981, but LeConte was home. "The lodge was our little homeplace," she said. "I wasn't motivated to stay in Wears Valley where I would be practically alone. So, am I going back to the lodge with him? Of course I am."

Nathan and Grace were born during the winter, and within a few weeks they were on their way to the top of the mountain in their parents' arms—venturing into a childhood that few kids could dream about.

Tim became the lodge handyman. "I had worked as a plumber's helper in college, so I knew a little about plumbing. There was no electricity up there, so I didn't have to worry about that. A lot of stuff you just learn on the job because there's no other way to do it. There was a lot of trial and error and a lot of worry and torture over not being able to get something fixed."

Tim retired as lodge manager in 2018. "I loved it and I don't regret a minute of it," he said. "But after 41 years—I guess I was about ready to retire. There are certain things I miss about it, but it's been great being retired. We can do anything we want to do, which is nice."

John and Bonnie Northrup: Snowbound

John Northrup climbed Mount Le Conte before he was born—his mom was five months pregnant—and made the trip on his own feet at age eight, so it's no surprise he fell in love *with* the Smokies. Then in 2010, he took a job at the lodge and fell in love *in* the Smokies.

Fresh out of the University of Michigan—where he majored in history and marched with the band in the 2007 Rose Bowl parade[6]—John was shoveling snow on the Alum Cave Trail when he met his bride-to-be, Bonnie Scott from Atlanta, who was hiking up to interview for the last vacancy on the crew.

The winter of 2009–10 was one of the snowiest seasons the lodge has ever seen, with accumulations up to 55 inches. As the crew prepared for opening day, they had to shovel paths day after day. "The first week, we knew we had families coming up, and the cables on Alum were still buried in snow. They asked the crew to go down there with a shovel or pick-ax. I grabbed a shovel and headed down to a corner where the snow had drifted nine feet high."

---

6. The Rose Bowl Parade is a six-mile march, and John was carrying a 30-pound bass drum, which trained him well for hauling supplies up to the lodge. The day after the Rose Bowl, the band rushed back to Michigan for the funeral of the 38th president, Gerald Ford.

"The first few hikers were starting to make their way up, and one was this girl. She wasn't dressed for the conditions—wearing cotton blue jeans. But she had a smile on her face." John recalls it as his "struck-by-lightning moment."

Not only did Bonnie and John turn out to be soulmates, but they were also well matched as hikers. Friends said that Bonnie was the only one fast enough to keep up

Lodge managers John and Bonnie Northrup visited the "other" LeConte Lodge on a 2023 trip to California's Yosemite National Park (courtesy John Northrup).

with John on the trail. She became one of the first women to complete the Tour de Le Conte, hiking all six trails in 24 hours. Bonnie has also served as llama wrangler.

On a 2011 hike to see the flame azaleas on Gregory Bald (the same place where Herrick and Myrtle Brown met), John gave Bonnie a ring. They were married in Pigeon Forge in June 2012 during their third season on the crew.

They intended to move on to other careers, until the Lines asked John and Bonnie if they might be interested in management opportunities. After Chris and Allyson Virden ended a 12-year tenure as site managers, and the Northrups transitioned into that role. The 2023 season marked John's 14th with the lodge. "I worked my way up," he said.

"The magic of Mount Le Conte"

The Virdens were site managers from 2003 through 2014, allowing the Lines to spend more time off the mountain managing the lodge's business. The Virdens met while through-hiking the Appalachian Trail. "The magic of Mount Le Conte never ceases to amaze me when it comes to bringing people together," Allyson wrote on the lodge blog in 2014.

Alan Householder and Chrissy Mann met as llama wranglers and were yoked in a mountaintop wedding in 2014 on Grassy Ridge in the Roan Mountains. Grassy Ridge is the highest bald along the Appalachian Trail, which Alan hiked in 1988.

Chrissy and Alan Householder, 2014 wedding at Grassy Ridge Bald (courtesy High on LeConte, blog of LeConte Lodge).

"A llama would have made a nice ring-bearer," the lodge blog said, "but it was not to be." The Householders served a total of 29 seasons with the lodge and totaled about 1,500 ascents before retiring in 2021, so Chrissy could pursue her calling as a travel nurse.

There is no logbook for weddings on Le Conte, but there have been several who followed the Huffs' example. In 1979, Clyde "Rusty" Nail and Deborah Ground were married at Cliff Top. They met while working on the lodge crew, where he was the site manager before Line.

In 2010, Pam Parkinson and Chuck Haggard were married at Cliff Top by a chaplain from Dollywood. According to Sam Venable of the *Knoxville News-Sentinel*: "The trip Chuck Haggard and Pam Parkinson made down the aisle was a bit longer and steeper than most. Right at 5.2 miles, one way. Straight up."

Myrtle Point weddings have included Kelly and Bill Pyle in 2012 and Lisa and Tim Parkinson in 2019. The Pyles were married at dawn, and as the clouds parted, birds broke into song, as if on cue. "There's no more perfect place on the planet to get married," Kelly said. Lisa hiked to her wedding with her dress in her backpack, and the lodge staff made a cake that was shared by all the overnight guests.

Others who met on the lodge crew were Jeremiah and Allison Donovan; Brad and Nicollette Graham; Josh and Kat Holsworth; and Beau and Courtney Belmont.

How about celebrating your golden anniversary at LeConte Lodge? Mae and Roger Snyder made their 208th ascent together on August 15, 2019, to mark their 50th anniversary.

Getting married on the mountaintop can be complicated, but Le Conte can be a romantic place to propose. In fact, two of Jack Huff's grandchildren proposed on the mountaintop.

8

From Moonshine to Moonshots

As LeConte Lodge guests look forward to pancakes hot off the griddle, few know that the syrup has its own off-the-grid backstory.

Herrick Brown, the lodge operator from 1960 through 1975, pioneered brewing syrup on the mountaintop. The story was shared on the lodge blog in 2014 with comments from Al Bedinger, who worked for the Browns and became the lodge historian: "You have to be a practical kind of impractical person to run the lodge. If you were a strictly practical person, you'd never live at the top of a mountain without electricity or a road. However, you have to find a way to make things work on Le Conte—a practical impractical person. Like all good LeConte managers, Herrick was always looking for better ways to do things at the top of Tennessee."

Pack horses hauled syrup along with other supplies to the lodge, until one day a crew member offered a suggestion: "Most of the weight in syrup is from water. Herrick, we've got the best water in the state from the Le Conte spring. Why don't you just order up some sugar and we'll make our own syrup from Le Conte spring water?"

Brown ordered several hundred pounds of sugar. Federal agents tend to be suspicious of mountaineers who buy sugar in bulk, so they tracked this shipment up to the mountaintop, where they determined that pancake syrup—not untaxed moonshine—was the strongest thing being distilled atop the Smokies.

To get the taste right, Brown's recipe called for imitation rum extract. This once caused confusion, when the crew included a Vietnam vet and his wife, who was from Thailand. Her English was limited, so when she went to the store, the extract she brought back was not alcohol-free. That was one batch of syrup that they didn't want the "revenooers" to sniff.

A federal agent once visited Paul Adams and asked him to be on the lookout for the smoke of moonshine stills when he made his daily fire patrols overlooking the valleys. Adams declined, telling the officer: "I hope to live a long time in the mountains, and I don't want to go out of my way to make enemies."

Legal alcohol finally came to the mountaintop in 1985, when the state of Tennessee permitted the lodge to serve wine. Sevier is a "dry county" (with municipal exceptions in Gatlinburg and Pigeon Forge), so state approval was required. As legislators debated the issue, they wondered if the bears had been polled. "You certainly don't have to worry about drunk drivers," said Rep. John Chiles.[1]

A "bottomless" glass of wine ($14 in 2023) can be ordered with supper, with last call at 7 p.m. Tip your glass to the memory of Prohibition, which was the law of the land when the lodge was founded.

"Hunger was good sauce for these meals"

Family-style supper and breakfast became a staple of the LeConte experience after Jack Huff opened the dining hall in 1939. In the early years, guests cooked their own meals over a campfire and dined *al fresco* around rough picnic tables.

The breakfast and supper menus are Huff legacies. Most guests find the meals plentiful and hearty. Site manager Chris Virden estimated he flipped 22,000 pancakes over the course of a season and each morning started by baking 53 biscuits.[2]

In 1926, John Willy of the trade magazine the *Hotel Monthly* wrote a review of the lodge. Huff gave him the VIP treatment. About the meals, Willy wrote:

> The cooking is mainly done in an open-air stone-constructed stove with sheets of iron laid on top for the pots, kettles, and skillets. There is food for sale, and the patrons are expected to do their own cooking; but mostly people bring their food and take advantage of the cooking facilities. The dining table also is outdoors, under the balsams; bare wood boards, with complete absence of style.
>
> The food sold, Jack Huff said, is charged just double what it costs in the village, because all of it has to be brought up man-back, and it is no easy thing to bring food a mile above the village man-back. For our evening dinner (or supper), the guide Will Ramsey, who acted as cook and waiter, provided tomato soup with whole wheat bread, bacon, fried eggs, canned peaches, coffee. For breakfast we had oatmeal with condensed milk, bacon, scrambled eggs, coffee. Hunger was good sauce for these meals.[3]

Newspaper columnist Ernie Pyle caused a stir after it was reported that Huff served him salmon croquettes[4] instead of the cold Spam that was the customary supper meat. One guest complained to park officials: "Cannot something be done about the dinners served at LeConte Lodge? We recognize the difficulties involved in packing food up the mountain, but it is very depressing to find a meal built around Spam when publicity such as Ernie Pyle's columns a few years ago has indicated something considerably better. Hot meat and fresh biscuit would go far toward making an otherwise dull menu palatable."

Huff said it was the first complaint about food he had received in nearly 20 years of operation. "Since Ernie Pyle was here on Oct. 11, 1940, we have served 10,299 meals, all of which were the exact meals that were served to Mr. Pyle. Except we served him salmon croquettes instead of Spam."

---

1. John G. Chiles of Nashville served in the state house 1976–1992. His family once had a home in Elkmont.
2. Morgan Simmons, "Life at LeConte Lodge," *Knoxville News-Sentinel*, May 4, 2008.
3. John Willy, "Editor Writes Glowing Story of Park Region," *Hotel Monthly* (reprinted in *Knoxville Journal*, Oct. 17, 1926).
4. There's actually no mention of Spam or salmon in a collection of Pyle columns published in 1951, *Gatlinburg and the Great Smokies*, published by Mountain Press of Gatlinburg, compiled by C.C. Callaway.

The original kitchen was a campfire, and the cabintry was hung between a couple of cabinet-trees (photo by Jim Thompson, courtesy Thompson Photo Products).

Huff reasoned that weary hikers digest Spam better than salmon. "Seventy percent of our guests when they reach our camp are exhausted, nervous, and their stomachs are weak," he wrote. "If we serve the Spam fried I am afraid we would get what we had with the croquettes—sick people each evening."

Family-style meals became a LeConte tradition after Jack Huff opened the dining room in 1939. This replaced a temporary mess hall and kitchen that was built around 1932. The dining room was expanded in the 1980s by moving the north wall (Huff family photo, courtesy Cookie Bowling).

Eventually, Spam was replaced by canned beef and gravy. Stewed apples, green beans, and a chocolate chip cookie have been added to the dinner meal, plus grits and biscuits for breakfast.

Eggs, of course, require fresh deliveries. When newspaperman Leo Hershfield visited the lodge in 1929, he marveled: "Young Huff brought all his supplies up on his back, and thought nothing of carrying a crate of eggs up the steep slope with nary an egg so much as nicked." Now, fresh eggs are brought up by the soft-stepping llamas.

In 1941, the lodge began selling sandwich lunches to day hikers. The crew used butter as a spread, because they had no way to refrigerate mayonnaise.

The crew looked forward to the days that Pauline Huff baked huckleberry pies. Many of the blackberries that grew around the lodge were too seedy for pies. The best huckleberries were found on Rocky Spur, along the Rainbow Falls Trail. "We'd be lucky if we got enough huckleberries for two pies," Pauline's daughter Cookie Bowling said.

Myrtle Brown was beloved for her blackberry cobbler.

Guests sometimes requested cakes for special occasions, so Mrs. Brown had to figure out the secrets of baking at a high altitude. Most commercial cake recipes include instructions for 3,500 to 6,500 feet, and the lodge is at the upper limit of that range. "When you would bake a cake, it would rise up, and then it would settle back down and run over the pan," she said.

A guest from Laramie, Wyoming (600 feet higher than the lodge), gave her a card with high-altitude tips on how to make a cake rise. In general, you have to add flour and an egg, decrease sugar, and cook for a shorter time at a higher temperature.

The first time she got it right, she said, "was the most thrilling thing I did working at LeConte."

She also found that the altitude made a difference in boiling potatoes, which took 50 minutes at the lodge, compared to 20 minutes at Gatlinburg.

In 1976, when the use of pack horses was restricted under the Wilderness Act, the kitchen began using powdered soup and potatoes as well as dried beans—staples that could be delivered by the ton aboard the preseason airlift.

Guests haven't always been enthralled by the quaint lodge experience. Back in 1962, some disappointed Floridians wrote Herrick Brown asking for a refund:

> Although we consider climbing LeConte one of the more fun spots of our vacation, we find that your cabin rates are quite exorbitant and we feel we should be forwarded a refund. It should be interesting for you to know that we have stayed in some lovely places and the best never charged us more than $14 for one night's lodging for our party.
>
> As your accommodations are crude (there were no facilities, a shower, or even running water, the toilets were 100 feet away from the log cabins) and, although we know your supplies are brought up on horseback, we feel that you are taking outrageous advantage of your position in the midst of a great national park and its "captive audience."
>
> We do not care to comment on the quality of your meals, excepting to say the quantity was adequate and the price in line.
>
> However, we were not prepared to be relieved of $24.50 plus tax for just one night's lodging. We request, therefore, that you refund a minimum of $12.50 to us.

Brown responded with a letter copied to the park superintendent and noted that one of the guests had visited the lodge two months earlier, so the rates and conditions should not have been a surprise. He said his crew went out of their way to accommodate these guests. "They are vegetarians and we did our best to feed them as they requested. However, they carried their arguments to the extreme, saying that it wasn't right to take milk from a cow."

Nowadays, guests can sign up in advance for vegetarian meals.

Brown sometimes grumbled about the challenges of complying with Occupational Safety and Health Administration regulations that were well intentioned but not written for backcountry accommodations. "When I retire," he vowed, "I'm going to write a book called *Far, Far from OSHA*."

Living the High Life

When former employees of LeConte Lodge reminisce about their adventures, they sometimes joke, "Somebody ought to write a book."

Well, somebody did—an introspective Californian musician named David Witherspoon,[5] who spent two seasons on the crew, plus two winters as the lodge caretaker. He turned his journals into a behind-the-scenes book, *Song of the Winter Wren*, which could have been subtitled *Black Bears in Bohemia*.

Witherspoon's tenure in the 1970s coincided with the 50th anniversary of the

---

5. David Witherspoon (1949–2010) graduated from UCLA, became a renowned flutist, and authored seven books.

lodge, the wilderness debate, and the ownership transition from Herrick Brown to Jim Huff, Jr. Middle-school librarians might object to some of the carnal content, as the national park bureaucracy did.

In 1976, the national park service cracked down on the "hippie look" and required men on the lodge crew to keep their hair cut above the collar. The *Knoxville News-Sentinel* ran the story on April Fools' Day, but in context, it appears to be genuine.[6]

The "hippies" played their own joke a few years later, when they started posting March 32 over the dining-room door on April 1. Manager Chris Virden said he met only one guest in five years who got the joke.[7]

Witherspoon described serving on the crew as "the hardest work I've ever done, to keep this place alive, sustaining tourists in a wilderness." He quoted Dick Ketelle on the challenge of managing the crew: "I learned a long time ago that you can't give orders up here. The crew can make it awfully hard on someone who does."[8]

Guests usually look forward to the isolation at the lodge, but from the perspective of the crew, the primitive lifestyle can get old. Employees live communally in cabins on the terrace below the dining room and work 22 days per month. In the 1960s, crew members got one hot shower a week, and on laundry day, they used a wringer washer and clotheslines.

Arriving hikers with April 1 reservations might have been dismayed by this April Fool prank (courtesy High on LeConte, blog of LeConte Lodge).

6. Carson Brewer, "Life on Le Conte," *Knoxville News-Sentinel*, April 1, 1976.
7. Morgan Simmons, "Life at LeConte Lodge," *Knoxville News-Sentinel*, May 4, 2008.
8. Witherspoon, *Song of the Winter Wren*, p. 42 and 62.

Obviously, a job at the lodge is unlike any other. But it's not a junket. Employment postings for 2023 declared: "THIS. IS. A. JOB. If you are passionate about the outdoors, working with a team to serve others, and living off-grid, then this is the opportunity for you!" For the 2023 season, crew members were hired at $15 per hour plus tips.

In 1975, by comparison, the going wage was $15 per day. The crew rebelled at the proposal by Jim Huff, Jr., of $12 per workday day with a $2 daily bonus for those who completed the season.

Generally, the crew is high-spirited. On July 4, crew and guests enjoy barbeque and watch fireworks down in the valley. Every fourth year, the crew stages the mock Le Conte Olympics, with events such as trail kayaking and hurdling the llama troughs. On Halloween, they have a pumpkin carving contest. And they celebrate the end of the season with a Thanksgiving feast.

Everyday activities, such as voting, can be complicated for those living at the lodge. For one primary election, the Browns made a 13-mile round-trip hike to Gatlinburg to cast their votes. Nowadays, the crew can take advantage of absentee ballots.

And what happens when a dad wants to send birthday flowers to his daughter who is working at the lodge? In 1987, when Michael Bridges called FTD in Cincinnati and ordered a bouquet of carnations to his daughter Melinda, Florist Steve Sanders contacted a friend, Paul Campbell, who regularly hiked to the lodge to visit his girlfriend on the crew. "We attached the flowers to his backpack and he

On his 911th ascent, Dave Scanlon lit a kerosene lamp at the ceremonial opening of the 2012 LeConte Olympics (courtesy High on LeConte, blog of LeConte Lodge).

This "Jack-o-Lantern," carved by Nathan Kirkham to celebrate Jack Huff's famous feat, won the crew's 2014 pumpkin-carving contest (courtesy High on LeConte, blog of LeConte Lodge).

took off," Sanders said.[9] Hopefully, the florist also sent an extra bouquet for Campbell's sweetheart.

Good Night, Johnboy

At the end of a work day in the 1970s, it was common for the crew to gather to watch television. On Thursday nights, they enjoyed *The Waltons*. Corny as it may sound, Walton's Mountain was must-see TV at 6,593.

"We had a little black and white TV," said Tim Line, who was then a member of the crew. "It ran on a 12-volt car battery and had about a 12-inch screen. Guests might every now and then see the reflection of the TV through the windows and ask about it. Or if a football game was on."

For the crew, part of the attraction was popcorn. "We ran out of popcorn one Thursday and didn't realize it until late afternoon," Line said. Starting at 5 p.m., he made a swift door-dash down the Alum Cave Trail, drove his yellow Volkswagen to the Mountain Market in Gatlinburg, bought popcorn and a six-pack of Budweiser, and made it back to the lodge 10 minutes before eight.[10]

---

9. "Mountaintop Delivery Spells Extra Legwork," *Memphis Commercial Appeal*, June 8, 1987.
10. Line held the unofficial record for running down the Alum Cave Bluff Trail in 33 minutes, until John Northrup did it in 26 minutes in 2012.

In the 1930s era—when the Waltons series was set—Jack Huff used a battery-powered Atwater Kent radio to stay in touch with the world. Thanks to the elevation of the lodge, he was able to tune in clear-channel AM stations hundreds of miles away. If the weather was favorable, he even picked up stations from New York, New Orleans, Denver, and Havana. In 1927, Huff tuned in the heavyweight boxing match from Chicago when Gene Tunney defeated Jack Dempsey after a controversial "long count."

After writer Ernie Pyle visited the lodge in 1940, he commented on how well informed Huff was, from listening to the radio and reading the daily newspapers brought up by hikers. Huff recycled the newspapers by using them as wallpaper to prevent drafts in his early log cabins.

College football on the radio added color to fall Saturdays. In 1928, the *Knoxville News-Sentinel* carried a front-page story headlined "High Sport":

> Six of Tennessee's most loyal fans received returns from the UT-Alabama football game on top of Mount LeConte Saturday afternoon.
> They had just arrived at the summit of the highest peak in the Smokies when Jack Huff, who has a cabin on the peak, began to pick up the game.
> The six were so winded from their climb that they could give nothing more than a feeble whoop when they heard that (Gene) McEver had returned the first kickoff 97 yards for a touchdown for Tennessee.
> In the party were Kyle Jenkins, Robert McClellan, Miss Mildred Ayres, Mr. and Mrs. Allen Robinson, and Sam Keener. "Jack Huff has an Atwater Kent in his shack on top of the mountain," Mr. Jenkins said today, and the reception is splendid.

Huff's radio provided an ironic perspective in 1930 when Horace Albright, director of the National Park Service, visited the lodge. Knoxville reporter John T. Moutoux wrote: "At the top, we went into Jack Huff's newest cabin. He and Dick Holt of Knoxville were sitting on a bench in front of a log fire in the grate. A radio was on, and the first thing we heard was an announcer saying that the program was being broadcast from the Manhattan Hotel, New York. The contrast was striking."[11]

The Highest Telephone in Tennessee

When you call LeConte Lodge for reservations, the phone rings in an office on Apple Valley Road in Sevierville. But that wasn't always the case. Back when phones required wires, Huff and Brown strung miles of lines to the lodge, where their wives and daughters took calls for room reservations.

Huff's original phone line ran down Bear Pen Hollow, the steep two-mile shortcut that he and Pauline climbed in 1934 for their wedding. Later he ran two lines down Mill Creek[12] (the general route of the original Rainbow Falls Trail). One was a hand-cranked line that gave him a direct connection to his supply barn in Cherokee

---

11. John T. Moutoux, "Albright Gets Thrill from LeConte Trip," *Knoxville News-Sentinel*, May 22, 1990. Moutoux (1901–1978) was a cub reporter who created a media spectacle in 1925, when he broke the story of the Scopes Monkey Trial in Dayton, Tennessee.
12. The park changed the name to Le Conte Creek to avoid confusion with multiple Mill Creeks in the Smokies.

Orchard. The other connected to the South Central Bell network at Twin Creeks on the outskirts of Gatlinburg.

In 1935, Jack Huff ran miles of telephone lines to connect the mountaintop with the Southern Bell network. Calls for reservations were answered at the lodge, and guests could use the phone to reassure their families that they had arrived safely (photograph by Tom Layton).

The lodge dining room still displays the old hand-cranked phone, and off-trail hikers still find strands of the old phone lines along Le Conte Creek. When the line was broken by a falling tree or a gnawing squirrel, Brown often could repair it within an hour.

In 1976, the lodge opened an office near Sevierville to handle reservations calls and sell souvenirs.[13]

After the Browns replaced the Huffs, they worked with Southern Bell to install a more modern telephone. That's how the Brown children kept up with their friends down in Gatlinburg and where Carson Brewer from the *Knoxville News-Sentinel* called for daily weather reports.

In July 1961, the *Southern Telephone News* told the story of the installation of what it called "Southern Bell's Highest Telephone."

When Installer-Repairman Dave Johnson picked up a service order recently at Gatlinburg, Tennessee, he didn't know it then, but he was about to swap his familiar green truck for a horse—at least temporarily.

Dave's assignment, as he soon learned, was to install a telephone near the top of 6,593-foot Mt. LeConte in the Great Smoky Mountains National Park. And there are no roads or sky lifts up the steep mountain—one of the highest points in Eastern America—only a horse trail.

So Dave traded his steering wheel for a leather rein and his brakes for a pair of stirrups and together with veteran mountain guide Carl Bohannon, and a pack horse, saddled up to Mt. LeConte Lodge to install Southern Bell's highest telephone.

Seven miles and three-and-a-half hours later, the party was at the lodge after a somewhat stiffening ride punctuated by beautiful forests, waterfalls, and breathtaking mountain views.

The new dial phone Dave installed is one of the few modern conveniences at the rustic but comfortable lodge where guests can go to "get away from it all."

---

13. Carson Brewer, "Life on Le Conte," *Knoxville News-Sentinel*, April 1, 1976.

An old magneto line had previously served the lodge. Owner Herrick Brown still uses it to communicate directly with a building he operates at the foot of the mountain. Mr. Brown, who strung a new line down the mountain to accommodate the new dial phones, maintains and makes all repairs on the line from the mountain down to a point where Southern Bell picks up the maintenance.[14]

This rainbow spans LeConte Lodge's vital infrastructure: a solar panel, one of the four fire hydrants, the llama hitching post, and the Ashberry cabin where some crew members live (courtesy High on LeConte, blog of LeConte Lodge).

---

14. Tom Sands, "He Traded His Truck for a Horse," *Southern Telephone News*, July 1971.

Thanks to solar panels, gasoline-powered generators, and batteries, the crew does have limited electricity available at the lodge. With wireless technology, they no longer have to hike off the mountain to watch a movie. Guests eager to check in with family or Facebook usually can get a signal from the cell towers near Sevierville, Jefferson City, or Morristown, 5,400 feet below.

On July 20, 1969, Herrick Brown set up a portable television in the dining room so guests could watch the historic Apollo 11 moon landing.

Brown was an avid ham radio operator and raised an antenna on a cabin occupied by four youths who worked for him. Sixty years later, that cabin is still known as "the radio shack." The radio required 120 volts, so it was only practical to use while the Onan generator was cranked up to power the laundry.

The Coronavirus Shutdown: Weeks, Not Years

The Covid-19 pandemic erupted just as the lodge was preparing to open for the 2020 season. The airlift was already complete, but the national park and its trails had to be shut down, so the lodge did not open on schedule.

While the lodge office scrambled to reschedule reservations, the only person on the mountain was manager John Northrup, who was rewriting all the housekeeping and sanitary protocols so that the lodge could reopen promptly and safely as soon as the park permitted. Chrissy Ponder, who has served 40 years in the reservation office, led the busy effort to reschedule guest visits.

The most significant change, in terms of the LeConte experience, was the closing of the 81-year-old dining room. The family-style table fellowship had to be sacrificed to safely reopen the lodge. The park reopened May 9, 2020; llamas made their first trip May 11, and overnight guests returned on May 18. Masks were required by the park service, and meals were delivered to the cabins by the crew in 2020 and 2021. The dining room was closed for meals for 908 days until it reopened May 22, 2022.

The office was open for check-ins and souvenir sales, but the informal evening gatherings were no longer allowed. Also, each cabin had to be carefully sanitized as part of daily cleaning and bed-changing routines.

The prompt reopening of the lodge after the pandemic should not be underestimated, as some national park facilities out West did not reopen for three years.

"We never had any mass breakouts or spreader events," Northrup said in 2021. "That's almost a small miracle. We've done our best to follow protocols, so our guests could enjoy what we've known and loved for 90-something years."

The Reservations Bottleneck

The pandemic did not slacken the public demand for reservations, which has been intense for decades. The number of overnight guests was down 26 percent during the shortened 2020 season but rebounded 30 percent in 2021, despite the closed dining room.

When the national park reopened after the Covid-19 shutdown, the first men on Myrtle Point were named Adam (Adam Gravett, front, Adam Ozment, center, and Adam Williamson, right). They playfully mocked the occasion with masks, which were required at the lodge but not on the trails (Up N' Adam Adventures).

Before the 1970s, the lodge was rarely full on weeknights. Demand skyrocketed about the same time as the lodge was made famous during the debate over the Wilderness Act. News coverage of those who cherished the lodge had the forbidden-fruit effect of attracting more visitors. Many who had a lodge trip on their bucket lists realized it was now or never.

In 1969, the lodge drew 5,200 guests over seven months, an average of 29 per night. Twenty years later, in 1989, the average was 43 guests per night—essentially full occupancy, given the environmental restrictions. For practical purposes, the limit now is 40 overnight guests.

Myrtle Brown remembers that the Rev. Rufus Morgan sometimes would show up without reservations, "and we had to find room for him and his group," even if it meant that someone had to sleep on a cot. When visitors asked the old preacher if there was anything they could do for him, he would ask them to take him to Le Conte. "He didn't think of calling to see if we had room," Mrs. Brown said. The Reverend Morgan was the oldest man to climb the mountain, celebrating his 93rd birthday at the lodge in 1978. Because his eyesight was failing, he couldn't drive to the trailhead, but he was able to hike with a guide.

Don't be like the Reverend Morgan and walk up to the lodge and ask for a room. This isn't Pigeon Forge—you can't just cruise by looking for vacancies. One night in the 1980s, a group of 20 showed up without reservations. "One man was really adamant," said Bill Rinearson, who was one of the managers at the time. "He said that as long as he had money, we ought to provide rooms for them." With no vacancies, the best Rinearson could do was to offer them flashlights for the hike back down the trail.

And if the weather prevents you from hiking, don't expect a last-minute refund, either. Because of the logistics involved in operating the lodge, cancellations require 30 days' notice. "There are no exceptions to our cancellation policy," the lodge website declares. "We are not responsible for medical or family emergencies, weather or weather-related trail conditions. There will be no refunds based on unavailable vehicle parking at trailheads."

The lodge once allowed guests to "grandfather" their reservations and carry them over to the following year. In 1998, almost half of the beds were booked that way. Then the park phased out standing reservations by 2018. "It was intentional to try to give more people the opportunity to experience LeConte Lodge," said lodge manager John Northrup. "We've had more first-timers in recent years."

In 1983, people camped out at the Sevierville office hoping to get reservations for the following season. One man drove from Atlanta to get in line. Walk-ins are no longer allowed.

The Huff and Brown families took "grandfathering" literally and held reunions at the lodge, with up to 60 Huff descendants one year. One church group from South Carolina came for 46 consecutive years. "End of a wonderful tradition," one member wrote in the 2018 logbook after her 17th visit.

How do you get a reservation? Start by entering an online lottery each August, listing your preferred dates. The lottery entries are processed on the first Monday in October, the same day that telephone reservations open. The lodge strives to handle lottery and phone reservations simultaneously, but if you want a particular date, you would be wise to call. Some guests speed-dial the lodge hundreds of times until they get through, and the volume of calls can overwhelm the phone bank. In a matter of hours, most of the preferred dates (spring and autumn) are filled.

Guests have discovered a few ways to work around the bottleneck.

If you have a large group, you can reserve one of the three larger cabins, which

Descendants of Jack Huff at their 2011 reunion (Huff family photo, courtesy Cookie Bowling).

accommodate up to 13 hikers, with most of them sharing double bunk beds. The large lodges do not fill up as fast as the individual cabins, which are designed for parties of five or smaller.

If your schedule is flexible, you may find last-minute vacancies posted on the lodge's Twitter account, after someone cancels a reservation. Also, the lodge opens a waiting list each November.

Once you get a reservation at LeConte Lodge, there's still sticker shock for those who discover they could stay and eat cheaper at the Parkview Hotel in Gatlinburg or at Dollywood's DreamMore Resort & Spa in Pigeon Forge.

The 2024 rate for a cabin for two adults was $415 (including taxes and fees). The larger three-bedroom lodges (accommodating 12 persons) went for $2,677 per night and the two-bedroom lodge (eight persons) for $1,618.

In 1925, Paul Adams charged $1.50 per night. By 1959, Jack Huff's last year, the rate was $8. Herrick Brown charged $12 in 1974 and had 8,140 guests, which would have generated nearly $100,000 in revenue. Still, that was barely enough to keep up with the bills for maintenance, staffing, supplies, and food. Brown counted 7,043 guests in 1972, which broke the old record by more than 200.

The Browns retired after the 1975 season, and the new owner, Jim Huff, Jr. (Jack Huff's nephew), said he and his partners realized that they needed to raise rates to keep up with maintenance expenses. Huff invested $300,000 in facilities and kept construction crews on the mountain during the winters of 1975 and 1976. In a 2021 interview, Jim Huff recalled how his crew numbered the timbers in the Old Lodge (now known as Cabin 1), took it apart, rebuilt the foundation, and replaced any logs that were rotten.

Even as the rates went up, the guests kept coming: 7,532 at $20 per person in 1979, 10,042 at $50 in 1989 (the year Stokely bought into the business), and a record 11,493 at $136 in 2016. Since 1989, the lodge has averaged over 10,600 guests per year, or 48 per night.

Steel braces support the buckled walls on the 1971 office and recreation building. This building was closed in 2024 and is scheduled to be replaced by 2027.

The National Park Service has tracked the number of guests since the 1970s, revealing an interesting ratio. Of the millions who visit the Smokies each year, about one in a thousand spend the night at the lodge. For example, the 2016 lodge total of 11,493 guests corresponded closely to the park attendance of 11,312,786.

Stokely Hospitality Enterprises has been operating the lodge on a series of short-term contracts, so long-term maintenance was deferred. In 2024, the park service solicited bids for a 10-year contract that will require an investment of $851,000 into the operations and facilities.

The contract specifies construction of a new office and an open-air pavilion where guests can socialize. These will be the first new guest facilities at the lodge since 1971. They will replace the existing office, which has structural problems and needs steel braces to support its log walls. For decades, the office was a popular place for guests to gather at night, but engineers will have to determine if it can be repaired.

The bid prospectus offered some insight into the revenue generated by the lodge, projected to reach $2.6 million in 2027. The park service will receive a franchise fee of 13 percent on revenue up to $2,250,000 and 22 percent on receipts above that threshold.

Fly Le Conte

Much of the food served at the lodge is canned and delivered by a helicopter airlift each March. Jack Huff experimented with helicopters as early as 1954, though it was the 1970s before they were used routinely. In 1976, a chopper chartered by Jim Huff, Jr., airlifted 30,000 tons of food, supplies, and equipment.[15] In recent years, the spring airlift may involve more than 50 flights.

During heat waves in 1975 and 2024, park officials permitted the lodge to fly summer airlifts to give the llamas a break.

In addition to food staples, flights bring in tanks of propane, construction materials, and the "I hiked it" T-shirts that are sold only at the lodge.

The airlift supplies are loaded into cargo nets at the Luftee Overlook just south of Newfound Gap, a three-mile hop from the lodge. The lodge charters a Sikorsky S-61 helicopter that can drop a five-ton sling of cargo at pinpoint locations around the lodge campus. If it is necessary to land, there is a helipad called "the blowdown" in a forest clearing east of the lodge.

During the winter of 1925, Adams received fresh meat and supplies tossed by the pilot of an army biplane that was being used to survey the Smokies.

In 1996, the lodge chartered a yellow Sikorsky that delivered 40 tons of supplies, including 3,600 T-shirts, new floorboards and windows for some cabins, an 800-pound stainless steel stove, and bundles that contained a season supply of cornmeal, sugar, flour, grits, and canned apples, not to mention concrete and tools for trail repairs.

---

15. Carson Brewer, "Life on Le Conte," *Knoxville News-Sentinel*, April 1, 1976.

Decades ago, three helicopters crashed while servicing the lodge.

In August 1969, a Pigeon Forge sightseeing helicopter was chartered to fly plumbing supplies to the lodge during a renovation of the water and sewer systems. Pilot Gene Henry picked up a load at Indian Gap and began to swing around to fly to Le Conte, but the chopper plunged into trees on the North Carolina side of the park. Henry, 30, died in the crash.

In the summer of 1983, two helicopters crashed while delivering construction supplies to the lodge. A Bell 206 was returning from the lodge with a sling filled with packing straps. One of the straps came loose and was sucked into the rear rotor, forcing the chopper to spin out of control into the trees. The aircraft was destroyed, but pilot Robert Bailey, 42, survived.

Each season begins with the March airlift, when a helicopter delivers tanks of fuel, tons of canned food, and T-shirts and other souvenirs that are sold at the lodge (courtesy John Northrup).

Two weeks later, a Sikorsky-58 helicopter from St. Louis was chartered to complete the airlift. As it lifted off from Indian Gap, it lost power and crash-landed on the road embankment. The pilot and two passengers escaped without injuries.

When medical evacuation is needed, the lodge crew can summon a helicopter. In 2021, a hiker stricken by a diabetic condition needed hospital treatment. The National Guard dispatched a rescue helicopter, only to find that thick clouds made it impossible to land on the blowdown.

The lodge crew moved the patient down the Alum Cave Bluff Trail to a spot where the clouds were breaking and the tree canopy was thin.[16] As the chopper hovered just above the treetops, a paramedic was hoisted down to the trail to stabilize the patient, and then they were lifted together into the cab for the 12-minute flight to a hospital in Knoxville.

---

16. Since the 1960s, many of the fir trees on Le Conte have been killed by an infestation of the Balsam Wooly Adelgid, a pest native to Europe, so ridgetop forests are marked by the still-standing carcasses of dead trees. The forests appear to be recovering, and there is hope that younger firs may have developed an immunity.

In the fall of 2022, a guest at the lodge tripped, broke bones, and needed to be evacuated. Helicopters were grounded by foul weather, so the injured hiker was brought down on horseback via the Trillium Gap Trail.

Throughout the Smokies, there have been dozens of plane crashes, including at least three on Le Conte.

On April 3, 1973, as horrified hikers watched from Cliff Top, a twin-engine Piper flying south from Cincinnati slammed into the mountainside a couple of miles below and burst into flames. Two men and two women died in the crash.

Incredibly, there was a survivor who wasn't found until six days later. Jim "Pop" Hollandsworth was hiking with students from Asheville School, and they bushwhacked down to

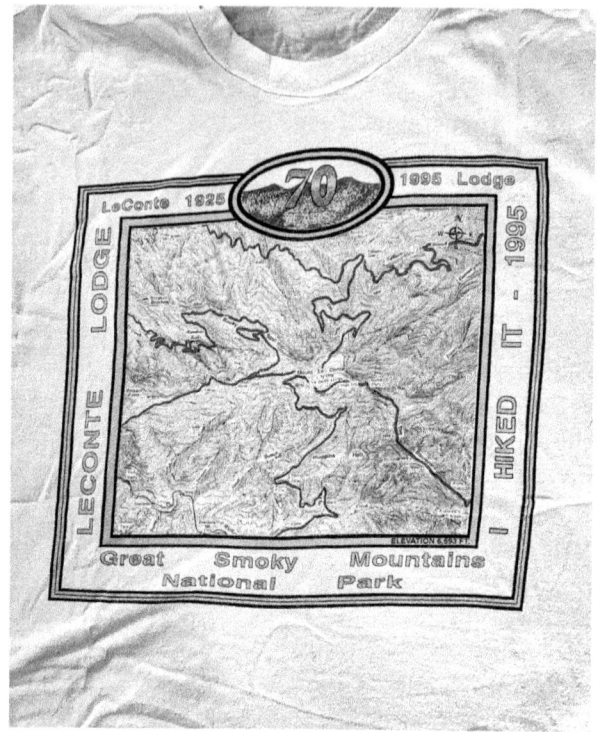

For decades the lodge has sold "I hiked it" T-shirts, which are sold only at the lodge, not online. This is the 1995 version, marking the lodge's 70th anniversary (courtesy John Woge).

the crash site from Alum Cave Bluff Trail. They were surprised to find a white Afghan hound curled up next to the wreckage. The dog was hungry but uninjured.

Evidently, the dog had been thrown free from the crash, retreated elsewhere while rescuers recovered the bodies, and returned to the scene out of devotion. After first aid from a local veterinarian, Ali Khzin was adopted by a friend of the pilot.

The day after Christmas 2016, three persons died when a Cessna flying from Florida to Pigeon Forge crashed into a ridgeline near West Point, barely a mile from the lodge.[17]

Not Quite a Lunar Landing

Jack Neiman, Jr., was one of the Navy's first astronauts, though he never made it into outer space. Raised in Gatlinburg, where his family ran Neiman's Good Food Restaurant, he participated in high-altitude simulations in 1958 to test and perfect the space suit that Alan Shepard wore when he became the first American in space in 1961.

---

17. Tyler Whetstone and Rachel Ohm, "National Park Service: Three dead in Smokies Plane Crash," USA TODAY network, *The Commercial Appeal*, December 28, 2010.

Neiman was a lieutenant commander in the Navy and a veteran of World War II and Vietnam who had logged more than 9,000 hours of accident-free flight. "This was the caliber of pilot who, rather than landing on the moon, landed instead on Mount Le Conte," wrote Jeff Wadley and Dwight McCarter in *Mayday! Mayday!*—their book about Smoky Mountain plane crashes.

A year after Shepard golfed on the moon[18] with Apollo 14 in 1971, Neiman was hired by lodge owner Herrick Brown to airdrop bags of feed for Blackie, the workhorse who lived at the lodge. On August 22, 1972, Neiman was flying a single-engine Cessna 182 for Smoky Mountains Aviation out of Sevierville. Neiman, 48, planned to make a low-speed pass over the blowdown, while his mechanic, Allen Moore, 25, would dump the 50-pound bags out the side door into the clearing. From his cockpit perspective, Neiman described the blowdown as "about the size of a tennis court."[19]

After Jack Neiman risked his life to test space suits for NASA, fate rewarded him by sparing his life in a crash landing on Mount Le Conte (U.S. Navy photo).

Neiman was approaching the drop zone at about 60 mph when the Cessna stalled. Rather than diving off the side of the mountain in a desperate attempt to regain lift, he opted for a crash landing on the helicopter pad. As Wadley and McCarter wrote: "He set the plane's nose high and allowed the tail to slowly touch the small trees and eventually slide into the forest." Neiman and Moore walked away with only scratches, and Blackie got fed.

The wreckage was removed and few traces remain of these crashes. The lodge crew recycled wheels and tires from Neiman's Cessna to make a cart for Blackie to haul logs.

---

18. Alan Shepard (1923–1998) became the first American in space on January 19, 1961, and was the fifth man to walk on the moon, February 5, 1971, on the Apollo 14 mission. He is remembered for hitting two golf shots on the moon, using a makeshift 6-iron.

19. Willard Yarbrough, "'Captain Crunch' Has 1st Crash in 31 Years," *Knoxville News-Sentinel*, Aug. 27, 1972. As small as the blowdown is, the lodge crew has to cut down saplings to keep the forest from encroaching. In the 2000s, manager Chris Virden transplanted many saplings from the blowdown along the railings at the lodge entrance, where they now form a Christmas tree corridor.

The notion of landing a plane on Le Conte had been proposed back in 1924, when federal commissioners were scouting the park. According to the *Knoxville Journal and Tribune*,[20] the Smoky Mountains Conservation Association hired pilot Buck Rawlings of Knoxville Aero to offer the commissioners an aerial tour and see if it was possible to land on the mountain.

As early as 1922, some daredevil pilots landed on Gregory Bald in the western Smokies.[21] But Le Conte lacks open fields or level plateaus like Gregory Bald, despite the fact that the sand myrtles look deceptively smooth from a distance.

---

20. "Park Commission Party Leaves on Inspection Tour," *Knoxville Journal and Tribune*, Aug. 7, 1924.
21. "Airports in Smoky Parks Area Seen By Commission," *Knoxville News-Sentinel*, Oct. 9, 1929.

9

Llamas, Canines and Bears

Close to 2,000 black bears roam the Great Smoky Mountains National Park and about two dozen llamas work rotating shifts on the trails of Mount Le Conte. Hikers keep their eyes peeled for a glimpse of these lumbering icons.

A century ago, black bears were nearly exterminated by hunting in the Smokies. Paul Adams saw only one bear during the summer of 1925. Yet today they are thriving.

It is estimated there are now about two bears per square mile in the park. So when you hike on Le Conte, bears are likely nearby. Just because you don't see them doesn't mean that they don't see you. If you're wanting to calculate your odds, consider that Margaret Stevenson had 20 bear encounters on her 718 Le Conte hikes, and only one was aggressive.

Since the 1960s, the park has documented over 1,000 human-bear conflicts (incidents involving injuries or property damage). Most of these happened along the roadsides and involved tourists feeding or petting a bear.

The only fatal bear attacks in the Smokies were far from the lodge. In 2000, a hiker on the Little River Trail was killed by a malnourished 113-pound bear, and in 2020 a backpacker on Hazel Creek was killed by a 240-pounder. In 2008, a family from Florida was hiking the Rainbow Falls Trail when their son was mauled by an 86-pound black bear. John Pala, 43, was able to pry open the bear's mouth to rescue his eight-year-old Evan.[1]

Until the 1970s, LeConte Lodge used garbage pits and counted on scavenging bears to get rid of food scraps. A 1976 study found at least 12 bears dining at the lodge. This problem was resolved under the Wilderness Act, when the garbage pits were replaced by an incinerator. Since then, guests are more likely to see deer rather than bears.

Even now that the lodge has reduced its waste, bears are occasionally attracted to the mountaintop meadow to feast on berries, to say nothing of snacks and trash discarded by careless hikers.

When park rangers deal with a bear, they tag it with a number. But the lodge crew knows many of the bears by name. One they called Goliath was a 500-pounder who frequently raided the food shed at the lodge. Jack Huff packed the food in steel drums that he buried and covered with rocks. That didn't stop Goliath, who dug up the drums and dragged them off.

---

1. Duncan Mansfield, "8-year-old Boy Survives Bear Attack," *The Tennessean*, Aug. 13, 2008.

Lodge guests got a special thrill in 2010 when they watched a national park ranger tag a tranquilized two-year-old bear (courtesy High on LeConte, blog of LeConte Lodge).

Tim Line remembers a bear called Ralph who opened the screen door one night and strolled into the kitchen after supper. Suddenly, he was surrounded by hollering crew members in every doorway. "He didn't have any way to get out," Line said. "I guess he thought: 'What do I do now?' So he took a big dump right in the middle of the floor."

One bear nicknamed Roxy (whose face was scarred after biting into a bottle of Clorox) became such a nuisance that rangers put him down with tranquilizers and buried him under logs, but somehow he survived and dug his way out.

Sheba came to the lodge every spring. "She knew when the dinner bell rang that everybody would be in the dining room and nobody was in the cabins," Line said. "That's when she would go in the cabins and make her rounds."

Sheba once broke into the cabin of Gracie McNicol, who was in her 80s. Gracie attempted to scare away the bear, and Line eventually ran it off with a pellet gun. Sheba remained a nuisance and had to be relocated to the Cherokee National Forest.

Jack Huff's daughter, Cookie Bowling, remembers one day when there were eight bears in camp, mostly foraging through the lodge's garbage dump. "Every time you came out the door, you had to look left or right, to see if there was a bear. I don't think there was a single cabin they didn't get into."

The Huffs and Browns strung a battery-powered electric fence around the kitchen to keep bears out. Mischievous crew members sometimes baited the fence with bacon to watch bears get buzzed. In moments of macho boredom, crew members would compete to see who could hold the wire the longest.

In the 1970s, the crew armored the window sills with nails and saw blades and kept a pitchfork to guard the door. In 1976, the crew took turns sleeping in the kitchen to guard against a marauding bear. They heard it crawling under the floor, "causing midnight earthquakes," according to crew member David Witherspoon.

As the bears were weaned off the garbage, a few turned aggressive. In 1979, more than a dozen boys on the Alum Cave Trail surrendered their backpacks to bears. At the lodge, one bear swiped a woman's backpack and clawed her arm when she tried to retrieve it.

The bear problem was worse at the back-country campers' shelter near the lodge. The park eventually enclosed the three-sided shelter in a steel mesh fence and added "bear cables" where hikers could hang their packs. Occasionally, the shelter is closed to avoid confrontations with aggressive bears. According to a 1988 story in the *Charlotte Observer*, one hungry bear broke into the shelter nearby sliding down the chimney, Santa style.[2]

In *A Natural History of Mount Le Conte*, Kenneth Wise and Ronald Peterson write:

> The black bear is as much a figment of lore and superstition as a creature of the forest. Much of the common knowledge of the black bear is a confused amalgamation of blatant anthropomorphism and horror stories with a slight leavening of biological fact.
>
> Contrary to popular assumption, black bears do not maintain homes in caves or dens. Black bears do, however, "den up" for long periods, usually in December. The den is likely to be at the base of a fallen tree, in a hollow log, underneath a rock shelter. Smoky Mountain bears apparently have a peculiar affinity for denning in cavities of mature trees, often as high as sixty feet above the ground.
>
> Black bears are not skilled hunters. They compensate for their lack of hunting prowess by being omnivorous. A Smoky Mountain black bear's diet might include berries, nuts, fruit, roots, bark, leaves, twigs, insects, eggs, honey, fish, frogs, salamanders, small animals, carrion, and garbage.
>
> Bears are smart and secretive and usually wary of humans. They can be irascible.

Pioneer hiker Paul Fink told the national park commission in 1924 that bears are cowards. "I wouldn't be afraid to go up and kick any bear in these mountains," he said. "But boys, I'll run any time from one of those tusked razorback wild boars."[3]

The lodge blog in 2013 reported on a nuisance bear:

> He is a stubborn bear that runs when we yell at him, but he doesn't seem too concerned. Unfortunately, we're going to have to catch him in our sturdy bear trap and let the Park Service guys do their job. They've been extremely successful in scaring the past bears to the point they do not come back around. That's the main objective for us—keep the bears wild and scared of humans. Once the bear is caught, the park service will put him under, like at the dentist office. He will then get a health check. The only difference is that when he wakes up, he will have a new earring. He will have a little hangover which will hopefully help him to realize he doesn't want any part of those two-legged creatures. If everything works according to plan, he will be on his way to greener pastures, or should I say, redder ash berries.

---

2. Jack Horan, "Outsiders Crimp Bears' Wild Living," *Charlotte Observer*, Feb. 26, 1988.
3. L.W. Miller, "Famous Professors Laud Smokies to Party on Trip," *Knoxville News*, Aug. 12, 1924.

In 1928, three youths were arrested for carrying pistols on Le Conte. "Were you intending to hunt some bears up there?" the judge asked them. "The next time you start to LeConte, don't take the guns along." The judge promised to dismiss the charges pending good behavior.[4]

One of the most tragic bear incidents on Le Conte involved an innocent yearling. In 1938, an 80-pound bear became too friendly around a Civilian Conservation Corps camp, and workers who were building the Trillium Gap Trail trapped it in a garbage pit and killed it with a four-pound hammer. A federal judge offered leniency if the pelt was returned, but instead the culprit was sentenced to five months in prison.[5]

Usually, bear encounters are harmless novelties, as long as guests stay at least 50 yards away, as recommended by rangers. After all, these are wild animals, and while black bears are not as ferocious as grizzlies, they are not teddy bears.

If a bear follows or approaches, you are advised to change your direction or stand your ground. Don't run, but back away, talking loudly. Make yourself look as large as possible (perhaps by standing on a rock). Usually bears will retreat, and bear spray is not necessary.

Smoky Jack: All Business

In the founding years of the lodge, the most respected and feared animal on the mountain was Smoky Jack, Paul Adams' German Shepherd. Trained as a police dog, Jack learned to carry supplies from Gatlinburg to the lodge and was known to snap at hikers who interfered with his business trips.

"When I was assured by Col. David C. Chapman in 1924 that I would be appointed by the Great Smoky Mountains Conservation Association to start a camp on top of Mount Le Conte, I started looking around for a grown, intelligent dog which might be a companion in my vigil," Paul Adams wrote in his book, *Smoky Jack*.[6]

Jack (1920–1935) was jet black, a stout 90 pounds, 26 inches tall at the shoulders. His registered name was Cumberland Jack of Edelweis II. He had been trained as a police dog in New Jersey and belonged to a Knoxville detective who was killed in a shootout. The officer's widow wanted $500, which was more than Adams could afford. When she was satisfied that Adams and the dog would be good together, she agreed to sell him for $50 down and $25 per month.

Smoky Jack turned out to be much more than a companion—a smart tracker, a hard worker, and brave enough to defy wolves and armed robbers.

Adams called him Smoky Jack during their year on Le Conte but then reverted to his formal name when they settled in the Cumberland Mountains of Tennessee.

---

4. "Youths Believe Pistols Needed on Mt. LeConte," *Knoxville Journal*, April 17, 1928.
5. "Bear Killing Brings Term of 5 Months," *Knoxville Journal*, Jan. 7, 1939.
6. Adams' manuscript, *Smoky Jack*, was not published until 21 years after his death, after it was substantially edited by Anne Bridges and Ken Wise. Cumberland Jack's LeConte Kitchen, a restaurant at 1019 Parkway in Gatlinburg, is a shrine to Jack and Adams.

Smoky Jack with guide Paul Adams, leading the Knoxville Rotary Club to his 1925 camp (photo by Jim Thompson, courtesy Thompson Photo Products).

As Jack became familiar with the mountain trails, Adams trained him to bring up supplies from Charlie Ogle's store in Gatlinburg. Adams found an army cavalry officer's satchel and had a harness maker adjust the straps to fit Jack. Adams determined that Jack could safely carry up to 30 pounds. When Adams ordered him, "Go to the store, Jack," the dog romped down the trail with a shopping list in his saddlebag and returned four and a half hours later with Adams' order, which might include nails, mail, and lemons for lemonade.

Adams wrote in *Smoky Jack* that one August morning, when he and his dog were on their way down the trail toward Gatlinburg, they were accosted by a disguised man who jabbed a revolver into his ribs and demanded his money. In a 1971 newspaper interview, Adams said he was carrying about $400 in receipts from a busy week at the camp. It happened again a few weeks later, but this time Adams had stashed the cash in the dog's saddlebag, assuming that the robber wouldn't look there, and that if he did, Smoky Jack would retaliate. This time, the robber got only $5 in personal cash from Adams.

Adams carried a .44 Colt revolver but never had a chance to defend himself. One friend later told Adams that he might have been killed if he had made a move. Adams knew that Jack could track down the robber, but he decided not to risk the pursuit, knowing that if there was a showdown, his dog might be shot.

The robber eventually stalked the camp on Mount Le Conte, and Adams was able to get shoe-prints to identify him. One day in Gatlinburg, Smoky Jack cornered the robber on the street, but Adams and Chapman declined to press charges. After that, Smoky Jack always carried the camp receipts, and no one ever stole the money.

Smoky Jack understood that he was on duty while he wore his saddle bags, and he would not let anyone approach him. Adams wrote:

> We sometimes had a few wounded hands and arms requiring first aid in camp. We had no way of knowing the dog had attacked anyone until that person walked into camp and told us about it. Jack came into camp without showing any signs of having encountered someone on the trail. He always came in with loaded saddle pockets. One of my boys or I would remove them, give him a couple of dog biscuits, and then he would run around by himself in the woods. But when those he had bitten came into camp, he would never have anything to

do with them. At these times, he would stay close by my side. If that person approached a little too close to me, according to Jack's way of thinking, he would growl or snarl and let it be known that he would protect me. On two occasions, men walked into camp and asked for guns to shoot the dog. We laughed about it and told those fellows that, if the dog tried to bite them, it was their own fault because we were certain they had tried to interfere with the dog's work.[7]

One hiker who arrived with a bloody hand vowed to kill Jack while Adams was making his evening fire patrol. Lodge workers warned the fellow that he might not make it home alive if anything happened to the dog. "Feuds have been started in the mountains over things more minor than the killing of a dog," Adams wrote. The next day, the wounded man kicked Jack, and Adams had to restrain his dog. "If I had allowed the dog to fight this young man, Jack would have jumped for the boy's throat and killed him in seconds. I did not want murder committed."

During one visit to Gatlinburg, Jack broke a leg while jumping down from Adams' car. Adams took him to a veterinarian in Sevierville, and Jack growled at the doctor, who recommended shooting the dog to put him out of his misery. Instead, Adams took Jack to Knoxville, where a vet was able to set the fracture. Adams subsequently learned that the Sevierville vet had been bitten by Jack on the trail near Rainbow Falls. "No wonder there was animosity between them," Adams wrote. Jack recovered, went back to work, and even worked briefly for Jack Huff.

After Adams left the lodge in 1926, Jack led search parties that helped track down and rescue several lost hikers in the Smokies. He lived until 1935, when he suffered a fatal heart attack while he was running home to greet his master.

Smoky Jack's era predated the national park. Since the 1930s, dogs have not been allowed on the park trails.

Before Jack Huff met his bride, an Angora cat named Beauty kept him company on the mountain. Beauty once followed a couple of hikers out to Myrtle Point, where they feared she might fall off the cliff. One of Huff's co-workers assured them, "Oh, it's all right. She sleeps out there all the time."[8]

The Browns had a cat named Velvet who was legendary among the crew. They swore her daddy was a bobcat and that she once treed a bear.

Mules and Horses

The early trails were too rugged for horses, so Adams, Huff, and their employees carried most of the heavy supplies on their backs. As guest traffic increased and the trails improved, pack animals were employed.

Huff first used mules to haul supplies from Newfound Gap. In 1933, he built a supply cart 32 inches wide that mules could pull up the Boulevard Trail. "Jack Huff has a load off his shoulders," the *Knoxville News-Sentinel* reported.[9]

---

7. Paul J. Adams, *Smoky Jack*, edited by Anne Bridges and Ken Wise (Knoxville: University of Tennessee Press, 2016).
8. "First Hike Up LeConte Inspires Artist to Produce Sketch of Sights," *Knoxville News-Sentinel*, Oct. 9, 1932.
9. "Mule Replaces Men," *Knoxville News-Sentinel*, April 7, 1933.

Jack Huff riding Old Joe at Cliff Top in the 1920s (Great Smoky Mountains National Park Archives).

In the 1920s, Huff led a horse named Old Joe up the Trillium Gap Trail, then saddled up for a photo at Cliff Top. "Taking a horse up Mount LeConte is rather an odd adventure," according to the *Knoxville News-Sentinel*. "Jack did it for pleasure, with a notion possibly that he might blaze a horse trail up the ascent—a notion he no longer holds. But perhaps the real reason was that he wanted 'Old Joe' to enjoy the heights."[10]

The ascent took eight hours. "I would say that one horse out of ten would make the trip," Huff said. "Joe is a horse that will do as you tell him or kill himself trying. Joe didn't seem to have much trouble going up, but he was in danger about all the way after leaving Brushy Mountain."

The reporter noted the back-to-back irony in Huff's story, since he had carried his mother up on his own back and now he reached the top on Old Joe's back. At least Old Joe (unlike Jack's mother) got to witness a sunset. "You can believe or not that horses have souls that respond to the magnificent and the beautiful, but there must be some feeling in Old Joe's heart, some memory of a clean, rare, lofty atmosphere in his nostrils and some sense of accomplishment in his lean legs that sets him spiritually apart from his less experienced brethren," the newspaper wrote.

Two months later, Old Joe made an encore trip up the same route, this time carrying the director of the National Park Service, Horace Albright. This was before the Smokies became a national park, and Albright (who had previously visited in 1925) wanted to tour the mountains as the park took shape. His party, which included a movie crew and guides Paul Fink and William Ramsey, rode eight miles from Gatlinburg to Brushy Mountain and then hiked the final three miles up to the camp.

---

10. "'Old Joe' Ascends the Heights," *Knoxville News-Sentinel*, March 30, 1930.

At breakfast the next morning, Albright penned a note to Joseph Nisbet LeConte, the California naturalist who had succeeded John Muir as president of the Sierra Club. He declared the top of Le Conte should be preserved in all its primitive beauty and that no horse trail should be built on the mountain.

Yet the park eventually permitted Huff to use pack horses to supply the lodge and also licensed stables to transport riders up the mountain. Usually they came up via Rainbow Falls. Riders paid $6 for a two-day saddle trip.

A draft horse named Blackie worked at the lodge during Herrick Brown's era in the 1970s. He replaced a mule named Ambrose who did much of the tractor work around the lodge. Blackie sometimes escaped from his barn at Cherokee Orchard, walked up in the dark, and greeted the lodge crew when they woke in the morning.

Blackie's pasture was off the Trillium Gap Trail in a clearing that has been reclaimed by forest. Blackie weighed a ton, and when his black winter coat grew thick, "he looked like a bison grazing in the field," said former crew member Al Bedinger.

For years, pack horses made four trips per week up the Rainbow Falls Trail. In 1976, helicopters made spring and mid-season flights, so the pack trips were cut to twice a week by 1978.[11]

Mules visited the lodge as recently as 2016, hauling tools for reconstruction of the Alum Cave Bluff Trail.

Llamas Tread Lightly on Le Conte

Horseshoes were hard on the trails, so the lodge needed alternative transportation in light of the Wilderness Act restrictions of the 1970s. Jim Huff, Jr., Jack's nephew, worked with the park service in the 1980s to transition from horses to llamas, who still make the trip three times a week. Huff acquired the first three in 1984 from a farm in Kokomo, Indiana, and their first trip was April 10, 1984. Two weeks later, Margaret Stevenson remarked in her journal, "the llamas are not doing well," but eventually they found their stride.

The llamas live at a ranch near the foot of the mountain and ride in trailers to the Roaring Fork trailhead. Each weighs about 300 pounds, and they are strong enough to carry up to one-third of their weight. They typically work in tethered strings of six to nine, bringing up fresh groceries (including eggs) plus laundered bed linens. On the return trip they carry down mail, dirty laundry, and garbage. Their working career is from age four to 18. All the pack llamas are males, to avoid distractions while they work.

The llama train makes three trips a week, typically on Mondays, Wednesdays, and Fridays. Individuals work in rotations so each one makes three trips every two weeks. The llamas follow the Trillium Gap Trail, which means they pass behind Grotto Falls.

---

11. Carson Brewer, "Le Conte Lodge Expected to Stay, but with Fewer Accommodations," *Knoxville News-Sentinel*, April 26, 1978.

Three times a week, the llamas make the trip on Trillium Gap Trail, which takes them under Grotto Falls (courtesy High on LeConte, blog of LeConte Lodge).

One beloved llama known as Clifford Cliff Tops made about 800 trips before retiring in 2017. Wrangler Alan Householder called Clifford "the smartest and strongest llama on the farm. If he sets his mind to it, he can get through any fence on the farm. He's also more tolerant of people than most of the other llamas."

Householder developed a strong working relationship with the llamas. "They don't want affection; they want respect," he said in a 2020 story in *Blue Ridge Outdoors* magazine. "At first, I'd bark orders at them, but that was the wrong approach."

Morgan Simmons of the *Knoxville News-Sentinel* described the scene at the lodge while the llamas were on their lunch break, feasting on alfalfa pellets and leftover pancakes to carb up for the three-and-a-half-hour trip down: "After an hour at the lodge, it was time to hit the trail. The packs were loaded with trash and dirty linen, and the llamas were ready to go. Still tied to their hitching post, they started making more noise than they'd made all day. Some chittered like squirrels, while others sneezed, coughed, and yawned. At one point, George, the last llama in the pack line, began to hum, and the others joined in, chanting like Buddhist monks."[12]

John Northrup worked on the llama farm before he became the lodge manager. "Some can be sweet," he said. "Some are hard workers. They are smart critters." Once they learn the routine, "they are pretty much set for their careers." Steve Cogdill, the original wrangler, was glad to find such a unique job. "I don't expect to do it more

---

12. Morgan Simmons, "Packed with Personality," *Knoxville News-Sentinel*, Aug. 15, 2004.

Larry Russell and Clifford the llama have been among the lodge's most frequent visitors in recent years. Clifford made about 800 trips before his retirement in 2017. Larry has made more than 500 climbs since retiring from law enforcement, including 115 in 2023—the busiest season by any LeConte hiker since 1998 (courtesy Chrissy Householder and LeConte Lodge).

than four or five years—then it's off to college," he said in a 1990 interview. "But for now, it's a good job—the pay is about $400 per week—and how many llama drivers do you know in Tennessee?"[13]

Jim Matthews was the wrangler in 1984. Following Cogdill, Jeff Hostler served

---

13. William Thomas, "Mountain Mecca," *Memphis Commercial Appeal*, July 15, 1990.

nine years as wrangler and Alan Householder 20 years (splitting duties with his wife Chrissy). Brad Graham took the reins in 2021.

The llamas are often muzzled when they work, to keep them from snacking on trailside plants that might not be healthy for them. Rhododendron and laurel are bad for their livers. In 1993, several llamas became sick (and one died) after eating dog-hobble.

The llamas prefer cooler temperatures, and the wranglers sometimes cancel trips on hot summer days. On a 77-degree July day in 2010, a llama named Woody suffered heat exhaustion and collapsed on the Trillium Gap Trail a mile below the lodge. The crew fetched cool water from the Basin Spring and called a veterinarian for advice, but nothing seemed to help. Members of the crew sat up with Woody during the night, guarding him against possible bear attacks and using an umbrella to shelter him from a hailstorm. The next morning, Woody was still immobile, and rangers were summoned by radio to come put him out of his misery.

Crew member Nathan Kirkham serenaded Woody with Willie Nelson songs and whispered a pep talk, telling Woody that he was one of the best llamas, and that if he ever wanted to walk again, now was the time. Woody stood up, wobbled, and collapsed again. Kirkham was encouraged enough to call off the rangers, as he encouraged Woody to keep trying. Later that night, Woody made it to the lodge, arriving to a huge ovation from the guests and crew. He spent a couple of days recovering at the lodge before walking back down the mountain. "He was honorably retired after that and lived a life of leisure," Kirkham said.

Squirrels, Snakes, and Wolves

On the first anniversary of the 1924 federal delegation, Paul Adams was notified that three VIPs were en route to the camp: Harlan Kelsey from the Southern Appalachian National Park Commission; Arno Cammerer, assistant director of the National Park Service; and G. Freeman Pollock, Jr., an influential lodge owner in the Shenandoah Mountains. Pollock doubted that Congress would approve two new national parks, so in his mind, it was a competition between the Smokies and Shenandoah, which he promoted as "a national park 90 miles from the nation's capital."

Adams understood that these men "could have more to do with the future of the Great Smokies than anyone else in the nation." He wanted to treat them to a special dessert with supper, so he mixed up a bowl of fruit jello with bananas, oranges, apples, and black walnuts. He placed the bowl in the Basin Spring to chill. Just before his guests arrived, he discovered that a dozen red squirrels—called "boomers" in the Smokies—had pulled off the lid and gorged on the jello. Adams mixed up a fresh batch of gelatin to fill the hole, put the bowl back in the spring, and put a heavy stone on the lid to make it boomer-proof.

Supper went delightfully well, and afterward the group went to Myrtle Point for sunset, where Kelsey had been part of the delegation that watched the sunrise in 1924. As dusk fell, Adams would describe the valley towns and landmarks by their lights. "It was a beautiful night, clear and just chilly enough," Adams wrote.

As the owner of the off-road Skyland Lodge in Virginia, Pollock understood how challenging it must have been to make jello without a refrigerator, and he offered his congratulations for dessert. One of Adams' workers muttered, "Hell, it should have been good, after the boomers had a hand in it."

The secret was out. "Mr. Kelsey asked us what part the squirrels played in preparing supper," Adams wrote. "So I told them. Everybody had a good laugh. And Mr. Pollock said again that the cooks, regardless of who they were, were to be congratulated."

It wasn't long until the boomers and park boosters got their just desserts. Cammerer, the first national park official to visit the Smokies, told the *Knoxville Journal* in 1925: "The Great Smoky Mountains national park area is in every way eminently worthy of being included in the national park system. From a purely scenic viewpoint, the park has few equals anywhere in the world. Its ultimate establishment is only a matter of time, and as far as I can predict, as an administrative official of the federal park service, it is an absolute certainty."[14] Four months later, the Smokies and Shenandoah were both nominated to become national parks.

Boomers are a northern species and are about half the size of the gray squirrels more common in the South. They chatter at lodge guests, have been known to unzip backpacks and steal snacks, and can be just as territorial as the bears. As Tim Line's son Jacob wrote in a 2019 poem, "Up here, it's only the squirrels that bite."

Jack Huff's daughter, Cookie Huff, was amused by the boomers. When cooks threw out a leftover pancake, one boomer would claim it, a second one would arrive to fight over it, and then a third squirrel would run off with the treat. "Number 3 got it every time," she said.

Guests are unlikely to see snakes at the lodge. Naturalists have identified 23 species of snakes (21 non-venomous) in the park, but being cold-blooded, they mostly avoid the chilly mountaintop. The park has never had a fatality attributed to snakebite. Paul Adams and Ron Valentine never saw rattlesnakes higher than Rocky Spur in the Rainbow Falls Trail.

Randy Ratliff, an amateur herpetologist who finds dozens of snakes in the park every year, has seen only two snakes at the lodge in 25 years of hiking. Both were harmless garters.

Paul Adams said in a 1963 interview that there was once a pack of wolves near Mount Guyot, and he saw one on Le Conte that was probably exiled from the pack: "As long as my dog could outrun it," he said, "I didn't mind it being around."[15]

Timber wolves were eradicated from the Smokies before the park was developed. The *Knoxville Journal* reported in June 1926 that Huff had to use a gun to chase away wolves circling the lodge.

Elk have multiplied since they were reintroduced to the park in 2001, but they prefer meadows in the North Carolina valleys and have not wandered to the lodge.

Bobcats are the largest cats in the Smokies, as there have been no verified panther sightings in more than 100 years.

---

14. John C. Ottinger, Jr., "Cammerer Says Park in Smokies Now Certainty," *Knoxville Journal*, Aug. 13, 1925.

15. "Strolling with Bert Vincent," Oct. 31, 1963, *Knoxville News-Sentinel*.

10

How Does LeConte Measure Up?

Jack Huff liked to promote LeConte Lodge as the highest inn in eastern America. In fact, it wouldn't have taken much qualification to justify even loftier superlatives.

If you limit the competition to *full-service facilities* (offering meals and beds) that are *off-road* and *on mountaintops,* LeConte is one of the highest in the entire nation—especially since most high-altitude lodges out West are nowhere near the peaks but are nestled in passes or on lower slopes.[1]

On the other hand, you could argue that LeConte Lodge is not technically on the mountaintop, since the cabins are a half-mile stroll from High Top. But none of the other contenders are within a mile of a summit.

The mountaintop elevation, "6,593," has become an icon of Le Conte, emblazoned on lodge souvenirs (including T-shirts and car decals) and even on tattoos.

A sign that declares "Elevation 6593" hangs next to the date over the dining-room door at LeConte Lodge, but the actual elevation for that photo-op is about 6,360 feet. Cabin 10 is the highest, where the top rafters reach almost 6,400 feet.

The 6,400-foot contour on the USGS topographic maps is south of the lodge campus and crosses the Boulevard Trail near the lodge's water tank. The park's back-country camping shelter is inside the 6,440 contour, so the primitive shelter outranks the lodge as the top bunk in eastern America.

Wherever you sleep on Le Conte will be higher than you can do along the Appalachian Trail, where the highest shelters are Roan High Knob (6,260 feet), Tricorner Knob (5,920), Icewater Springs (5,900), and Mount Collins (5,870).

Across the nation, the highest comparable hike-in lodges are the Vogelsang Camp in California's Yosemite National Park at 10,300 feet and the Barr Camp halfway up Colorado's Pikes Peak at 10,200.

Vogelsang is the highest of six lodges along the High Sierra loop, a 51-mile trail in Yosemite National Park. Yosemite is thousands of miles from the Smokies, but the parks are connected through none other than Joseph Le Conte, who became a professor at the University of California after his pioneering scientific research in the Southeast.

---

1. We're disregarding Colorado ski lodges that are on roads and on the power grid, such as Telluride's Tempter House (elevation 12,000) and Vail's Game Creek Chalet (10,500).

The Le Conte backcountry hikers' shelter is run by the national park and is not part of the lodge. It has been open since the 1960s (courtesy Stephen "Sid" Sidbury).

The LeConte Memorial Lodge,[2] the original visitor center in Yosemite National Park, was built by the Sierra Club in 1904 in memory of Joseph Le Conte, who suffered a fatal heart attack at age 78 in 1901 as he was preparing for a Yosemite hike. His son, Joseph Nisbet "Little Joe" LeConte, drew the first maps of the High Sierra, so if you trek to Vogelsang, you are following the footsteps of the Le Contes.

Vogelsang has 12 tent cabins located in a pass through the majestic Cathedral Range, whose peaks tower more than 2,000 feet above the camp. To get reservations, you enter a lottery just like at LeConte. Unlike LeConte, the High Sierra lodges were closed for three years following the pandemic and then by record snowfall. So be prepared for long waiting lists and pent-up demand.

Colorado's Barr Camp is also celebrating a centennial, as it still uses the original log cabin built by Fred Barr in 1924. Like LeConte, Barr is renowned for its pancakes, but it doesn't have llamas to nosh on the leftovers. Barr is resupplied by an ATV driven alongside the adjacent Pikes Peak cog railway; Vogelsang, by pack mules. Barr is open year-round, but bring your sleeping bag because there are no blankets and there is no overnight heat. The 15 bunks go for $40 a night, which includes breakfast.

The national parks feature several high-altitude hotels that are accessible by car.

---

2. Because the Le Contes owned slaves, the lodge was renamed in 2016 as the Yosemite Conservation Heritage Center.

Yellowstone has four inns higher than LeConte, including the classic Old Faithful Inn at 7,360 feet, where a suite with a geyser view costs $1,200 per night.

The Grand Canyon Lodge built in 1937 on the remote North Rim sits at 8,200 feet and is a relative bargain at $160 per night. The South Rim hotels are higher in price and a little lower in elevation. At the bottom of the canyon is the century-old Phantom Ranch (elevation 2,550), where a cabin and meals costs about $300 per couple. The hike (15 miles round-trip) is as formidable as the wait-list.

In Colorado's Mesa Verde Park, you can drive up to the Far View Lodge (built 1974, elevation 8,000) and be a cliff dweller for $200 per night.

Sequoia & Kings Canyon National Park in California has three lodges higher than LeConte, though they are not situated on mountaintops. At the Sequoia High Sierra Camp, you can drive most of the way and glamp at 8,500 feet with hot showers, chef service, and 100-mile views, for $1,200 for a two-night minimum. About 20 miles away, the Bearpaw High Sierra Camp (7,800 feet) has been closed in recent years because of water problems. The Wuksachi Lodge (7,200 feet, accessible by car) opened in 1999 and offers rooms for $260.

California also has the Muir Trail Ranch (elevation 7,600 feet) in a valley near the midpoint of the John Muir Trail. The ranch has eight log cabins and is often booked by groups who pay close to $9,000 per night for 15 people—who enjoy meals, showers, horseback rides, and natural hot springs. If you can afford that, getting there is a breeze, via a boat across Florence Lake and a three-mile amble.

Glacier National Park in Montana has two hike-in chalets that are at almost the same altitude as LeConte. The Sperry Chalet (elevation 6,550) requires a hike of 6.8 miles climbing 3,360 feet—comparable to Le Conte via Trillium Gap. Sperry burned in 2017 but has been rebuilt, and rooms go for $473. Granite Park Chalet is at elevation 6,650, or 535 feet below Swiftcurrent Pass on the Continental Divide. It has 12 bunkrooms and a kitchen, but guests are responsible for their own cooking. Rooms are $315 per couple.

The eastern version of the High Sierra loop is in New Hampshire, where the Appalachian Mountain Club operates a series of "huts" along the Appalachian Trail. The highest is Lakes of the Clouds Hut, built in 1915 at 5,012 feet, above the tree line in the notch between Mount Washington and Mount Monroe. It's open June through September, at $717 per couple. Bring your sleeping bag, because the 96 bunks don't have bed linens.

On the Georgia end of the Appalachian Trail is the Len Foote Hike Inn, which offers bunks, showers, and family-style supper and breakfast, at 3,100 feet. It's a five-mile hike and is usually full, at $200 per couple. Built in 1998, this lodge is not strictly off-road, as it has a driveway for workers and deliveries.[3]

Out West, dozens of mountaintop fire towers can be rented as campsites,[4] including Mestaa'ėhehe Peak[5] in Colorado (11,500 feet) and Spruce Mountain in Wyoming (10,000). You get a bunk, extreme solitude, and in some cases electricity, but meals are on your own.

---

3. Leonard E. Foote (1918–1989) was a Georgia conservationist.
4. The Forest Fire Lookout Association lists tower rentals at firelookout.org/lookout-rentals.html.
5. Mestaa'ėhehe was formerly known as Squaw Peak and was renamed in 2022.

The Hawaiian island of Maui has three hike-in cabins in the crater of the dormant Haleakala Volcano. The highest is the 12-bed Kapalaoa Cabin, 7,250 feet above sea level, which requires a climb comparable to Le Conte's Alum Cave Trail. On the big island of Hawaii, you can drive up to the Volcano House (altitude 3,750), a national park inn on the rim of the active Kilauea crater. The inn includes 33 rooms and several cabins, and if you are lucky enough to get reservations, you'll pay more than $400 per night.

In Alaska, the Sheldon Chalet on Denali sits at 5,800 feet, not quite as high as LeConte and still almost three vertical miles below the summit of North America's tallest peak. Enjoy the three-night minimum for $35,500 per couple, which includes a helicopter ride up to the chalet.

In Canada, Skoki Lodge sits at 7,100 feet on the slopes of Skoki Mountain (8,881). The lodge is a seven-mile hike (climbing 1,500 feet) from Lake Louise in Banff National Park, with five bedrooms and three cabins that go for about $250 per guest. Accommodations are comparable to LeConte. The Skoki lodge, built in 1931, was listed in 1982 as a national historic site in Canada.

The Cloudland Hotel: High and Half-Dry

When Jack Huff was born in 1903, the highest inn in eastern America was the Cloudland Hotel, a three-story, 166-bed facility on Roan Mountain, built in 1885 by John T. Wilder, a Union general in the Civil War who became an industrialist in Tennessee. Wilder advertised "the highest human habitation east of the Rocky Mountains" at 6,394 feet. That elevation was based on a primitive measurement of nearby Roan High Knob, though the ridge where the inn stood crests at 6,200.

The Cloudland took its name from the damp clouds that frothed up as westerly winds swept over the Roans. It was so chilly that Wilder kept fireplaces burning all summer. In the era before air conditioning, tourists eager to escape from summer heat boarded the original Tweetsie Railroad (East Tennessee and Western North Carolina Railroad) to the Roan Mountain station[6] and then rode in horse-drawn carriages 15 bone-jolting miles to the mountaintop. A room and three meals cost $2 per day, $10 per week, or $30 per month. The Cloudland was an elegant destination popular with honeymooners.

The dining room featured a white stripe on the waxed maple floor that marked the state line. It was legal to buy and drink alcohol on the Tennessee side but not in North Carolina, where Mitchell County was and is "dry."[7]

It was said that when the gales thundered, the Cloudland "rocked like a ship at sea," making it a challenge to operate and maintain. Wilder shut it down after he turned 80 in 1910, and within five years the building collapsed. Only a few traces remain, just off the Appalachian Trail.

---

6. The Roan Mountain station was at elevation 2,545. The ET&WNC continued to Boone, and the track crested near Grandfather Mountain at 4,045 feet.

7. As of 2023, North Carolina still had three dry counties: Mitchell, Graham, and Yancey (the home of Mount Mitchell). The town of Spruce Pine in Mitchell County negotiated an exception in 2009 and allows alcohol sales.

Before LeConte Lodge, the Cloudland Hotel (1885–1910) on Roan Mountain reigned as the highest inn in eastern America (courtesy Mitchell County, NC, Historical Society).

The Roan highlands—featuring vast grassy balds and pink rhododendron gardens—were promoted in 1924 as a possible national park, contending with the Smokies and Shenandoah. Botanist Asa Gray[8] described Roan as "the most beautiful mountain east of the Rockies." The Cloudland was long gone before then, and who knows if the park commissioners might have voted differently if they had been feted at the Cloudland bar after roughing it on Le Conte. Sunrise at Cloudland could have been a worthy rival for the show they saw at Myrtle Point.

Harsh weather doomed other mountaintop accommodations across the South. In 1896, the year after George Vanderbilt finished the Biltmore House near Asheville, he built the Buck Spring Lodge for his highfalutin guests on a 5,000-foot shoulder of Mount Pisgah. His engineers used a hydraulic ram to pump water a half mile from Buck Spring to supply the lodge and fill the highest swimming pool in the East.

Vanderbilt, 52, died following an appendectomy in 1914, and his widow Edith sold much of the mountain estate to the federal government to establish the Pisgah National Forest. Yet she kept the lodge and often stayed there until her death in 1958. Buck Spring Lodge fell into disrepair and was dismantled in the early 1960s during

---

8. Gray (1810–1888) also climbed Grandfather Mountain but probably never saw the Smokies. He was a scientific associate of professors John and Joseph Le Conte.

the construction of the Blue Ridge Parkway across Mount Pisgah. Foundations and other relics, including the stone walls of the old pool, can still be seen along the trail from Buck Spring Gap.

Less than a mile from Buck Spring Lodge, the Pisgah National Forest Inn opened in 1918 on a 4,930-foot ledge. Weather-beaten by 1964, it was replaced by the 51-room Pisgah Inn, and the original lodge was used for staff housing until it was torn down in 1990. Newspapers have mistakenly described Pisgah Inn as the highest hotel in eastern America, yet its elevation is a quarter-mile lower than LeConte Lodge. A room at Pisgah is $250 or more, plus meals.

Mount Mitchell has also had some high-altitude accommodations. In 1914, J.W. Dunn opened the Log Cabin Inn on a plateau near the 6,684-foot peak (evidently the site of the summit parking lot, elevation 6,580). Dunn advertised meals and lodging for up to 20 guests, plus wireless communications with Asheville. Governor Locke Craig visited in 1914 as part of his initiative to establish Mount Mitchell State Park, riding up the Perley and Crocket logging railroad to Camp Alice, an old logging camp at 5,800 feet.

Dunn's inn and the railroad were gone by 1921, when the tracks were converted into the Black Mountain Turnpike. Camp Alice became an inn and restaurant for adventurous motorists. Traffic was one way, up in the mornings and down in the afternoons, for $3 per car. On the other side of the mountain, Ewart Wilson operated the "Big Tom Wilson Road," named for his bear-hunting grandfather, which led to the Mt. Mitchell Inn at Stepps Gap (elevation 6,100), now the site of the state park office. Wilson kept a black bear in a pen to attract tourists. The Blue Ridge Parkway accessed Mitchell in 1939.

Mount Mitchell State Park opened a restaurant in 1954 at 6,200 feet, where motorists can dine at an altitude almost as high as the LeConte dining hall. The park once proposed a 50-room hotel (similar to Pisgah Inn) but decided the project was not practical.

There are a couple of well-elevated private inns in North Carolina. The luxurious Swag (up to $1,100 for a two-night minimum) is drivable at 4,920 feet on the Cataloochee Divide, and the Cabins at Sandy Mush Bald ($50 per bunk) is a primitive hike-in lodge at about 4,700 feet, about 30 miles east of LeConte Lodge. The Swag opened to the public in 1982 as a gateway for tourists headed to the Knoxville World's Fair.

Seizing the Higher Ground

In the years before North Carolina and Tennessee teamed up to create the Great Smoky Mountains National Park, the states were at odds over which of them could claim the highest mountain in the eastern United States. Newspapers portrayed the rivalry as a war, and both sides maneuvered and finagled in an attempt to seize the higher ground.

North Carolina made its claim on behalf of Mount Mitchell, which had supplanted New Hampshire's Mount Washington as the highest point in the United

States. Mitchell reigned as America's rooftop until 1845, when Texas[9] became the 28th state. Yet 100 years ago, there were no definitive surveys of the Smokies, so no one knew if Le Conte or other peaks might outrank Mitchell as the highest in the East.

Tennesseans vouched for Mount Le Conte, oblivious to the fact that Clingmans Dome (now known as Kuwohi) stood a little taller.[10] After an 1858 survey, John LeConte reported that "Smoky Mountain" (presumably Clingmans Dome) topped out at 6,737 feet, which outranked New Hampshire's Mount Washington as the highest peak east of the Mississippi.[11]

Paul Fink of Jonesborough, Tennessee, led a 1921 survey on behalf of the Appalachian Mountain Club[12] of Boston, to investigate whether Le Conte might be the highest mountain in the eastern United States. The club president, Harlan Kelsey, grew up in the North Carolina mountains and climbed Le Conte in 1924 with the national park commission.

Fink wrote in the club journal, *Appalachia*:

> For several years, there has been a controversy as to which of the Southern Mountains is the highest, many claiming that Le Conte, the monarch of the Smokies, possesses greater altitude than Mitchell, in the Black Mountains. The U.S. Geological Survey was not able to settle the dispute, for their maps of the region surrounding Le Conte were merely reconnaissance maps and no precise instrumental survey had been done in this area.

Fink climbed Le Conte on his 29th birthday in June 1921 and used barometers to measure the mountain. His readings were inconclusive, but Fink felt confident that Le Conte reached at least 6,675 feet, which would rank next to Mitchell (then listed at 6,711) and its subpeak, Mount Craig (6,647). Fink expressed confidence that future federal surveys of Le Conte "may prove higher than Mount Mitchell."[13]

Mount Mitchell had become the standard despite its own uncertain measurements, as Professor Elisha Mitchell and his former student Thomas Clingman disputed each other's findings. Mitchell measured the peak (originally known as Black Dome) at 6,476 feet in 1835 and 6,708 feet in 1844. Clingman measured 6,941 in 1855.

At age 63, Mitchell returned to the Black Mountains in 1857 to try to verify his claim, but on his hike down, he slipped over a waterfall and fell to his death. He was vindicated in 1858 when Arnold Guyot's survey registered 6,709, almost exactly what Mitchell found in 1844.

In 1859, J.C. Turner, the chief engineer for the Western North Carolina Railroad,

---

9. The original 1845 map of Texas included a swath of Colorado that encompassed several 14,000-foot peaks. So did the Louisiana Purchase in 1803, if you want to count that unexplored territory as an extension of the states. When California became the 31st state in 1850, it brought in a new national highpoint, Mount Whitney, though its height was not documented until 1928. Some early 20th century atlases showed Washington's Mount Rainier as the nation's highest peak. Rainier, like Le Conte, has great prominence, rising 11,000 feet above its base.

10. Smoky Dome became known as Clingmans Dome after General Thomas Clingman measured it at 6,660 feet using a single barometer, according to Charles M. Yeates of Sweetwater, Tennessee, who led an 1882 survey. T.H. Alexander, "I Reckon So," *The Tennessean* (Nashville), Sept. 26, 1931.

11. "Black versus White," *Bangor Daily Whig & Courier*, Oct. 19, 1859.

12. The Appalachian Mountain Club proposed a southern affiliate in Asheville, which was organized as the Carolina Mountain Club and celebrated its centennial July 23, 2023.

13. Paul Fink, "A Barometric Survey to Determine the Height of Mount Le Conte," *Appalachia*, Volume XV, December 1922.

ran a spirit-level survey (considered more precise than barometers) and measured Mount Mitchell at 6,711. That became the accepted height for Mitchell until 1930, when the U.S. Geological Survey declared it to be 6,684.

The Smokies were unmeasured until the 1850s. In 1859, Arnold Guyot measured the Central Peak of Bullhead, which he labeled "Mt. LeCompte," as 6,612—within 20 feet of the modern measurement. Guyot usually spent more than 24 hours on a summit to take a series of measurements to minimize barometric fluctuations caused by changing weather.

In 1922, Knoxville sponsored another survey on behalf of Mount Le Conte. Confident that tourists would flock to see the highest mountain in the East, the city hired engineer Clem L. Garner from the U.S. Coast and Geodetic Survey to settle the question.

Triangulating from the bell tower at Ayres Hall at the University of Tennessee in Knoxville, Garner and his team measured Le Conte at 6,580 feet. Since they were sighting with sun-lit mirrors called heliographs, it's likely that they measured Cliff Top, which offers a clear line of sight toward Knoxville, rather than tree-shrouded High Top, which is about 40 feet higher.

The brightness of the heliograph dazzled Wiley Oakley, who was guiding the survey party. "It looked like Knoxville was on fire with a bright mirror," he said.

On June 22, 1922, the *Knoxville News-Sentinel* declared victory with this headline: "Finds Mt. LeConte Highest Peak." The story lacked documentation or quotes and seems to have been based on rumors and wishful thinking.

A week later, on June 29, 1922, the *Asheville Citizen-Times* dismissed the Tennessee claims in a story headlined "Mount Mitchell Remains King of Eastern Peaks." The story said:

> A stir of no small consequence has been created in Knoxville and in Washington over the height of Mount Mitchell compared with the height of Mount LeConte in Tennessee, not far from Knoxville. Believing that LeConte is higher than Mount Mitchell, long reputed to be the loftiest mountain east of the Rockies[14] and in eastern America, citizens of Knoxville asked for a survey by official engineers.
>
> Authentic advice has been received in Asheville that from the survey it was found that Mount LeConte is not the highest mountain in East Tennessee, but that Mount Guyot on the Tennessee and North Carolina line is 117 feet higher than the former. A complete report of the survey is expected to be filed in Washington soon, it is understood that engineers have found that Mount Mitchell is still the highest point in the eastern half of the United States.[15]

David Chapman, a leading booster for Le Conte and the Smokies, took up the cause for Mount Guyot after a 1929 barometric reading there topped 7,000 feet.[16]

> If the recent survey finally determines that Mount Guyot is 297 feet higher than Mount Mitchell, people would have to visit the national park to make good their boast that once they "stood higher than anyone else in the eastern states of the union," or that "they were looking down on everybody."

However, Mount LeConte is far more impressive than Mount Guyot and will continue, of

---

14. "East of the Rockies" is a problematic description, because there are higher mountains in Texas and South Dakota that are east of the main Rockies range.
15. "Mount Mitchell Remains King of Eastern Peaks," *Asheville Citizen-Times*, June 29, 1922.
16. "Approval Sought of Mount Guyot as Highest Peak," *Knoxville Journal*, July 25, 1929.

course, to be one of the principal attractions of the park area. Mount Guyot is just one of several high peaks in a massive range. On its top you do not have the feeling of awe and solemnity that is experienced on LeConte because of its sheer drop of almost a mile below you.

A 1930s-era topographic map indicates that there was a U.S. Geological Survey surveyor's benchmark, engraved "Mount Le Conte." It is no longer evident on the mountain and has been removed from the USGS database, although replica benchmarks are sold as souvenirs.

The *Raleigh News and Observer*'s Washington reporter wrote in 1930:

> There have long been those who believed that one or more of the Smoky Mountain peaks towered above Mitchell, and fresh fuel was added to the flame of controversy when altitude tests with an aneroid barometer showed Mt. Guyot at 7,025—with Mitchell's 6,711.
>
> At last the U.S. Geological Survey, doubly interested in the controversy due to the establishment of the Great Smoky Mountains National Park, took official cognizance of it and started the labors which today ended in definitively settling the argument.[17]

The 1930 survey listed Mount Mitchell at 6,682 feet, Clingmans Dome at 6,643, Mount Guyot at 6,620, and Le Conte at 6,593. The official figures were later revised to 6,684 for Mitchell and 6,621 for Guyot.

"There is not the slightest doubt that Mitchell is the highest peak in eastern America," said George Otis Smith, the director of the U.S. Geological Service, who had climbed Le Conte with the 1924 park commission. "In the meantime, the remains of Dr. Elisha Mitchell, who lost his life while measuring the peak that is named for him, can continue to rest in peace upon its top. It is still the highest peak in eastern America, as he said it was."[18]

The neighboring states came to terms by 1929, when newspapers from Asheville and Knoxville sent delegations to meet at Clingmans Dome and exchange letters from the governors. Tennessee's Henry Horton wrote to North Carolina's Max Gardner:

> Accept from myself and the people of Tennessee cordial greetings and good wishes to you and your party on the exploring expedition in the Great Smoky Mountains and for an exchange of opinions and greetings between the people of the two states.
>
> Nothing is dearer to the heart of the people of Tennessee than the preservation of this great National Park in all of its unrivaled beauty, to the honor of both states and the Nation and as an inspiration for coming generations.
>
> Tennessee is working steadily ahead to carry out her pledges made both to the sister State of North Carolina and to the Federal Government of the United States, and we pledge to you and the people of North Carolina our united and enthusiastic efforts to the final consummation of this great Park.[19]

Raising the Mountaintop?

Tennesseans weren't content to let federal surveyors have the last word. In 1948, the Gatlinburg American Legion Post proposed bringing stones from around the

---

17. "Mount Mitchell Retains Laurels," *Raleigh News and Observer*, Jan. 22, 1930.
18. "Says Mitchell Is Highest Peak," *Raleigh News and Observer*, July 6, 1929.
19. Lee Davis, "Fellowship Is Pledged by States Above Clouds," *Knoxville News-Sentinel*, June 10, 1929. Walter S. Adams, "Times Explorers Tell Experiences in Great Smokies," *Asheville Times*, July 5, 1929.

world to build a new summit on Clingmans Dome to make it the highest peak east of the Rockies.[20] Instead, the national park built a 45-foot concrete tower on the dome in 1959, which reaches the same natural height as Mount Mitchell, 6,684 feet.[21] Tourists can stand a little higher atop Mitchell, where North Carolina built an eight-foot platform in 2009 to replace a weathered 30-foot concrete tower.

In 1964, Ralph Davis of Delray Beach, Florida, pointed out that a seven-foot stack of rocks would elevate Le Conte to a tidy 6,600 feet—exactly 1.25 miles above sea level. Lodge guests and hikers started stacking rocks on High Top as a sort of slate offering to exalt the mountain.

Adherents of leave-no-trace hiking derisively knock down such rock cairns, but occasionally the stack on Le Conte reaches 6,600 feet above sea level. The lodge blog encourages guests: "Be sure to add a rock to our cairn so we can catch Clingmans Dome." It's a far-fetched dream, but if the pile ever rises 50 feet, Le Conte would stand eye to eye with its neighbor.

When David Witherspoon was on the crew in the 1970s, he climbed the fir trees on High Top and said, "They lift you higher than Clingmans Dome." Of course, the dome has trees, too.

Surveyors ignore trees and manmade structures when measuring mountains, so Le Conte is not officially growing. If Le Conte's official elevation changes, it will be because of more precise surveying. Since 2011, the national park has been working on a satellite survey, and in one case the surveyors added five feet to the elevation of West Point, on the flanks of Le Conte. As of 2023, High Top had not been re-measured.

In 1928, Tennessee state senator A.J. Graves proposed a 100-foot obelisk on Le Conte in memory of Governor Austin Peay,[22] who was a strong advocate for the national park. Editors of the *Knoxville News-Sentinel* rejected the idea as an intrusion upon the wilderness—to say nothing of the impossibility of construction:

> Senator Graves' desire to honor Governor Peay is laudable but he has not studied the national park idea very closely or he would not make such a suggestion. A national park is no place for shafts, statues, or even bronze tablets. It is itself a monument—a monument to the primeval nature which would be gone from the earth but for these national parks.
>
> There is no place in a national park for any man-made structures except the shelters which are necessary for the comfort of the people who go to enjoy the beauties of nature there.
>
> Mt. LeConte especially shows nature in one of her grandest moods. It should be reserved as a "wilderness area" and forever be unmarred by any hotel or road. It should remain as a challenge to the young and strong to try their youth and strength in the climb. When hundreds now climb it, thousands will come from all over the world to climb it after the area has been made into a national park. These nature lovers want to find LeConte just as it was before the white man came to America. We must not disappoint them.[23]

---

20. "Clingmans Dome May Get 'False' Summit," *Kingsport News*, July 26, 1948. The proposal may have been inspired by the Masons Marker at Polls Gap (25 miles southeast of LeConte), built in 1938 with stones from various states and 41 countries.

21. The original timber tower built in 1938 on Clingmans Dome was 46 feet high, and as Carlos Campbell pointed out, "makes the highest point in the park 6,688." "LeConte and Other Monarchs Stand Out Above Clouds Like Islands in the Sea; New Trail to Tower from End of Skyway," *Knoxville News-Sentinel*, March 14, 1938.

22. There were subsequent proposals to rename Blanket Mountain (near Elkmont) after Governor Peay.

23. "Not on LeConte," *Knoxville News-Sentinel* editorial, Oct. 24, 1928.

10. How Does LeConte Measure Up?

For 60 years, hikers have piled stones on High Top to elevate the peak to 1.25 miles above sea level (Up N' Adam Adventures).

Graves' proposal was made during a political campaign where he said: "Austin Peay did more for East Tennessee than any governor." Graves (1880–1951) was among 81 legislators who visited the Smokies in 1928 as they considered a $2.5 million appropriation to purchase park land.

The Vertical Mile

Even if Le Conte is not the highest, some describe it as the tallest mountain in the east, because the summit stands more than a vertical mile above its base in downtown Gatlinburg. In fact, Le Conte is the one place in the Southeast where it is practical for a day hiker to climb a vertical mile.

Starting at elevation 1,313 near Ripley's Aquarium, it's a climb of 5,280 feet to High Top. Customarily, hikers start and finish the vertical mile by dipping a toe into the Little Pigeon River. The round-trip hike is a little over 20 miles. To make a similar ascent on Mount Mitchell would require 25 miles one way from the town of Old Fort, North Carolina.

Vertical milers usually follow the road up to Cherokee Orchard and then hike up via the Rainbow Falls or Bullhead trails. Luke Bollschweiler ran Bullhead in 2021 when he set the course record, 3:11:51 on a 21-mile round trip.

Dozens have conquered the vertical mile. On April 18, 1930, Nick Robinson of Knoxville started at the Andrew Johnson Hotel on Gay Street in Knoxville and walked 51 miles to LeConte Lodge. That's a gain of more than 5,400 feet. He averaged three miles per hour along the roads and finished strong, zipping up the old Rainbow Falls path (4.1 miles) in 1:48. The *Knoxville News-Sentinel* said Robinson, 32, "claims to be Knoxville's champion hiker and challenges any doubter to equal his record."[24]

On Armistice Day 1922, Frank Machamer, Jr., signed a logbook at the summit with this comment: "Made it in 3½ hours from Gatlinburg. It's hell, but it's great."[25]

Larry Russell did the vertical mile three times in 2022, when he turned 79. Completers are listed at lecontest.com/vertical-mile.

Getting Away from It All?

If trails had turnstiles, Le Conte would be one of the busiest mountains in America. Over the course of a season, the lodge attracts close to 30,000 visitors—an average of 10,600 overnight guests since 1989, plus day hikers by the hundreds. That's just counting the summit traffic—not including multitudes who turn back at the caves or the waterfalls.

New Hampshire's Mount Washington counts 250,000 visitors annually via road, cog railway, or hiking trails. New Mexico's 10,679-foot Sandia Crest is accessible via a road (built in 1927) and a tramway (1966) that conveys 200,000 passengers per year.

In California, foot traffic is restricted on Mount Whitney and Half Dome. Whitney issues 30,000 permits annually, with about 10,000 hikers successfully attaining the highest point in the lower 48 states. Yosemite National Park limits Half Dome climbers to 350 per day.

---

24. "Claims Hiking Crown," *Knoxville News-Sentinel*, April 22, 1930.
25. J. Frank Machamer, Jr. (1904–1941) was training British aviators in Albany, Georgia, when he died in a crash on October 30, 1941. It's not clear where he started his hike. If he began at the Mountain View Hotel, that would be slightly less than a vertical mile.

Washington's Mount Rainier sees about 10,000 climbers annually, while about 1,200 try Alaska's Denali.

Colorado's Pikes Peak may have the spacious skies that inspired "America the Beautiful," but the 14,115-foot summit tends to get crowded, especially since a $65 million visitors center opened in 2021. More than 500,000 visitors drove up in 2021, plus about 300,000 passengers on the renovated Broadmoor Manitou & Pikes Peak Cog Railway and 25,000 hikers on the 13-mile Barr Trail—comparable to the annual total of day-hikers on Le Conte's six trails.

Japan's Mount Fuji is probably the most frequently climbed mountain in the world, with about 160,000 summiteers every summer, about five times busier than Le Conte. Four trails lead to the summit of Fuji, and there are several stations where hikers can nap until the 1 a.m. wake-up call to make it to the 12,388-foot summit by sunrise.

Snowdon, the highest summit in England and Wales, averages more than 2,000 visitors daily. Snowdon has a cog railway plus six trails, like Le Conte. In the summer, there is often a 45-minute queue at the trailheads.

11

The GOATs of Le Conte

In the 1970s, a retired nurse and an Episcopal pastor made headlines in their rivalry to see who could climb Mount Le Conte the most.

Gracie McNicol (1891–1991) made 244 ascents, 155 on foot plus 89 on horseback after she suffered a stroke, finishing on her 92nd birthday in 1983. The **Rev. Rufus Morgan** (1885–1983) made his 174th climb on his 93rd birthday in 1978. He kidded her that he had the most hikes, after subtracting her saddle trips.

Paul Dinwiddie surpassed them in 1986, when he wrote in his logbook, "As far as I know, I am the first park visitor to hike Mt. LeConte 300 times. Nearest to me is **Margaret Stevenson** with 249 trips." Dinwiddie retired with 750 and Stevenson with 718.

Their records would be trampled by the next generation: **Ron Valentine** with about 3,000 and **Ed Wright** 1,310.

Wright (1925–2009), a mechanical engineer at the Oak Ridge National Laboratory, developed mtleconte.com, where he posted his trip reports and the hiking totals of his peers. He published his journals in a book, *More Than 1,001 Hikes to Mount LeConte*. Yet he never knew for sure how he measured up against Valentine, whom he called "a mountain goat"—years before "GOAT" came to mean "Greatest of All Time."

Their paths crossed frequently, including Wright's final summit hike in October 2008. "I asked him about his total hikes," Wright wrote. "My hearing is marginal at best, but I think that he said that he had made 798 hikes to LeConte since January 1, 2000. I think he said that he had about 3,000 hikes before that. I asked him when he was going to come clean and tell the world of his accomplishments. He replied that he would give the number after I died. I told him that I was not half dead yet." Wright died in 2009, and Valentine continued summiting until 2015.

Valentine wasn't just being coy. He couldn't be certain about his total, having lost decades of records in a 1999 fire. His post-fire journals document 1,183 ascents, and it's reasonable to estimate that he made at least 3,000 climbs.

Valentine and Wright specialized in day hikes up the Alum Cave Bluff Trail. In fact, Wright never spent the night at the lodge! His daughter said that was partly because he was frugal, but mostly because he preferred to sleep in his own bed.[1] When Valentine stayed overnight, it was usually as a guest of his hiking partner, Ray Ogle, whose brother Hugh Ogle was co-owner of the lodge in the 1970s.

---

1. Wright's book, *More Than 1,001 Climbs to Mt. LeConte*, is available at mtleconte.com.

11. The GOATs of Le Conte

In 1991, as Wright turned 66, he "decided to set a mark for hiking Mount Le Conte in one calendar year, which would only be broken by someone with lots of determination"—and he climbed the mountain 230 times. That's more than double Valentine's best year, 113 in one of his lost years in the 1990s.

To make the most of the long drive from Oak Ridge into the Smokies, Wright made two laps in a day 125 times. "Ed was tough as nails," Valentine said.

Born the same year Paul Adams welcomed the first paying guests on Mount Le Conte, Wright climbed Le Conte in 160 consecutive months and kept that streak alive even in 1999 when he was diagnosed with congestive heart failure. He hiked up on April Fool's Day, then went into the hospital to have five bypasses and a mitral valve replacement, and he was back on the summit in six weeks.

Valentine usually hiked on Wednesdays, Saturdays, and holidays, starting at dawn and finishing in four hours so he could be in his Cosby real-estate office in the afternoon. He carefully tracked his mileage in his journal, which totals 27,000 trail miles hiked since 2000—enough to circle the globe!

Valentine and Wright are among six men who climbed Le Conte more than a thousand times. Lecontest.com lists 22 women and 97 men with at least 100 summits at the end of the 2024 season. The 20th-century forerunners, McNicol and Morgan, have been squeezed out of the Top 20 among Le Conte's most prolific climbers.

Ed Wright was the first hiker to document more than 1,000 Le Conte climbs. He retired in 2008 with 1,310 (courtesy Ron Valentine).

Ron Valentine is Le Conte's all-time leader with an estimated 3,000 climbs (courtesy Ron Valentine).

Jack Huff (1903–1985) kept count of his trips when he built the lodge, and a 1937 story in the *Knoxville News-Sentinel* credited him with 1,043 climbs. By the time journalist Ernie Pyle visited the lodge in 1940, Huff said he had lost count. Assuming that Huff maintained the same pace through 1949 and continued occasional trips in the 1950s (while he operated the family hotel in Gatlinburg and his wife managed the lodge), it's safe to estimate that he climbed the mountain close to 2,500 times.

Tim Line, who had the longest tenure of any lodge manager when he retired in 2018, estimates he made 1,500 climbs, averaging a trip per week for 41 years.

Alan Householder, who worked 20 years as llama wrangler and also worked stints on the crew, estimated more than 1,200 trips. He averaged 40 miles per week in his heyday.

Graham "Cracker" Dinwiddie Cooper (1929–2013), a farmer from Greenback, Tennessee, told Wright in 1994 that he had about 1,000 climbs but he did not keep an exact count. He continued hiking frequently through 2002.

Dave Scanlon (1936–2014) made weekly climbs and was approaching a thousand before cancer stopped him at age 78, after 982 climbs. Dave's first ascent in 1966 coincided with the last climb by Harvey Broome, the Knoxville lawyer who was a co-founder of the Wilderness Society and helped write the 1964 Wilderness Act.

Paul Dinwiddie's total of 750 ascents ranks third in his family, compared to his son **David Dinwiddie** with about 800 and his cousin Cracker Cooper with more than 1,000. David worked several seasons on the lodge crew. David and his brother Wally were with Paul when he died at age 80 in 1995. As their dad exhaled his last breath, they inhaled. The next day, they climbed Le Conte. "We carried his soul back to the mountain," David said.[2]

Stevenson was 48 when she first climbed Le Conte, and she counted 718 ascents at age 84 when she retired from the mountain because of fading eyesight. The year she turned 79, she made 78 climbs. She was the first female member of the 900 Club, hiking every mile of trails in the park, a feat since duplicated by several members of her Wednesday Hikers group. The thrifty daughter of missionaries who served in China, Margaret hiked in sneakers until friends bought her a pair of hiking boots, which were bronzed and are displayed at the lodge.

Margaret Stevenson made her 718th and final Le Conte hike in 1997 (courtesy Julie Dodd).

Stan Wullschleger, also from Oak Ridge, had 570 climbs as of 2018 and set the speed record with a 46-minute ascent of Alum Cave Bluff Trail. His horizons are not limited to the Smokies, as he has also climbed all 57 of the 14,000-foot peaks in Colorado.

Al Bedinger joined the lodge crew in the 1970s and became the de facto historian of the lodge. He counted 532 hikes as of 2024, and his fellow crewman **Richard Ketelle** would have a comparable total if he had kept count.

Henry Neel, a veteran of the Iraq war who worked 25 seasons at the lodge, estimates close to 600 ascents.

Paul Adams (1901–1985), the co-founder of the lodge, hiked up in 1975 to celebrate the 50th anniversary of the lodge and closed his era with 523 ascents. Others who estimated 500 climbs were **Herrick Brown**, the lodge manager between the Huff eras, and **Wiley Oakley**, the legendary "Roamin' Man of the Smokies."

Registering 500 in recent years have been **Larry Russell**, a retired police officer living in Sevierville, **Ed Jones**, a physician for the Veterans Administration in

---

2. Jim Bulloch, "Two Toes, Part of Hiker's Right Foot Amputated," *Knoxville News-Sentinel*, Jan. 22, 2005.

The leading active hikers on Mount Le Conte in 2024 were Ed Jones (left) and Larry Russell, who both have registered more than 500 climbs (photograph by Tom Layton).

Knoxville, and **John Northrup**, manager of LeConte Lodge. That's 17 hikers who have at least 500 trips—the threshold for the International Peak-Baggers Hall of Fame (sites.google.com/view/baggerswithoutborders/home).

Mount Rush More

Has any other mountain been climbed so frequently by so many? Mountain-climbing records are inherently hard to document, but websites devoted to "peakbaggers"[3] list few hikers as relentless as the pilgrims of Le Conte.

The de facto national champions are from Phoenix, Arizona. A Holocaust survivor named Sam Wagman claimed 34,000 ascents of 4,912-foot Camelback Mountain—three times a day,[4] six days a week, from 1975 through 2012, when he turned 75. Also on Camelback Sandy Kloch counted 10,000 ascents. On nearby Piestewa Peak, Nick Palmares had 6,000.

There are also at least three men with more than a thousand climbs of Grand Monadnock, a 3,166-foot hikers' mecca in New Hampshire, where Henry David Thoreau once enjoyed the panoramic view of Boston, 60 miles southeast. The rocky trail has been trod 7,600 times by Larry Davis, a pony-tailed Florida native who climbed Grand Monadnock on 2,850 consecutive days.[5] That's nearly eight years without missing a day.

Anyone who has hiked to Le Conte Lodge (10.4 miles roundtrip via Alum Cave, gaining 2,763 feet) might scoff at Camelback (3.8 miles, 1,280 feet) or Monadnock (4.4, 1,715).

In the same way, Colorado hikers might look down on Le Conte. Most of the state's famed "14ers"[6] require climbs more than 3,000 feet. Pikes Peak via the Barr Trail gains 7,500 feet with the round-trip mileage of a marathon. The lifetime record on Pikes Peak is 985 ascents by Edwin Paget, an eccentric professor who liked to be called "History's Most Significant Man."[7]

Out West, it's not uncommon to find hikers who have repeated the same hike hundreds of times. At the end of 2023, John Kirk had 1,040 trips up Stafford Hogback, and his wife Alyson had 1,039 on Green Mountain.[8]

Mount Fuji in Japan requires a climb of at least 5,000 feet over four miles—substantially steeper than any trail on Le Conte. A Japanese proverb says, "A wise man will climb Mount Fuji once; a fool will climb Fuji twice." Jitsukawa Yoshinobu, born during World War II, has been Fuji's fool more than 2,000 times, including an annual record of 248 trips—18 more than Wright's best year on Le Conte.

---

3. Peakbagging has become something of a competitive sport, as hikers vie online to complete lists on Peakbagger.com, ListsofJohn.com, SummitPost.org, and Peakery.com. Baggers Without Borders (sites.google.com/view/baggerswithoutborders) includes a Hall of Fame for those who have climbed the same mountain at least 500 times.

4. Three ascents in a day is not uncommon on Le Conte. Dozens have done it in the course of completing the Tour de Le Conte. Ed Wright made three trips in a day three times and two trips 125 times. The single-day record on Le Conte is seven ascents by John Northrup in 2012.

5. The records for consecutive days climbing Le Conte are 15 by Tillroe Smith of Moody, Alabama, in 2002 and 11 by Paul Dinwiddie in 1991.

6. https://www.14ers.com/php14ers/14ers.php.

7. Edwin Paget (1903–89), a speech professor at North Carolina State University, believed serious runners could reach their physical peak at age 140. He spent his summers in Colorado climbing Pikes Peak, and in 1988 he announced plans to make his 1,000th ascent on his 100th birthday, accompanied by a brass band. Yet his heart failed him, and his final trip was #985 at age 85, unless you count the day friends spread his ashes on Pikes Peak. As for his audacious title, "Most Significant Man" was the headline on his obituary, and he counted 78 authorities who vouched for his claim. "I have no rivals," he said. "Nobody else has effrontery enough to accept a title like that." *Raleigh News & Observer*, July 11, 1989.

8. https://listsofjohn.com/PeakStats/Content/mrepeat.php.

For Old Times' Sake

No one knows who the first person was to climb Mount Le Conte. We can be reasonably certain it was neither of the namesake brothers. Based on their journals, we have no reason to believe John Le Conte (1818–1891) or Joseph Le Conte[9] (1823–1901) ever conquered the mountain, though Joseph may have visited Alum Cave during the Civil War. Surveyor Samuel Botsford Buckley would have been among the first to seek out the actual summit (now known as High Top), measuring it at 6,613 feet in the 1850s and eventually bestowing the name Le Conte.

In the 1940s, Philip Huff (son of Jack and Pauline Huff) found a piece of slate near Basin Spring that was carved with the date July 27, 1880. Known as the Walker Stone, it includes the names of John Walker, T.F. Walker, and L.L. Houser and an etched scene of a hunter shooting a deer. Assuming the date is authentic, it documents one of the earliest ascents.

The "Walker Stone" documents an 1880 climb by the father of the famous "Walker Sisters" (courtesy LeConte Lodge).

John N. Walker (1841–1921) was a former Union artilleryman who hunted in the Smokies. Thomas Walker (1861–1942) was his brother and was credited with carving the deer-hunting scene.[10] John Walker had 11 children, including the famous Walker sisters, who were among the last residents inside the national park. The last of them, Louisa, died in 1964. The Walker Sisters' cabin is preserved in the Little Greenbrier Cove section, more than 20 miles from Le Conte. The Walker Stone was displayed for decades at the lodge, but since 1990 it has been in the archives at the University of Tennessee.

The *Knoxville News-Sentinel* reported five climbers in 1912 (including professor S.H. Essary on back-to-back days) and put out a call for anyone who might have preceded them: "If there is anyone now living in Knoxville who climbed Le Conte prior to August, 1912, the News-Sentinel would like to learn who it is." Evidently, no one came forward.

The tradition of a summit logbook is even older than the lodge. In 1922, Charles

---

9. Even if he never climbed his namesake mountain, Joseph Le Conte was an accomplished mountaineer who climbed Mount Mitchell (then known as Black Dome) in 1858 and explored the High Sierra of Yosemite, where he died on a hiking trip at age 78.

10. Carson Brewer, "Father Carved Walker Stone," *Knoxville News-Sentinel*, Oct. 28, 1962.

Baum placed a journal in a copper canister that he hung on a tree at the summit. He wrote on the first page: "This book was placed on top of Le Conte Mountain for records on June 6, 1922, by C.L. Baum, at that time said to be the oldest man to climb to the top, age 61." Baum was a florist in Knoxville who had a nursery in Cherokee Orchard.

Knoxville columnist Bert Vincent was shown Baum's journal in 1951, and he wrote about some of the early climbers:

> Climbing Mount Le Conte today is not so much to rave about, what with the way the Park Service has trails built. You can ride a horse right up there, even, in case you don't want to hike it. You can sleep in warm hotel beds, too, and eat as fine a meal as down in Gatlinburg.
>
> But 25 and 30 years ago, climbing this 6,593-feet high mountain in the Great Smokies was something to talk about for all the next week, and often for months!
>
> It was good enough to put in the paper. Even when I came to the *News-Sentinel* 23 years ago, these hardy souls would start calling the paper Monday morning, or dropping by in person to tell about climbing Mt. Le Conte the Sunday before, and who they saw up there, and what happened to them.[11]

Hundreds signed Baum's book. "As you would expect, different people had different reactions," Vincent wrote. "Some turned poetic, some philosophical, some recorded matter-of-fact data on the weather, some bragged a little about climbing, and some, wet and cold, wrote down their gripes. Hundreds merely signed their names."

Bill Dance (perhaps the grandfather of the famous Tennessee fisherman) left this message: "A man's a man when he tops Mt. Le Conte."

Baum's claim as the eldest hiker[12] didn't last long. Willis Davis was 64 in 1924 when he climbed Le Conte with the national park commission. So was white-bearded A.R. Brown when he made the climb at Easter 1927 along with three other state legislators who were preparing to vote on an appropriation for the national park.[13] That was before the lodge had a dining room, so their Easter dinner was a can of pork and beans.

In 1925, Dutch Roth photographed 76-year-old "Uncle" Ike Carter at Paul Adams' camp. Carter told Roth he previously made the climb as a boy, before the Civil War (photograph on page 25).

In 1927 Knoxville machinist Samuel Simcox raised the seniority bar to 80. According to the *Knoxville News-Sentinel*: "Mr. Simcox loves to walk, and all last summer he heard the young men at the plant talk about the mountains and climbing LeConte. Just before the summer ended, about the middle of September, he decided to go to Gatlinburg and see what it was all about. While there he climbed LeConte and spent the night. His guide, W.R. Ramsey, told him he was the oldest man ever to scale the mountain."[14]

---

11. "Strolling with Bert Vincent," *Knoxville News-Sentinel*, Jan. 21, 1951.
12. According to the dates on his gravestone, Baum was 59 in 1922, so it may have been 1924 when he placed the logbook.
13. Eighty-one legislators toured the Smokies but only four of them dared to climb Le Conte. Charles Moss, "Legislators Back from Trip," *Nashville Banner*, April 18, 1927.
14. Catherine Hooper, "Sam Simcox, at 80 Climbs LeConte, Works Regularly," *Knoxville News-Sentinel*, Jan. 9, 1927.

Simcox emigrated from England as a boy and went to work on the railroad rather than fight in the Civil War. He became a master mechanic for the East Tennessee and Western Carolina Railroad, nicknamed "Tweetsie." At 80 he was still working daily at the Fulton Sylphon plant in Knoxville. Simcox's record stood until 1966, when the Rev. Rufus Morgan made his 81st climb on his 81st birthday.

Who were the first women to climb Le Conte? Knoxville friends Maisy Pomeroy Graves and Mollie Kimball climbed the Bear Pen Hollow Trail with two guides in 1916. "Mountaineers living near their camp told them they were the first women ever to attempt the arduous climb," according to the *Knoxville News-Sentinel*. The story later makes the distinction of "white women," evidently allowing for the possibility that Cherokees might have preceded them.[15] To celebrate the 2016 centennial of that hike, Maisy's granddaughters Mary Pom Claiborne and Olwen Claiborne repeated the feat along with Jack Huff's granddaughter, Lorie Huff Matthews.

The Fountain of Youth

Is there something medicinal or magical about the waters of Basin Spring? Many who have sipped Le Conte's cold elixir are remarkably long-lived. At least six 90-year-olds have made it up to the lodge. Lecontest.com/lecontest-records tracks octogenarians who have made the climb (22 men and 12 women through 2024).

The oldest climber was Rufus Morgan, an Episcopal pastor known as "Moses of the Mountains," who made his 174th climb on his 93rd birthday in 1978. He was mostly blind but had memorized the trails like the Scripture he recited on each visit to Cliff Top. He made his final hike up Trillium Gap with his hand on the shoulder of a guide and a flower pinned to his lapel. Morgan made 100 ascents after he turned 80 and 22 after he turned 89, and he was 97 when he died in 1993. One hiker who met him on his final Le Conte hike described him as "aged but not old." At 89, he performed a sunset wedding[16] at Cliff Top.

Gracie McNicol celebrated 30 birthdays at the lodge, and at 97 she had a sprightly notion to saddle up and return to the lodge, but she couldn't get her doctor's permission. In her biography, *Gracie and the Mountain*, friend Anita Crabtree said Gracie "had grown young hiking the mountain." She told reporter Bill Hart: "Keep walking and you'll stay young."[17] She also owed her longevity to good genes, as she had a 104-year-old brother and a 100-year-old sister.

Dr. Jesse "Kip" Miller was 90 and his wife Jean Ann was 87 when they made their 255th ascent in 2022. Despite his age, he climbed the Alum Cave Trail in less than three hours. Miller made his 100th ascent in 2000, just 24 days after heart surgery.

George Fritz, Jr., was 90 and his wife Carol was 85 when they made it to the

---

15. William T. Finley, "First Women to Conquer Mount Le Conte Spent Night in Driving Rain Under a Ledge," *Knoxville News-Sentinel*, April 15, 1928.
16. The wedding was August 26, 1974, between two medical students from Pennsylvania, Patricia O'Meara and Jack Martin Thome. The Rev. Morgan's niece said that day, "He wants to die up here." Witherspoon, *Song of the Winter Wren*, p. 47. Morgan (1885–1983) rarely made reservations to stay at the lodge, but optimistically booked a night for his 94th birthday. However, his health did not permit any more hikes.
17. William A. Hart, *3000 Miles in the Great Smokies* (Charleston, SC: The History Press, 2009).

11. The GOATs of Le Conte

The Rev. Rufus Morgan was portrayed as "Modern Moses" by watercolor artist Marjarie Ostborg (1923–2008). Morgan (1885–1983) climbed Le Conte on his 93rd birthday in 1978 and was inducted into the Appalachian Trail Hall of Fame in 2014. Morgan and Ostborg were both descendants of Jesse Siler, a 19th-century settler who was the namesake of Silers Bald (courtesy of Albert Rufus Morgan III).

lodge in 2022. They are members of the Nantahala Hiking Club, which was founded by the Reverend Morgan.

Lenore "Gundy" Costello, from Florida, climbed Le Conte to celebrate her 90th birthday in 2006 and turned 108 in 2024.

Ed Iler from Greenville, South Carolina, made 92 climbs, starting in 1945, and he was 103 when he died in 2022. "We just kept going," he said. "We prayed for snow. We wanted to hike in the snow—the thrill of doing it nature's way."

Dr. John Adler of Rockford, Tennessee, regularly climbed Le Conte until he was about 90 (often delivering the mail) and was 101 when he died in 2022. A World War II veteran, he was in the army honor guard at Newfound Gap in 1940 when President Franklin D. Roosevelt dedicated the Great Smoky Mountains National Park. Adler offered to buy LeConte Lodge when the Huffs retired in 1959. After that deal didn't work out, he built a similar hikers' destination in North Carolina—the Cabins at Sandy Mush Bald, a mountaintop lodge 30 miles east of Le Conte.

Anne Springs Close was 87 in 2013, the year she climbed Mount Le Conte as well as New Hampshire's Mount Washington. She joked that she outlived the "Old Man of the Mountain," a rock formation that collapsed in 2003 after being featured on

Gracie McNicol on her 92nd birthday in 1993, with Paul Dinwiddie, who eventually broke her record for the most ascents by a LeConte guest. Dinwiddie envied the fact that Gracie usually spent two nights at the lodge. "It's not how many trips you make," he wrote, "but how much time you spend on the mountain" (courtesy Edwin C. Jones).

the New Hampshire state quarter in 2000. She also outlived the Hindenburg, having crossed the Atlantic as an 11-year-old passenger in 1936, a year before the zeppelin's horrifying crash in New Jersey. She climbed Le Conte 42 times over 50 years, and her Mount Washington climbs spanned 75 years. Five of her great-grandchildren accompanied her on her last Le Conte hike. Her name is synonymous with fitness in Fort Mill, South Carolina, where walkers enjoy the Anne Springs Close Greenway. She was pushing 96 when she died in 2021.

Margaret Stevenson retired from Le Conte at 84 and Ron Valentine at 82, but even then they kept active for years hiking in the valleys.

James "Pop" Hollandsworth climbed Le Conte into his mid–80s and was nearly 98 when he died in 2013. He was the founder of the mountaineering program at Asheville School and was the first director of the North Carolina Outward Bound School.

The early owners of the lodge were blessed with longevity. Paul Adams lived to 84, and Pauline and Jack Huff reached 93 and 82. Myrtle Brown and Gracie McNicol concurred that relentless walking was the secret to longevity. They were in step with renowned western mountaineer Finis Mitchell, who once declared: "We don't stop hiking because we grow old. We grow old because we stop hiking."[18]

---

18. Finis Mitchell (1901–1995) hiked solo in Wyoming's Wind River Mountains until he was 84.

Myrtle Brown made annual climbs with her family until she turned 81 in 2007. That marked 80 years since her husband Herrick first climbed the mountain as a boy. She turned 97 in 2023.

Jim Thompson, whose photographs documented the early history of the lodge and the park, was 95 when he died in 1976.

Beatrice McClenaghan, one of the first women to make the round trip hike in a day (along with Dorothy Fonde), became a Girl Scout leader in Georgia and lived to 97.

At least four retirees have "climbed their age," meaning that their annual ascents outnumbered their birthday candles—the hikers' equivalent of a golfer shooting his age.[19]

Wright was the first to do it with 69 climbs the year he turned 64, and in 1991 as he turned 66 he set the annual record with 230 climbs. He continued to hike his age each year until he turned 74 and needed heart bypass surgery. Wright made 1,114 climbs after he turned 65, 489 after hitting 70, 122 after his heart surgery, and 43 after double knee replacements. His replumbed heart kept ticking to age 84.

Valentine's best years were 113 and 109 when he was in his sixties. He made 911 ascents after he turned 70. Twelve years after he retired from climbing Le Conte, he was still hiking more than a thousand miles a year on valley trails.

Paul Dinwiddie hiked his age three times: 76 as he turned 73 in 1988, 88 as he turned 75 in 1990, and 102 as he turned 76 in 1991. Dinwiddie made 707 of his 750 hikes after his 65th birthday. He died of cancer at age 80. In 2023, when Larry Russell turned 80, he hiked up 115 times—the most by anyone since Wright.

Can You See the Stars from Here?

As the most visited national park, the Smokies have quite a guest list, but celebrities rarely go the extra miles to visit the lodge.

If you're looking for "stars" on Le Conte, you're usually better off looking up at the Milky Way—or at least gazing at the moon. That's what several guests were doing in 1989, when one of them introduced himself as Charlie Duke, an astronaut from the Apollo 16 mission—one of the 12 men who set foot on the moon.[20]

You never know whom you might meet up at the lodge. LeConte could have its own Hollywood Hike of Fame, as a couple of Golden Globe nominees have visited: David Keith, a University of Tennessee graduate who played opposite Richard Gere in *An Officer and a Gentleman*, and Andie MacDowell, a South Carolinian whose films include *Groundhog Day*.

In a 2023 interview with the *New York Times*, MacDowell described the Le Conte hike as one of her favorite memories. "My sister Beverly was a teacher, and when she retired at 65, she started leading backpacking trips. We did Mount LeConte, the third tallest mountain in the Smokies. It has an old historic lodge and

---

19. Professional golfers who have shot their age in competitive tournaments include Arnold Palmer, who shot 71 when he was 71, and Sam Snead, with a 66 at 67.

20. *HIgh on LeConte*, March 30, 2021 (comment by Joe Hendrick), highonleconte.com/daily-posts/march-30-2021.

cabins from the 1930s. No roads there, you hike in. No electricity. Beautiful hardwood forest streams. Wildflowers. Views to make you weep along the way."[21]

Supreme Court Justice William O. Douglas stayed at the lodge in June 1959 while hiking with Harvey Broome. Douglas timed his trip to see rhododendron and laurel in bloom, after camping in the Smokies in 1957 during the fall colors. "I learn something new each time in the Smokies," Douglas told Broome.[22]

Hall of Fame coaches have also made the trek. Pat Head Summitt of the University of Tennessee climbed Le Conte in the summer of 1990 while she was pregnant with her son Tyler. "I was well into my third trimester when I led our team on a strenuous hike to the top of Mount LeConte," she wrote in her 2013 memoir, *Sum It Up*. "You should have heard the Lady Vols huffing to keep up, trying to avoid the humiliation of being out-climbed by the pregnant lady."[23] The exercise paid off for her team, which climbed another metaphorical mountain that season when they won the third of her eight national championships.

Another UT icon, Johnny Majors, a member of the College Football Hall of Fame, once spent the night at the lodge, according to former owner Jim Huff, Jr.

Stock-car racing fans may meet the pit crews of Trackhouse Racing, who hike to LeConte Lodge as an annual retreat. Trackhouse features drivers Ross Chastain and Daniel Suarez. The crews make the hike to LeConte to escape the roaring engines and social-media noise. The team's coach, Shaun Peet, said,

> I'm a big believer that when you do hard things together it binds you together. There's not a free pass to the top. You have to earn it.
>
> I guarantee you it's probably the only time during the year that our guys will sit and watch the sunset. I know that doesn't sound like much, but when you have everyone there, it's a neat experience. And it's brand new for some guys. I have guys on the team who say it's the first time they've ever been in the woods.

In the state that is "Birthplace of Country Music," at least two Nashville performers have stayed at the lodge: Helen Cornelius in 1992 and Ira Wolf in 2017.[24] Memphis songwriter Jimmy Davis visited the lodge and used a photograph of the cabins on his 2006 CD, *Campfire Songs*. Jimbo Whaley, who wrote "The Legend of Jack Huff" (see Chapter 2), said he has climbed Le Conte a number of times.

Acclaimed photographer Ansel Adams visited the Smokies in 1948 during a tour of the national parks. He published only four prints from this trip, including one that shows Mount Le Conte on the horizon. "The Smokys are OK in their way, but they are going to be devilish hard to photograph," he wrote. Since Adams' first

---

21. MacDowell also has climbed Mount Snowdon (the highest peak in England) and Mount Stromboli (a live volcano in Italy). Kathryn Shattuck, "Andie MacDowell still scaling new heights," *New York Times*, February 27, 2023.

22. Douglas (1898–1980) was an avid hiker and a strong voice for the environmental movement, even arguing that trees have legal standing in a court of law. "It is only by foot that one can really come to know the nation," he wrote in his autobiography. John Parris, "Douglas Gathers Buckeyes for 'New Frontier' Symbol," *Asheville Citizen-Times*, Sept. 26, 1962.

23. Pat Head Summitt and Sally Jenkins, *Sum It Up* (New York: Three Rivers Press, 2013), p. 194.

24. Another musician moved by Le Conte was Charles A. Garratt (1848–1938), who directed the Knoxville High School orchestra and wrote an organ composition inspired by a view of the mountain from a roadside overlook. Professor Garratt previously was an organist at the royal chapel in Britain's Windsor Palace. Maude Waddell, "LeConte Inspires Him," *Nashville Banner*, Feb. 19, 1931.

job was at the LeConte Memorial Lodge in Yosemite National Park, this LeConte Lodge might have attracted him. Alas, there is no photographic evidence that he visited the lodge.

Directors of the National Park Service who have visited the lodge include Arno Cammerer in 1925, Horace Albright in 1930, and Newton Drury in 1940.

Myron Avery, chairman of the Appalachian Trail Conference, stayed at the lodge in June 1931, after hiking 170 miles from Mount Oglethorpe in Georgia, on his way to attend the ATC's fifth annual convention in Gatlinburg.

Even the campaign trail has led to LeConte Lodge. Sen. Bill Frist and Congressman Bob Corker visited the lodge in 2003, and Sen. Estes Kefauver (who campaigned for president in 1952 wearing a coonskin hat) once rode up on horseback. When Sen. Lamar Alexander spoke at the national park's 75th birthday in 2009, he recalled that when he was 14, he made a Christmas hike from Newfound Gap to Gatlinburg.

Dolly Parton grew up at the foot of Le Conte, and her grandparents lived in the Greenbrier community not far from the Brushy Mountain Trail, but if she ever hiked, she did not mention it in her autobiography.[25] When she headlined the 75th anniversary celebration of the park at Newfound Gap in 2009, she gestured toward Le Conte as she sang, "These are my mountains, this is my home." Hikers have nicknamed a ridgeline above Huggins Hell as the "Dolly Parton peaks."

---

25. Dolly's smile was seen at the lodge in 2020, when Jevin Hooper and Jeff Conyers wore Dolly jerseys while they completed the Tour de Le Conte in support of her Imagination Library.

Who's Who
A Biographical Index

Adams, Paul (1901–1985) built the tent camp on Mount Le Conte that served as the original lodge in 1925. Born in Paxton, Illinois, he was the elder son of the Rev. Clair Stark Adams (1862–1938), who served as a pastor for Presbyterian churches in Elwood, Paxton, and Bement, prairie towns southwest of Chicago, and later at Christ Church in Alpine, Tennessee.

Adler, John (1920–2022), a physician in Rockwood, Tennessee, climbed Le Conte more than 100 times in the 1950s, made a bid for the lodge concession contract as the Huffs retired in 1959, and built the Cabins at Sandy Mush, a hikers lodge in North Carolina.

Albright, Horace (1890–1987) was the second director of the National Park Service and visited LeConte Lodge in 1930. Namesake: Albright Grove, an old-growth stand of hemlocks and tulip poplars 10 miles northwest of Le Conte.

Alexander, Lamar (born 1940 in Maryville) served Tennessee as governor, 1979–87, and senator, 2003–21. Namesake: Lamar Alexander Rocky Fork State Park in Unicoi County.

Avery, Myron (1899–1952) was chairman of the Appalachian Trail Conference from 1931 to 1952 and worked with Paul Fink to route the trail through the Smokies. Namesake: Maine's Avery Peak (elevation 4,088).

Brewer, Carson (1920–2003) returned from World War II and spent 40 years telling Smokies stories as a columnist for the *Knoxville News-Sentinel*. His books include *Day Hikes of the Smokies*, *Hiking Trails of the Smokies*, *A Wonderment of Mountains*, and *Just Over the Next Ridge*. Namesake: Carson Brewer Trail, near Lake Norris.

Broome, Harvey (1902–1968), a Knoxville attorney, was co-founder of the Wilderness Society, along with three men he met at a 1934 forestry conference in the Smokies: Bob Marshall (1901–1939), Benton MacKaye (1879–1975), and Bernard Frank (1902–1964). He climbed Le Conte more than 60 times, including one hike in 1959 with Supreme Court Justice William O. Douglas. Namesake: the Knoxville chapter of the Sierra Club is known as the Harvey Broome Group.

Brown, Herrick (1913–1986) was a Knoxville businessman who operated LeConte Lodge from 1960 through 1976, along with his wife Myrtle Graybeal Brown (born 1926). Brown built the office and brought flush toilets to the lodge.

Buckley, Samuel Botsford (1809–1884) surveyed peaks for Arnold Guyot and later became state geologist for Texas. Namesake: Mount Buckley (elevation 6,560), a sub-peak of Clingmans Dome.

Burroughs, John (1837–1921) was a naturalist who accompanied Henry Ford (1863–1947), Thomas Edison (1847–1931), and Harvey Firestone (1868–1938) on a glamping trip to the Smokies in 1918. They called themselves "The Vagabonds." Namesake: Burroughs Mountain (elevation 7,828) in Mount Rainier National Park.

Cammerer, Arno B. (1883–1941), assistant director of the National Park Service under Stephen Mather, declared that a national park in the Smokies "is a certainty" after climbing Le Conte in August 1925 and staying in Paul Adams' camp. Cammerer worked with John D. Rockefeller to secure a $5 million grant that was vital for the park campaign. Namesake: Mount Cammerer (elevation 4,928, formerly known as White Rocks).

Campbell, Carlos (1892–1978) served more than 20 years as secretary of the Great Smoky Mountains Conservation Association, climbed Le Conte more than 100 times, and wrote the book, *Birth of a National Park in the Great Smoky Mountains.*

Chapman, David (1876–1944) was vice-chairman of the Great Smoky Mountains Conservation Association under Willis Davis. He was known as "Colonel" for his army service, where he was aide-de-camp to Brigadier General Leonard Wright Colby. His unit, the 3rd Tennessee Volunteer infantry, was preparing for deployment to Puerto Rico in 1898 when an armistice ended the Spanish-American war. Namesake: Mount Chapman (elevation 6,417 feet, the sixth highest peak in the Smokies) on the Appalachian Trail; Chapman Highway (U.S. 441 from Knoxville to Sevierville).

Clingman, Thomas (1812–1897) was a congressman from North Carolina, a Confederate general, and a rival of his college professor, Dr. Elisha Mitchell. Namesake: Clingmans Dome (elevation 6,643) in the park (name officially changed to Kuwohi in September 2024), Clingmans Peak (6,460) near Mount Mitchell.

Cooper, Graham Dinwiddie "Cracker" (1929–2013), a farmer from Greenback, Tennessee, climbed Mount Le Conte more than 1,000 times.

Crouch, Brockway (1896–1971), a Knoxville florist, was a co-founder of the Smoky Mountain Hiking Club. His Gay Street shop, Flowercraft, became a popular gathering place for Smokies hikers.

Davis, Willis (1859–1931), president of the Knoxville Iron Company, was the founding chairman of the Great Smoky Mountains Conservation Association. His wife, Anne Patrick Davis (1875–1957), was regarded as the mother of the Great Smoky Mountains National Park. The Davises were married in 1902 in Louisville and moved to Knoxville in 1915. On the train ride home from a 1923 vacation in Yellowstone, she told her husband: "We have seen some beautiful country. Grand mountains but nothing more majestic than our own great Smokies. Why should there be national parks in the West and only one tiny one (Arcadia [sic] in Maine) in the east?" Mr. Davis replied, "If that is the way you feel about it, I will see what I can do." He pitched the idea to Hubert

Work, secretary of the interior under President Warren Harding. Shortly after becoming a grandmother, Davis was elected to the Tennessee state assembly, and she propelled the park movement with a 1925 bill that authorized the state to purchase 76,000 acres from the Little River Lumber Company. Namesake: Mount Davis (elevation 5,040) and Davis Ridge (4,640) along the Appalachian Trail west of Clingmans Dome.

Dearing, Gene (1902–1963) was a banker and hiker in Knoxville who worked with David Chapman on securing the Laura Spelman Rockefeller grant to fund land purchases for the national park.

Dinwiddie, Paul (1915–1995) climbed Le Conte 750 times, including 605 ascents after he turned 65 and 14 after surgery for an aneurysm in 1992. Dinwiddies are famous on Le Conte: Paul's cousin Graham Dinwiddie Cooper made more than 1,000 climbs, and son David Dinwiddie worked on the lodge crew for Herrick Brown and made nearly 800 ascents.

Douglas, Justice William O. (1898–1980) was a strong voice for environmentalism during his 36 years on the Supreme Court. Raised in Washington state within view of Mount Rainier, he climbed Le Conte in 1959 and was delighted to discover in eastern America "natural splendor that compares with any in the world." He wrote in his autobiography: "It is only by foot that one can really come to know the nation." Namesakes: Douglas Falls in the Craggy Mountains, 60 miles east of Le Conte; William O. Douglas Wilderness Area in Washington state.

Eakin, Ross (1880–1946) was the founding superintendent of the Great Smoky Mountains National Park. He served 24 years with the National Park Service and was also superintendent at Grand Canyon and Glacier. He was a topographical engineer who served with the army in World War I and is buried in Arlington National Cemetery. Stopped here

Everhardt, Gary (1934–2020) was appointed by President Gerald Ford as the ninth director of the National Park Service and later served 23 years as superintendent of the Blue Ridge Parkway.

Fink, Paul (1892–1980) was an attorney, banker, and historian in Jonesborough, Tennessee, who preferred the title "woods loafer," according to the *Knoxville Journal* in 1931. He was an influential advocate for the Great Smoky Mountains National Park, and he and Myron Avery (1899–1952) worked to route the Appalachian Trail through the Smokies. He published a memoir, *Backpacking Was the Only Way*, in 1974. "Nobody knew about Mount Le Conte until he began talking about it," friend David Wise said in 2005.

Guyot, Arnold (1807–1884, pronounced GHEE-oh) was a professor at Princeton College who explored and measured the mountains of eastern America. His books included *Creation, or the Biblical Cosmogony in Light of Modern Science* and *Earth and Man*, which became controversial for promoting scientific racism. Namesakes: Mount Guyot on the Tennessee–North Carolina line (elevation 6,621), Colorado's Mount Guyot (13,376), New Hampshire's Mount Guyot (4,560), Alaska's Guyot Glacier, and the Guyot Crater on the moon. Undersea plateaus are known as guyots.

Hanlon, Russell Wallace, Sr. (1894–1963) was a Knoxville businessman and army veteran of World War I who served as secretary of the Great Smoky Mountains Conservation Association.

Hartt, Rollin Lynde (1869–1946) was a clergyman who became a journalist, writing for magazines including *TIME, Atlantic Monthly, Century Magazine, The Literary Digest*, and *World's Work*.

Householder, Alan (born 1959) served 20 years in two stints as llama wrangler for LeConte Lodge. His hiking accomplishments include the Appalachian Trail, the Pacific Coast Trail, the Australian Alps Walking Trail, and the first through-hike of North Carolina's Mountains-to-Sea Trail. He became known as "the Mayor of Trillium Gap" since he was there three times a week.

Huff, Andrew Jackson "Andy" (1878–1949) was a lumberman who transformed his boarding house into the prestigious Mountain View Hotel and helped make Gatlinburg a destination. The national park's original offices were at the Mountain View, and the park headquarters are on land where Huff once operated a sawmill. He invested in the facilities at LeConte Lodge after his son Jack was appointed to manage the camp in 1926. He was the son of Noah Hauff (1838–1922) of Greene County, Tennessee.

Huff, Estel Carl "Jack" (1903–1985) operated LeConte Lodge from 1926 through 1959 and built most of the cabins. He was the oldest of five children of Andrew Jackson Huff (1878–1949) and Martha Whaley Huff (1876–1933). He and Pauline Whaling Huff were married April 29, 1934, at Myrtle Point and had two children: Philip (1935–1986) and Cookie Bowling (born 1944).

Huff, James Andrew, Jr. "Jim" (born 1939) led a partnership with Bill Rinearson and Hugh Ogle that managed LeConte Lodge during the adaptation to Wilderness Act requirements. The nephew of Jack Huff and grandson of Andy Huff, he developed several local restaurants, including the Burning Bush in Gatlinburg and the Applewood Farmhouse in Sevierville.

Huff, Pauline Whaling (1905–1999) came to the Smokies in 1932 as a teacher, married Jack Huff at Myrtle Point on April 29, 1934, and managed LeConte Lodge through the 1950s.

Ijams, Harry P. (1876–1954) was a commercial artist who founded the Ijams Nature Center in Knoxville in 1910. Ijams accompanied Paul Adams on an eagle-watching trip to Le Conte in 1925 and recommended him to David Chapman as manager for the original camp.

Kelsey, Harlan P. (1872–1958) led the federal national park commission which visited Mount Le Conte in 1924 and returned in 1925 with Arno Cammerer, the assistant director of the park service. He was the son of Samuel Kelsey, the founder of Highlands, North Carolina, which was advertised as the highest incorporated town (elevation 4,118) in eastern America. After moving to Boston, Kelsey became president of the Appalachian Club, which sponsored a survey to determine if Le Conte might be the highest peak in eastern America. He established the Kelsey Arboretum in Boxford, Massachusetts, to exhibit plants from the southern Appalachians.

Kephart, Horace (1862–1931) was called "the Apostle of the Smokies" and was influential in the creation of the national park. A librarian in St. Louis, he left his family and moved to the Smokies, making his home near Bryson City, North Carolina. He wrote: "I took a topographic map and picked out on it, by means of the contour lines and the blank space showing no settlement, what seemed to be the wildest part of these regions; and there I went." He published *Our Southern Highlanders* in 1913 and *Camping and Woodcraft* in 1921. *Back of Beyond: A Horace Kephart Biography*, by George Ellison and Janet McCue, was published in 2019. Namesakes: Mount Kephart (elevation 6,217), Kephart Prong Trail, and the Kephart Prong CCC Camp (1933–1942), which built the Newfound Gap highway on the North Carolina side.

LeConte, John (1818–1881) assisted Arnold Guyot on his 1858 surveying trip in the Smokies, and later served two terms as president of the University of California. Namesake: Tennessee's Mount Le Conte (6,593 feet).

Le Conte, Joseph (1823–1901) was a Georgia native who became a geology professor at the University of California and published *Theories on the Origin of Mountain Ranges* in 1893. His name has been removed from several California institutions because of concerns about his family's slaveholding legacy. Namesake: California's Mount Le Conte (a 13,936-foot sub-peak of Mount Whitney), Washington's Le Conte Mountain (7,762, a snow-covered peak in the Cascades), and Le Conte Glacier in Alaska.

LeConte, Joseph Nisbet "Little Joe" (1870–1950), son of Joseph Le Conte, succeeded John Muir as president of the Sierra Club. He was a professor of mechanical engineering at the University of California and an accomplished photographer and mapmaker. He spelled his surname differently than his father, removing the space.

Lindenkohl, Adolph (1833–1904) produced some of the earliest maps of the Smoky Mountains. Born in Germany, he became a U.S. citizen in 1857 and served as the army's senior draftsman during the Civil War. Namesake: Lindenkohl Canyon, a deep-sea fishing destination off New Jersey.

Line, Tim (born 1953) spent his entire 41-year career at LeConte Lodge, was the manager from the 1980s through 2018, and remains a managing partner.

MacKaye, Benton (1879–1975) was the father of the Appalachian Trail. Namesake: Benton MacKaye Trail in Georgia, North Carolina, and Tennessee.

McNicol, Grace (1891–1991), an Alaskan nurse who retired in Maryville, Tennessee, started climbing Le Conte at age 63 and retired with 244 trips. Her biography, *Gracie and the Mountain*, was written by Emilie Ervin Powell. Namesake: Gracie's Pulpit (5,280) on the Alum Cave Bluff Trail.

Miller, Loye W. (1899–1979) was the reporter who covered the 1924 national park commission hike for the *Knoxville News-Sentinel*. A native of Indiana, he served 26 years as editor of the newspaper. He barely survived the Labor Day flood in 1951 that deeply scarred the Smokies. He was swimming in Elkmont when water surged down the Little River. He clung to a tree until he was rescued by his sons.

Morgan, the Rev. Rufus (1885–1983) served as pastor of 11 Episcopal churches in western North Carolina and built St. John's Church in the Cartoogechaye Valley near Franklin. He was founder of the Nantahala Hiking Club, personally maintained more than 50 miles of the Appalachian Trail, and celebrated his 93rd birthday with his 174th climb of Le Conte. Namesake: Dining-room table at LeConte Lodge, Rufus Morgan Falls in Nantahala National Forest, Rufus Morgan Shelter on the Appalachian Trail, Rufus Morgan Trail at Kanuga Conference Center in Hendersonville, North Carolina.

Morrell, John Ogden (1901–1982) first climbed Le Conte in 1913 on a seven-day hike from Elkmont. He earned a law degree from the University of Tennessee and worked decades for the national park as an administrator and a ranger. His three-year-old daughter Mary became the youngest child to climb Le Conte. Namesake: The Great Smoky Mountains National Park administration building.

Muir, John (1838–1914) was the founder of the Sierra Club and was known as the "Father of America's National Parks." He never explored the Great Smokies but saw them from a distance in 1867 during his epic thousand-mile walk from Indiana to Florida. "The scenery is far grander than anything I have ever beheld," he wrote. His route may have crossed Waucheesi Mountain, which has a view of the southern Smokies. Namesake: Mount Muir (elevation 14,018), a jagged peak near California's Mount Whitney; the John Muir Trail, 211 miles in the Sierra Nevada range; and the John Muir National Recreation Trail, tracing his 1867 route for 21 miles along the Hiwassee River in Tennessee.

Neiman, Jack, Jr. (1923–2004) crash-landed an airplane on Le Conte in 1972. He grew up in Knoxville and Gatlinburg, became a Navy pilot, and received a special commendation from the secretary of the navy after he volunteered to test space suits for NASA. He spent 44 hours in a low-pressure chamber at Norfolk, Virginia, that simulated altitudes up to 105,000 feet—16 times higher than the thin air on Le Conte. It was Mother's Day weekend, and his mother in Tennessee nervously awaited his call, knowing that her son's life depended on the integrity of the experimental space-suit.

Oakley, Wiley (1885–1954) was a hiking guide and craftsman in Gatlinburg known as "the Roamin' Man of the Mountains" and "the Will Rogers of the South." Namesake: Wiley Oakley Drive, Gatlinburg. He climbed Le Conte hundreds of times but did not keep records.

Ogle, Earnest (1906–1979, grandson of pioneer settler John Ramsey) married Lucinda Oakley (1909–2003, daughter of Wiley Oakley) and they were selected as the "Typical Southern Highland Family" for the 1940 World's Fair in New York City. "They grew up in the shadows of Mount Le Conte," Gatlinburg mayor Steve Whaley said. Earnest helped Paul Adams set up his camp in 1925 and later worked for the national park in the construction of the Newfound Gap highway. Lucinda became known as the "Queen of the Smoky Mountains." Married in 1926, they lived in a century-old cabin in the Sugarlands community.

Overly, Fred (1907–1973) was the fifth superintendent of the Great Smoky Mountains National Park. His administration (1958–1963) opened the Roaring Fork Motor Nature Trail (a project advocated by Jack Huff) and halted the Fontana North Shore Road.

Pollock, G. Freeman, Jr. (1869–1949) was the Jack Huff of the Shenandoah Mountains, building Skyland Lodge on Stony Man Mountain and leading the campaign for a national park 90 miles from the nation's capital. A showman known for snake-handling and bugling, he served on the Southern Appalachian National Parks Commission and camped at Mount Le Conte in 1925. Namesake: Pollock Knob (3,580 feet), Pollock Dining Room at Skyland.

Rinearson, William III (1916–1986) was an army veteran and ski instructor in Gatlinburg who became co-owner of LeConte Lodge in the 1970s with Jim Huff, Jr., and Hugh Ogle.

Roth, Albert G. "Dutch" (1890–1974) was a prolific photographer who was a founding member of the Smoky Mountains Hiking Club and climbed Le Conte 120 times. Harvey Broome called him "a pint-sized juggernaut … oblivious of fatigue, weather, thicket, or steep, and who went climbing with me when no one else would go."

Scanlon, Dave (1936–2014) was a forester in Liberia for Firestone Rubber Corporation and retired from TVA in Norris, Tennessee. He hiked Le Conte weekly in the 1990s and finished with 982 trips.

Schantz, Orpheus (1864–1951) was president of the Illinois Audubon Society and treasurer of the Geographic Society of Chicago. When Hotel Monthly published the first story on the lodge, editor John Willy described Schantz as an authority on the Great Smokies, "having made several journeys through them, hunting with the camera. His enthusiasm for this territory brought a year ago, a request from the Geographic Society of Chicago, that he lead excursions to the Smoky Mountains; which he did, taking a party of 61 people, which was the first organized excursion party to what is now the Great Smoky Mountains National Park." His obituary in the *New York Times* said he was "instrumental in establishing the Great Smoky Mountains National Park."

Spence, Cary (1869–1943) was a national champion sprinter and won the army's Distinguished Service Medal for his leadership of the 117th infantry, which broke the Hindenburg Line to crush Germany in World War I. He became the Knoxville postmaster, served on the city council and the University of Tennessee board of trustees, and ran Spence Shoes, the largest independent shoe store in the Southeast.

Stevenson, Margaret (1912–2006), born to missionaries in China, settled in Maryville, Tennessee, and climbed Le Conte 718 times, starting at age 48. In 1976 she became the first woman to hike all 900 miles of trails in the Smokies. Namesake: Margaret Stevenson Wednesday Hikers Club. Her bronzed hiking boots are displayed at the lodge.

Thomas, Colonel William (1805–1893) was adopted as a teenager by Cherokee chief Yonaguska and negotiated to prevent the extradition of the Eastern Band of the Cherokee from the Qualla Boundary. In the Civil War, he commanded Thomas' Legion, which included 400 Cherokee soldiers who fought for the Confederacy, built a wagon road across the Smokies, and mined Alum Cave. Namesake: Thomas Divide (elevation 5,000).

Thornburgh, Laura (1885–1973) was a naturalist who wrote frequently of the Smokies in the Knoxville newspapers. She accompanied the 1924 national park commissioners on their hike to Gregory Bald after they had visited Mount Le

Conte. She wrote five books under the name Laura Thornborough, including *The Great Smoky Mountains* in 1937.

Wilder, General John T. (1830–1917) operated the Cloudland Hotel on Roan Mountain. Raised in New York's Catskill Mountains, he had a distinguished career with military, industrial, and government service. His "Lightning Brigade" made a decisive stand in the Battle of Chickamauga, and six years after the Civil War he was elected as the Yankee mayor of Chattanooga. He was also an inventor who held several hydraulic patents, which was helpful since his hotel (much like Le Conte Lodge) depended on water pumped up from a spring. His 1884 home in the town of Roan Mountain and his 1904 house in Knoxville are on the National Register of Historic Places. Namesake: Wilder Tower at Chickamauga and Chattanooga National Military Park.

Wright, Ed (1925–2009) was an Auburn graduate and an army veteran of the Korean War who became a mechanical engineer for the Atomic Energy Commission at Oak Ridge. Born the year that Paul Adams opened his Le Conte camp, Wright was 66 in 1991 when he set a one-year record with 230 climbs, and after 26 years of hiking, he retired with 1,310 trips. He launched the website mtleconte.com. His family holds memorial hikes each September.

Your Personal Logbook

Keep count of your hikes and log them online at LeContest.com. After you visit the lodge, you can help update LeContest.com by emailing snapshots of logbook pages to *LeConteLog@gmail.com*.

Date	Trail	Trip #	Cabin #	Memories

Your Personal Logbook

Date	Trail	Trip #	Cabin #	Memories

Your Personal Logbook

Date	Trail	Trip #	Cabin #	Memories

Your Personal Logbook

Date	Trail	Trip #	Cabin #	Memories

References

Adams, Doris, and Bruce Adams, *Stretching into the Mysterious and Dark Green Tunneled Sanctuary of Mt. LeConte*, journal, Calvin M. McClung Historical Collection, East Tennessee History Center, Knox County Public Library (Knoxville).
Adams, Paul J., *MT. Le CONTE* (1996, Knoxville: Holston Printing Company).
Adams, Paul J., *Smoky Jack* (edited by Anne Bridges and Ken Wise) (2016, Knoxville: University of Tennessee Press).
Bennett, Jenny, *Endless Streams and Forests* (streamsandforests.wordpress.com/).
Brewer, Carson, *Hiking in the Great Smokies* (1962, Knoxville: Holston Printing Company).
Brill, David, "Cumberland Jack: K-9 King of Mt. Le Conte," *Smokies Life*, Vol. 1, No. 1 (Gatlinburg, TN: Great Smoky Mountains Conservation Association).
Brill, David, *Into the Mist: Tales of Death and Disaster, Mishaps and Misdeeds, Misfortune and Mayhem in Great Smoky Mountains National Park*, Volume 1 (2017, Gatlinburg, TN: Great Smoky Mountains Conservation Association).
Brill, David, "A Mountain of Memories: Tim Line and the Legendary Lodge on Mount Le Conte," *Smokies Life*, Vol. 13, No. 2, Fall 2019 (Gatlinburg, TN: Great Smoky Mountains Conservation Association).
Broome, Harvey, *Earth Man* (1970, Knoxville: Greenbrier Press).
Broome, Harvey, *Out Under the Sky of the Great Smokies* (1975, Knoxville: Greenbrier Press).
Brown, Margaret Lynn, *The Wild East: A Biography of the Great Smoky Mountains* (2000, Gainesville: University Press of Florida).
Campbell, Carlos, *Birth of a National Park in the Great Smoky Mountains* (1960, Knoxville: University of Tennessee Press).
Catton, Theodore, *A Gift for All Time* (2008, Gatlinburg, TN: Great Smoky Mountains Conservation Association).
Catton, Theodore, *Mountains for the Masses* (2014, Gatlinburg, TN: Great Smoky Mountains Conservation Association).
Coggins, Allen R., *Place Names of the Smokies* (1999, Gatlinburg, TN: Great Smoky Mountains Natural History Conservation Association).
Davis, Timothy, *National Park Roads: A Legacy in the American Landscape* (2016, Charlottesville: University of Virginia Press).
Davis, Timothy, Todd A. Croteau, Christopher H. Marston, *America's National Park Roads and Parkways: Drawings from the Historic American Engineering Record* (2004, Baltimore: Johns Hopkins University Press).
Fink, Paul, *Backpacking Was the Only Way* (1975, Johnson City: Research Advisory Council, East Tennessee State University).
Fink, Paul M., *Mountain Days: A Journal of Camping Experiences in the Mountains of North Carolina and Tennessee, 1914-1938* (1960, Chapel Hill: University of North Carolina Press).
Frome, Michael, *Strangers in High Places: The Story of the Great Smoky Mountains* (1966, Knoxville: University of Tennessee Press).
Giddens, Elizabeth, "Something Unusual in Hotel Accommodations," *Smokies Life*, Vol. 4, No. 2 (Gatlinburg, TN: Great Smoky Mountains Conservation Association).
Hart, William A., Jr., *3000 Miles in the Great Smokies* (2009, Charleston, SC: The History Press).
Hoover, Greg, *Paths Less Traveled* (2017, CreateSpace).
Kephart, Horace, *Our Southern Highlanders* (1913, New York: Outing Publishing Company).
Krol, J.P., "Wintering on Mount Le Conte," *Smokies Life*, Vol. 10, No. 2 (Gatlinburg, TN: Great Smoky Mountains Association).
Lanois, Lindsay D., *The LeConte Lodge: A Lens for the Evolution and Development of the Great Smoky Mountains National Park* (2014, Clemson, SC: Clemson University).
Le Conte, Joseph, *The Autobiography of Joseph Le Conte* (1903, New York: D. Appleton).

Le Conte, Joseph, "Theories on the Origin of Mountain Ranges," *Journal of Geology,* September–October 1893.
Linzey, Donald W., *A Natural History Guide to Great Smoky Mountains National Park* (2008, Knoxville: University of Tennessee Press).
Lix, Courtney, *No Place for the Weary Kind: Women of the Smokies* (2016, Gatlinburg, TN: Great Smoky Mountains Association).
Mathis, Amy, *A Survey of Visitors to Mount Le Conte in the Great Smoky Mountains National Park* (2004, Knoxville: University of Tennessee Press).
Maynard, Charles W., "Paul Fink: Forgotten Founding Father of the Smokies?" *Smokies Life,* Vol. 11, No. 2 (Gatlinburg, TN: Great Smoky Mountains Association).
Nichols, Rosemary, *The Ecological Effects of LeConte Lodge in the Great Smoky Mountains National Park* (1977, Gatlinburg, TN: Uplands Field Research Laboratory).
Oakley, Harvey, *Rememberin' the Roamin' Man of the Mountains* (2000, Gatlinburg, TN: Oakley Books).
Oakley, Wiley, *Roamin' and Restin' with the Roamin' Man of the Smoky Mountains* (1986, Sevierville, TN Oakley Enterprises).
Parton, Dolly, *My Life and Other Unfinished Business* (1994, New York: HarperCollins).
Pollock, George Freeman, Jr., *Skyland: The Heart of the Shenandoah National Park* (1960, Baltimore: Chesapeake Book Company).
Porter, Eliot, and Edward Abbey, *Appalachian Wilderness: The Great Smoky Mountains* (1973, New York: Ballantine).
Powell, Emilie Ervin, *Gracie and the Mountain* (1981, Signal Mountain, TN).
Scott, David L., and Kay W. Scott, *The Complete Guide to the National Park Lodges* (2015, Guilford, CT: Globe Pequot).
Shealy, William, *Preserving the Experience: A Low Impact Approach to Landscape Management at LeConte Lodge in the Great Smoky Mountains National Park* (2005, Athens: University of Georgia).
Solnit, Rebecca, "Unfinished Business: John Muir in Native America," *Sierra Magazine,* Vol. 106, No. 2, March/April 2021.
Summitt, Pat Head, AND Sally Jenkins: *Sum It Up* (2013, New York: Three Rivers Press).
Wadley, Jeff, and Dwight McCarter, *Mayday! Mayday! Aircraft Crashes in the Great Smoky Mountains National Park, 1920–2000* (2002, Knoxville: University of Tennessee Press).
Wise, Ken, *Hiking Trails of the Great Smoky Mountains,* Second Edition (2014, Knoxville: University of Tennessee Press).
Wise, Kenneth, and Ron Petersen, *A Natural History of Mount LeConte* (1998, Knoxville: University of Tennessee Press).
Witherspoon, David, *Songs of the Winter Wren* (2001, Bloomington: Xlibris Corporation).
Wright, Ed, *More Than 1,001 Hikes to Mount LeConte* (2011, self-published).

Collections

"Chimney Top 2 Fire Review, "National Park Service, August 31, 2017 (wildfiretoday.com/documents/ChimneyTops2Report.pdf).
Database of the Smokies (dots.lib.utk.edu/), University of Tennessee Library, Knoxville.
Great Smoky Mountains Colloquy (.lib.utk.edu/smokies/colloquy/), University of Tennessee Library, Knoxville.
High on LeConte, the lodge blog (highonleconte.com/daily-posts), where crew members and winter caretakers have posted daily details and snapshots since 2010.
Newspapers.com archives (*Asheville Citizen-Times, Atlanta Journal Constitution, Greenville News, Charlotte Observer, Chattanooga Times, Knoxville News-Sentinel, Knoxville Journal, New York Times*).
Smoky Mountains Ancestral Quest (smokykin.com).
A Strategic Plan for Managing Backcountry Recreation in Great Smoky Mountains National Park (1995, Gatlinburg, TN: Great Smoky Mountains National Park).

Index

Abbey, Edward 75, 83
Abrams Creek 54
Adams, Ansel 84, 179
Adams, the Rev. Clair Stark 13
Adams, Paul 1, 13–31, 50, 68, 85, 99, 104, 120, 144–6, 151–2, 167, 169, 176, 181
Adler, Dr. John 50, 175, 181
Ahwanhee Hotel 51
Ailes, Milton 16
Albright, Horace 3, 14, 59, 68, 128, 147, 179, 181
Alexander, Lamar 181
Alpine TN 31
Alum Cave Bluff Trail 16, 19, 71–75, 116, 127
American Chestnut Foundation 64
American Entomological Society 7
Anakeesta Knob 67
Anderson, Scott 71
Andrews, Zachary 77–78
Apollo 11 131
Apollo 14 138
Apollo 16 177
Apollo 17 107
Apollo Point 107
Appalachian Mountain Club 15, 155, 159
Appalachian Trail 63, 67, 118, 155, 156
Aramark 51
Arch Rock 72, 74
Arthur, Blanch Huff "Boots" 109
Ashberry Cabin 130
Asheville NC 15, 56, 57
Audobon Society 24
Aurora Borealis 95
Avent Cabin 89
Avery, Myron 63, 179, 181
Ayres Hall 160

Bald Mountain 57
Balsam Lodge 51
Balsam Point 74, 101, 103
Barber, Charles 43, 75

Barnett, Betty Jean 74
Barr, Fred 154
Barr Camp 153–4
Bartram, William 84
Basin Spring 1, 15, 22, 23, 68, 82, 93, 98, 151, 174
Baum, Charles 173
Bean, Ellen 105
Bear Pen Hollow 25, 37, 62, 64, 109, 128
Bearpaw High Sierra Camp 153
Bedinger, Al 99, 107, 120, 169
Beeler, David 95
Behrend, Fred 59
Bennett, Jennie 60
Bice, Daniel 71
Black Mountain KY 67
Black Mountain Turnpike 158
Blackie (horse) 139, 148
Blitzkrieg 59
Blue Ridge Parkway 54, 59, 78, 158
Bohn, Frank 25, 54
Bolinger, John McCallie 96
Bollscheiler, Luke 164
Boone, Daniel 84
Boulevard Trail 54, 67
Bowling, Bruce 111
Bowling, Cookie Huff 45, 74, 108–111, 142, 152
Bowling, Parker 53
Braden, Bennie 102
Brasstown Bald GA 67, 106
Bratton, Susan Power 88
Brewer, Carson 85, 181
Bridges, Anne 28
Bridges, Michael 126
Brignance, Albert 97
Bristol TN 57
Broome, Harvey 59, 61, 80, 178, 181
Brown, A.R. 173
Brown, Carolyn 112–114
Brown, Glenn 112–114
Brown, Herrick 41, 45, 50, 66, 82, 83, 84, 91, 93, 94, 95, 98, 103, 105, 106, 108, 112–114, 120, 124, 181

Brown, Myrtle Graybeal 66, 108, 112–114, 123, 177
Brownlee, Wiley 16
Brunk, Kathryn 71
Brushy Mountain Trail 75–76
Bryan, Jack 34
Bryan, William Jennings 22
Bryson City NC 40, 56
Buck Spring Lodge 157
Buckley, Samuel Botsford 5, 11, 172, 182
Bullhead Mountain 11, 23, 101
Bullhead Trail 70, 102, 103
Burnsville NC 13
Burroughs, John 57, 182
Burtt, E.E. 16, 20

Cabins at Sandy Mush Bald 158, 175
Cades Cove 20, 54–55, 59, 90
Callaway, Lea 96
Camelback Mountain 171
Cammerer, Arno 14, 52, 151, 179, 182
Camp Alice 158
Camp David Chapman 76
Camp H.A. Morgan 70
Camp LeConte 13
Campbell, Carlos 14, 25, 42, 54, 58, 84, 86, 94, 182
Campbell, Paul 126
Cape Canaveral FL 107
Carolina Mountain Club 24
Carter, Ike 25, 173
Cataloochee 90
Cates, Reuben 65
Cathey, Col. Joseph 5
Champion Fibre Company 29, 30, 33, 50, 103
Chapman, David 8, 13–31, 54, 76, 144, 160, 182
Charlies Bunion 56, 103
Cherokee nation 3, 9, 10, 11, 40
Cherokee Orchard 16, 23, 37, 52, 65, 68, 79
Chiles, John 121
Chimney Rock 57
Chimney Tops 40, 101

Index

Civilian Conservation Corps 60, 70, 76, 144
Claiborne, Olwen 174
Clarkson, Philip "P-Nut" 100
Cliff Top 15, 16, 24, 25, 28, 39, 44, 62, 103, 106, 119, 138, 160, 174
Clingman, Thomas 5, 10, 159, 182
Clingmans Dome (see Kuwohi) 9, 19, 40, 54–55, 59, 89, 159, 161, 162
Close, Anne Springs 175
Cloudland Hotel 156
Cogdill, Steve 149
Cole, Alex 20, 60
Cole Branch 62
Conner, Dock 56
Continental Divide 155
Coolidge, Pres. Calvin 21
Cooper, Graham "Cracker" 168, 182
Cornelius, Helen 178
Costello, Lenore "Gundy" 175
Covid-19 pandemic 131
Cox, Stella Sue Huff 109
Crabtree, Anita 71, 174
Craig, Gov. Locke 158
Crater Lake National Park 83
Crouch, Brockway 13, 61, 95, 182
Cumberland Mountains 31

Dance, Bill 173
Darrow, Clarence 22
Davenport, Philip 97
Davenport Gap 13, 67
Davis, Anne 14
Davis, Larry 171
Davis, Ralph 162
Davis, Willis 14, 16, 19, 20, 173, 182
Dayton TN 22
Dearing, Gene 60, 183
Delaware North 51
De Soto, Hernando 84
Dickerman, Ernest 93
Diehl, Walter 61, 63
Dinwiddie, David 168
Dinwiddie, Paul 60, 73, 74, 97, 166, 171, 176, 177, 183
Douglas, Justice William O. 178, 183
Drury, Newton 8, 179
Duck Hawk Ridge 73
Duke, Charlie 177
Dunn, J.W. 158
Dure, Leon III 86

Eakin, Ross 52, 61, 183
East Lodge 42, 89
Edison, Thomas 57
Eisenhower, Pres. Dwight 57
Ekaneetlee Lodge 59

Elevation 6593 153
Elkmont 4, 19, 20, 23, 61, 90
Ellis, Vincent 85
Emerson, Bert "Wildcat" 100
Essary, S.H. 172
Everett, Robert 180
Everhardt, Gary 86, 183
Evison, Boyd 86, 88

Fink, Paul 15, 16, 60–61, 63, 143, 159, 183
Fisher, Jack 16
Fitified Spring 75
Fonde, Dorothy 177
Fontana Dam 89
Ford, Clara 58
Ford, Pres. Gerald 81, 116
Ford, Henry 57
French Broad River 22
Fritz, Carol 174
Fritz, George, Jr. 174

Gamble, Jim 98, 107
Ganier, Albert 22
Gardner, Gov. Mas 161
Garner, Clem L. 160
Garrett, Charles A. 178
Gatlinburg TN 15, 23, 35, 55, 63, 108, 124, 161, 173, 179
Gillette, Scott 99
Glacier National Park 103, 155
Glacier Point Hotel 103
Golden Gate National Recreation Area 78
Gracie's Pulpit 74
Graham, Brad 119, 151
Grand Canyon National Park 51, 58, 79, 103, 155
Grand Monadnock 171
Grand Teton National Park 95
Grandfather Mountain 15
Granite Park Chalet 155
Grassy Patch 20
Grassy Ridge 118
Graves, A.J. 162
Graves, Maisey Pomeroy 174
Gravett, Adam 132
Gray, Asa 157
Great Smoky Mountains Conservation Association 4, 18, 28, 29, 30, 32, 50, 140
Great Smoky Mountains National Park 48, 51, 77, 162
Great Smoky Mountains Wilderness Advocates 85
Green, Lucien 61
Greenbrier Cove 38, 60, 76
Greeneville TN 112
Gregory Bald 20, 112, 118, 140
Greystone Mountain 112
Groft, Anthony 77
Groft, Elias 77
Grotto Falls 22, 148–9
Grove Park Inn 60, 89

Grubb, Jimmy 97
Guyot, Arnold 3, 5, 7, 10, 159–60, 183

Hague, Geoffrey 98
Haiman, Richard 74
Half Dome 7, 164
Hallelujah Turn 16, 72
Hanlon, Russell 14, 16, 29, 184
Harding, Warren 15, 21
Harmon, Mike 97
Hartt, Rollin Lynde 54, 184
Hazelwood, Barbee 70
Henry, Gene 137
Henry, Shirley 74
Herschfield, Leo 4, 34, 65, 123
Hickok, Lorena 59
Hicks, Mitchell 9
High Sierra Loop 155
High Top 22, 62, 160, 162–3
Highlands NC 15
Hindenburg 176
Hogback Mountain SC 106
Hollandsworth, Jim "Pop" 96, 138, 176
Holt, Dick 128
Horton, Gov. Henry 161
Hostler, Jeff 100
Hotel LeConte 38, 75
Hotel Monthly 38, 41
Householder, Alan 118, 149, 168, 184
Householder, Chrissy Mann 118
Houser, L.L. 172
Howard, Erin 101
Hudson, Lucinda 76
Hudson Bay blankets 43
Huff, Andy 15, 17, 20, 29, 58, 60, 184
Huff, Cade 53
Huff, Billie 112
Huff, Jack 1, 15, 29, 30, 32–53, 55–57, 60, 64, 81, 95, 99, 104, 106, 108–11, 121–3, 127–8, 134, 136, 146, 153, 168, 176, 184
Huff, James 109
Huff, Jim, Jr. 42, 87, 89, 99, 106, 112, 126, 134, 148, 184
Huff, Henrietta McCutchan 112
Huff, Martha Whaley 32, 32–37
Huff, Neal 112
Huff, Pauline Whaling 1, 33, 43, 49, 64, 85, 91, 105, 108–111, 123, 176, 184
Huff, Philip 45, 108–112, 172
Huggins Hell 60, 62, 179
Hughes, Alex 100
Hummell, Edward 80
Hurricane Florence 94
Hurricane Ian 94
Hurricane Ida 94
Hurricane Irma 94

Index

Hurricane Ivan 94
Hurricane of 1928 36
Hurricane Opal 74, 94
Hurricane Sandy 94
Huskey Gap 20, 62

Icewater Springs 153
Ijams, H.P. 22, 38, 184
Iler, Ed 175
Indian Gap 20, 25, 30, 40, 51, 55, 57, 61, 67
Ingraham, Susanna 98
Inman, Martin, Jr. 93

Jackson, Pres. Andrew 11
Jackson, Dot 33, 109
Jeffries, LeRoy 75
Jett, Harry 70
Johnson, Dave 129
Johnson, Pres. Lyndon 80, 81
Jolly, Terri 105
Jones, Dr. Ed 169
Jonesborough TN 58

Keith, David 177
Kelsey, Harlan 15, 16, 21, 151, 159, 184
Kephart, Horace 4, 8, 55, 56, 67, 184
Kephart Prong Camp 61
Kesterson, Dr. R.N. 16, 20
Ketelle, Dick 99, 125, 169
Kimball, Mollie 174
Kipling, Rudyard 5
Kirby, Rusty 100
Kirk, Alyson 171
Kirk, John 171
Kirkham, Nathan 97, 151
Kitchen, Dan 99
Kloch, Sandy 171
Knoxville & Augusta "K&A" Railroad 61
Krol, J.P. 99, 100, 101
Kuwohi 9, 67, 106, 159

Lacy, Jordan 64
Lake of the Clouds Hut 155
Laurel Falls 79
Lawson, Mattie Huff 109
Lawson, Ralph 109
LeConte, John 5, 159, 185
Le Conte, Joseph 5, 7, 8, 9, 153–4, 185
LeConte, Joseph Nisbet 5, 68, 148, 154, 185
Le Conte backcountry shelter 154
Le Conte Creek 16
LeConte Ltd. 51
LeConte Memorial Lodge 11, 90, 117, 154, 179
Le Conte Star 76
Lee, Robert Ernest 58
Len Foote Inn 155

Lewis, Bill 95
Lewis, Lee 76
Lindenkohl, Adolph 85
Lindsay, Barbara Brown 108
Lindsley, Charles 96
Line, Felix 114
Line, Gracie 91, 108
Line, Jacob 108, 152
Line, Lisa 91, 99, 108, 114–6
Line, Nathan 91, 108
Line, Tim 51, 86, 88, 91, 99, 101, 108, 114–6, 142, 168, 185
Linville Gorge 15
Little Pigeon River 22, 62, 164
Little River Railroad 61
Little River Road 79
llamas 88, 119, 148–151
Locomobile 57
Log Cabin Inn 158
Longwell, Horace 16, 21
Look Rock 89
LuAllen, Ernest 74, 96
Ludgate, Roswell 61, 65

MacDowell, Andie 177
Machamer, Frank, Jr. 164
MacKaye, Benton 185
Maddox, R.S. 16
Majors, Johnny 178
Maloney, Frank 16
Mammoth Cave National Park 21
Mansfield, Donna 100
Mansfield, John 100
Many Glacier Hotel 50
Maples, Bruce 23
Maples, Isaac 37
Maples, Rellie 23
March, Frank 26
Marshall, Bob 59
Masa, George 56
Mather, Stephen 3
Mathes, Hodges 61
Mathews, Lori Huff 174
Maxon, Robert L. 61
McCarter, Lewis 22
McClenaghan, Beatrice 177
McFalls, Doug 100
McFarland, Russell 44
McNicol, Gracie 66, 71, 74, 86, 142, 166, 174, 176
Mesa Verde National Park 153
Mill Creek 16, 43, 65
Miller, Jean 174
Miller, Dr. Jesse "Kip" 174
Miller, Loye 16, 19, 185
Miller, Roger 86
Mitchell, Elisha 159
Model T Ford 57
Moore, Allen 139
Morgan, Rick 92, 100, 166, 175
Morgan, the Rev. Rufus 69, 133, 166, 174, 185
Morrell, John Ogden 16, 186

Mount Cammerer 89
Mount Collins 153
Mount Fuji 165
Mount Guyot 5, 18, 19, 40, 160
Mount Jackson 11
Mount Kephart 54, 67
Mount Mitchell 13, 57, 158–61, 162, 164
Mount Oglethorpe 179
Mount Rainier 165
Mount Rogers 67
Mount Snowden 165, 178
Mount Washington 57, 158, 164, 176
Mount Whitney 159, 164
Mountain View Hotel 15, 29, 30, 49, 58, 59, 60, 65
Muir, John 5, 68, 153, 186
Muir Trail Ranch 153
Murie, Margaret 81
Museum of East Tennessee History 36
Myers, Jim 69
Myers, Willie 59
Myrtle Point 18, 25, 32, 39, 64, 67, 109, 157

Nail, Deborah 99, 119
Nail, Rusty 99, 119
National Register of Historic Places 89
Neel, Henry 97, 100, 169
Neilson, Keith 82
Neiman, Jack, Jr. 138, 186
Nelson, Paul Wilbur 16
Newfound Gap 32, 40, 54, 55, 57, 59, 67, 74, 77, 79, 175, 178
Newman, Bruce 100
Nichols, Rosemary 87
Northrup, Bonnie Scott 116–118
Northrup, John 75, 78, 108, 116–118, 131, 149, 170
Norwood, J.L. 87

Oak Ridge TN 31
Oakley, Wiley 16, 17, 58, 60, 72, 98, 160, 186
Oconaluftee 56, 59, 90
Ogle, Barney 73
Ogle, Birdie 104
Ogle, Charlie 23, 145
Ogle, Earnest 23, 186
Ogle, Hugh 89
Ogle, Rosie 104
Old Cabin 92, 109
Old Faithful Inn 51, 155
Old Joe (horse) 147
Old Sugarlands Trail 71
Orme, Seth 88, 100
Ostborg, Marjarie 175
Overly, Fred 186
Ozark Mountains 13
Ozment, Adam 132

Packard automobile 57, 58
Paget, Edwin 171
Palmares, Nick 171
Park It Forward 77
Parton, Dolly 178
Peay, Gov. Austin 20, 162
Pegler, Westbrook 34
Peterson, Ronald 11, 60, 143
Phantom Ranch 51, 155
Pi Phi Settlement School 35, 58, 108
Piestewa Peak 171
Pigeon Forge 3, 133
Pikes Peak 57, 165, 171
Pisgah Inn 158
Plymouth automobile 55
Pollock, G. Freeman 151, 186
Polybaggers Hall of Fame 171
Ponder, Chrissy 131
Porter, Eliot 75
Porter Creek 67
Povia, Mike 76
Preston, George 70
Price, Dr. H.H. 37
Pyle, Bill 119
Pyle, Ernie 9, 34, 121
Pyle, Kelly 119

Qualla Boundary 10

Rabun Bald 106
Rainbow Falls 16, 64
Rainbow Falls Trail 16, 17, 25, 33, 37, 61, 64, 128, 152
Ramsey, William 17, 23, 29, 30, 31, 33, 39, 60, 64, 173
Ratliff, Randy 152
Reconstruction 11
Rinearson, Bill 51, 94, 133, 187
Roan High Knob 153, 156
Roan Mountain 15, 157
Roaring Fork 25, 29, 68, 90
Robertson, Reuben 51
Robinson, Nick 164
Rocky Mountain National Park 79
Rocky Spur 22, 65, 123, 152
Roosevelt, Eleanor 59
Roosevelt, Pres. Franklin 4, 59, 175
Rose Bowl Parade 116
Ross, Diana 108
Roth, Albert "Dutch" 6, 17, 42, 46, 61, 95, 187
Russell, Larry 150, 169, 177
Rutherford, Boyd 93

Sandia Crest 164
Scanlon, Dave 126, 168, 187
Schantz, Orpheus 24, 26, 39, 64, 187
Scheidt, Frances 87
Schlatter, Joe 96
Scopes Monkey Trial 22

Scratch Britches TN 16
Sehorn, Si 16
Sequoia & Kings Canyon National Park 153
Sequoia High Sierra Camp 153
Sharp, Bill 97
Sheldon Chalet 156
Shenandoah National Park 13, 15, 21, 151
Shepard, Alan 138
Shulley, F.J. 61
Sierra Club 8
Silers Bald 20, 54
Simcox, Samuel 173
Simmons, Morgan 149
Skoki Lodge 156
Skyland Lodge 57, 152
Skyway 54
Slusher, Dewey 102
Smith, George 16, 160
Smith, Ray 56
Smith, Tillroe 171
Smokemont NC 55
Smokey Bear 104
Smoky Jack 1, 23, 25, 28, 30, 104, 144–6
Smoky Mountain Hiking Club 24, 61, 75, 104
snakes 152
Sneddon, Lee 82
Snyder, Mae 119
Snyder, Roger 119
Soco Gap 54, 59
Spence, Carey 16, 19, 187
Spence Field 82
Sperry Chalet 103, 153
squirrels "boomers" 152
Stanley Steamer 57
Stevenson, Margaret 68, 106, 148, 166, 169, 176, 187
Stokely, William III 51
Stokely, William IV 51
Styx Branch 20 72
Sugarland Mountain 62
Summit, Pat Head 178
Swag 158

Tack House 26
Temple, Henry 16
Thomas, Col. William 187
Thomas Road 55
Thompson, Jim 24, 61, 177
Thoreau, Henry 31, 171
Thornburgh, Laura 65, 187
Thorne, Victor 97
Tinnell, Terry 69
Tour de Le Conte 53, 71, 76, 118, 178
Townsend, George 98
Townsend, Rosa 98
Trackhouse Racing 178
Trails Forever 66
Tri-Corner Knob 153
Trillium Gap 20, 75, 153

Trillium Gap Trail 25, 68, 144, 148, 174
Trout Branch 22
Turner, J.C. 159
Tweetsie Railroad "ET&WNC" 156, 174

Udall, Stewart 80
Underwood, Ron 100
University of California 7, 153
University of South Carolina 11
U.S. Weather Bureau 94
USGS benchmark 161

Valentine, Ron 152, 166–8, 177
Vanderbilt, Edith 157
Vanderbilt, George 157
Venable, Sam 119
Vertical Mile 164
Vincent, Bert 60, 110, 173
Virden, Allyson 95, 118, 121
Virden, Chris 118, 125
Vogelsang Camp 153–4

Wade, Karen 70
Wagman, Sam 171
Walasi'yi 10
Walker, John N. 172
Walker, Ronald 84
Walker, Thomas 172
Walker sisters 172
Walker Stone 172
Walland TN 61
Weaver, William 110
Webb, Tim 99
Welch, William 16
West Point 16, 138, 162
Whaley, Austin 56
Whaley, Jimbo 36
Whaley, Martha Cole 56
Whaley, Lavator 23
Whaley, Tillery 70
Whitaker, Paul L. 88
Whitesburg KY 106
Wilder, John T. 156, 188
Wilderness Act 50, 80–90, 125
Wilderness Society 81
Williams, Bill 26
Williamson, Adam 132
Willy, John 39, 64, 121
Willys, John North 39
Wilson, Big Tom 158
Wilson, Ewart 158
Wilson, Marshall 61
Wise, Ken 5, 11, 28, 60, 143
Witherspoon, David 50, 73, 82, 98, 99, 103, 105, 124, 143, 162
Wolf, Ira 178
Wonderland Hotel 13
Work, Hubert 15, 16
Wrangell-St. Elias Wilderness 81
Wuksachi Lodge 153
Wullschleger, Stan 74, 169

Index

Wright, Ed 71, 75, 92, 98, 166–7, 171, 177

Xanterra 51

Yellowstone National Park 14
Yosemite National Park 7, 11, 79, 84, 103, 153, 164, 179
Yoshinobu, Jitsukawa 171

Zahniser, Alice 81
Zahniser, Howard 81
Zion Lodge 51

www.ingramcontent.com/pod-product-compliance
Ingram Content Group UK Ltd.
Pitfield, Milton Keynes, MK11 3LW, UK
UKHW050525150426
5217IPUK00026B/1809